The Terms of Cultural Criticism: The Frankfurt School, Existentialism, Poststructuralism

1740 1814
SADE
afin que ... les traces de ma tombe disparaissent de dessus de la surface de la terre,
comme je me flatte que ma mémoire s'effacera de l'esprit des hommes... D.A.F. SADE.

THE TERMS OF CULTURAL CRITICISM

The Frankfurt School, Existentialism, Poststructuralism

RICHARD WOLIN

COLUMBIA UNIVERSITY PRESS
New York

Columbia University Press
New York Chichester, West Sussex

Library of Congress Cataloging-in-Publication Data

Wolin, Richard.
The terms of cultural criticism : the Frankfurt School, existentialism, poststructuralism / Richard Wolin.
p. cm.
Includes bibliographical references (p.) and index.
ISBN 0–231–07664–9
ISBN 0–231–07665–7 (pbk.)
1. Critical theory. 2. Existentialism. 3. Structuralism. 4. Postmodernism–Social aspects. 5. Pragmatism. I. Title.
HM24.W655 1992
301′.01–dc20 92–2624
CIP

Casebound editions of Columbia University Press books
are printed on permanent and
durable acid-free paper.

Printed in the United States of America

c 10 9 8 7 6 5 4 3 2
p 10 9 8 7 6 5 4 3 2 1

Cover illustration and frontispiece:
Man Ray, *Portrait imaginaire de D. A. F. de Sade* (1938).

For my dear friend Ulysses Santamaria
born, New York City, 1952; died, Florence, Italy, 1991

Brother, your death has left me sad and lone;
Since you departed all our joys have gone,
Which while you lived your sweet affection fed;
My pleasures all lie shattered, with you dead.
Shall I ne'er speak to you, or hear your voice?
Or see your face, more dear than life to me?
At least I'll love you to eternity. —Catullus

Contents

With Sade . . . private vice constitutes an anticipatory chronicle of the public virtues of the totalitarian era. Not to have glossed over or suppressed but to have trumpeted far and wide the impossibility of deriving from reason any fundamental argument against murder ignited the hatred which progressives to this day direct against Sade and Nietzsche . . . . Inasmuch as their merciless doctrines proclaim the identity of domination and reason, they are more merciful than those of the moralistic lackeys of the bourgeoisie.

—Horkheimer and Adorno, *Dialectic of Enlightenment* (1944)

Preface

> The immanent procedure [is] the more essentially dialectical. It takes seriously the principle that it is not ideology in itself which is untrue but rather its pretension to correspond to reality. Immanent criticism of intellectual and artistic phenomena seeks to grasp, through the analysis of their form and meaning, the contradiction between their objective idea and that pretension.
>
> —Theodor W. Adorno, "Cultural Criticism and Society" (1955)

In the mid-1950s, Theodor Adorno published *Prisms*, the first of four volumes on the theme of "cultural criticism and society"—*Prisms'* subtitle as well as the title of its programmatic introductory essay.[1] It would be difficult to find a more accomplished master of the genre. Nevertheless, our present social situation seems separated from Adorno's by a considerable remove. In many respects, the presuppositions of his approach to cultural criticism are no longer our presuppositions.

For example, Adorno finds the very term "cultural criticism" to be inherently problematic. His skepticism has to do with the peculiarities of the German context, where the term *Kulturkritik* is redolent of the values of the professorial mandarinate—those of the "unpolitical man" as described in Thomas Mann's 1916 tract.[2] As such, its connotations are integrally bound up with the infamous *Kultur/Zivilisation* dichotomy: that is, with Germany's self-understanding as a *Kulturnation* in opposition to the soulless and sordid commercialism of the western nations, England, France, and the United States. In the German sense, then, cultural criticism means less "criticism of culture"—exposing the latter's failings, inadequacies, and so forth—than criticism that is rendered from the ethereal standpoint *of* "culture": criticism of everything in life that is unexalted and base, *Kulturfeindlich*, or "hostile to culture." Thus: "Where there is despair and measureless misery, [the cultural critic] sees only spiritual phenomena, the state of man's consciousness, the decline of norms."[3] Understandably, Adorno feels a profound need to differentiate the contemporary tasks of cultural criticism from some of the more problematical constructs of German intellectual history.

Historically, we know that the arguments for German cultural superiority meshed all too seamlessly with contemporary arguments for the preponderance of Germany's continental geopolitical aims. And thus, as one critic has remarked, "With reference to the 'zero-hour' of 1933, it was only a short step from the ideology of the German professors to that of the fascists, and many were so enthusiastic that they made a quick leap into a brown uniform."[4] But, of course, the avowedly ideological definitions of culture that were being disseminated during the 1930s by the various ministries of Agitation and Propaganda—be it that of Goebbels or of Zhdanov—hardly constituted an improvement. In this respect, Walter Benjamin's well-known definition of the difference between fascist and communist aesthetics—whereas the former aestheticizes politics, the latter responds by politicizing aesthetics—presents us with a truly meaningless distinction.[5] But if the political events of our century have shown that Matthew Arnold's idea of culture as a bulwark against "anarchy" cannot be upheld—that is, if the putatively innate incongruence between "culture" and "barbarism" has indeed proved illusory—where does this leave the cultural critic with a conscience? In a type of intellectual no-man's-land, perhaps—which is indeed the terrain upon which Adorno elected to make his stand.

A dialectician's dialectician, he plays the apparent antagonism between culture and barbarism for all it is worth. He tries to stake out a position between the aesthete or *Kulturmensch*, who invokes cultural privilege as a sign of social superiority, and the modern-day philistine, who, upon hearing the word "culture," immediately reaches either for his revolver (reputedly, Göring) or checkbook (Hollywood). Both extremes must be forsworn—though one can hardly blame Adorno if, when forced to choose between the two, he betrays an affinity for the aesthete:

> For it is only in the process of withdrawing itself, only indirectly that is, that bourgeois culture conceives of a purity from the corrupting traces of a totalitarian disorder which embraces all areas of existence. Only in so far as it withdraws from a *praxis* which has degenerated into its opposite, from the ever-changing production of what is always the same, from the service of the customer who himself serves the manipulator—only in so far as it withdraws from Man, can culture be faithful to man.[6]

In Adorno's view, the only concept of culture that is viable in the aftermath of the German catastrophe would be an aesthetic corollary of negative dialectics: an *aesthetic of determinate negation*, which rejects any and every pretension that the blandishments of lyric poetry, tonality, or harmonious literary closure would be anything other than *ideology*. "Neutralized and ready-made, traditional culture has become worthless today," he tells us, refusing to mince words. But, of course, this insight hardly justifies making alliances with self-professed "enemies of culture." And thus, "Cultural criticism finds itself faced with the final stage of the dialectic of culture and barbarism."[7]

But Adorno's abandonment of culture may have been precipitate. To declare its "worthlessness" (an epithet he reserves for "traditional culture," rather than "modernism," though we know that, in the meantime, modernism has been made to endure the same fate: it, too, has become "neutral and ready-made") threatens to cede too much ground to what the ideologues and politicos have said about culture all along: that the only culture worth tolerating is that which furthers a specific political tendency or cause. Adorno believes that the position of the *Kulturmensch* or aesthete must be materialistically unmasked. "For no authentic work of art and no true philosophy, according to their very meaning, has ever exhausted itself in itself alone, in its being-in-itself."[8] It is precisely the claim of being above the fray that constitutes ideology. And in this regard, the "dialectic of culture and barbarism" remains indebted to one of Benjamin's better known aperçus: "There is no document of civilization that is not at the same time a document of barbarism."[9]

However, in contrast with Adorno, Benjamin had greater confidence that the semantic potentials of the cultural past could still be mobilized or redeemed by the historical materialist or critic. It falls due to the critic to rescue cultural history from the grasp of both historicism, which seeks to embalm it, thereby divesting it of its true radical potential—its *Aktualität*—as well as from that of the "victors," who seek to instrumentalize it as a testimony to their ill-gotten historical prerogative. For Benjamin, the materialist critic is aware that "*even the dead* will not be safe from the enemy if he wins." Hence, he must seize hold of the past "as it flashes up at a moment of danger." "For every image of the past that is not recognized by the present as one of its own concerns threatens to disappear irretrievably." The materialist critic is convinced that "the past carries with it a temporal index by which it is referred to redemption." And that "only a redeemed mankind receives the fullness of its past—which is to say, only for a redeemed mankind has its past become citable in all its moments." Citable not "the way it really was," but as a "now-time": a moment that has been rescued from the continuum of historical catastrophe in which it had been previously embedded. The materialist critic, therefore, views cultural history as "a revolutionary chance in the fight for the oppressed past," just as for Robespierre, "ancient Rome was a past charged with the time of the now which he blasted out of the continuum of history."[10]

The problem with Adorno's approach is that he prematurely relinquishes prospects for immanent critique. Instead, his cultural criticism assumes the all-too-aloof standpoint of a transcendent criticism. Among the epiphenomena and detritus of a society of total reification, the critic leaves him or herself without an immanent foothold. In the aftermath of the global conflagration that was responsible for Benjamin's death and Adorno's own exile, he can find little or nothing left to redeem: "All phenomena rigidify, become insignias of the absolute rule of that which is. There are no more ideologies in the authentic sense of false consciousness, only advertisements for the world through its duplication and the provocative lie which does not seek belief but commands silence."[11] The whole has become the untrue, and, as Adorno freely admits, "even the immanent method is eventually overtaken by this. It is dragged into the abyss by its object."[12] But with these words, negative dialectics comes close to proclaiming its own standstill, thereby threatening to seal its own fate. The conclusion that "only the mind which, in the delusion of being absolute, removes itself entirely from the merely existent, truly defines the existent in its negativity" cannot rise above the suspicion of sanctimoniousness, of arrogant self-justification.[13]

■ ■ ■ ■ ■ ■

The title of the present study, *The Terms of Cultural Criticism*, may imply an inclusiveness that is potentially misleading. At issue are three influential schools of twentieth-century continental cultural criticism—the Frankfurt School, existentialism, and poststructuralism. All three have enjoyed a fairly vigorous reception in post-war North American intellectual life. Despite their commonalities—as well as their considerable differences—seldom have they been treated as an ensemble. The origins of both existentialism and poststructuralism may be found in the work of Martin Heidegger. In truth, however, both currents have sought intellectual guidance from a very different Heidegger: for existentialism (e.g., Jean-Paul Sartre), the Heidegger of *Being and Time*; for poststructuralism, the later Heidegger qua critic of metaphysical reason. To be sure, traces of Heidegger's influence may be detected among the critical theorists as well, especially in the case of Herbert Marcuse, a former student.[14] But for the Frankfurt School, Heidegger's intellectual affinities with that "German ideology" that was about to wreak so much havoc on the world remained too profound; affinities that seemed rudely confirmed by the alacrity with which Heidegger, in 1933, joined in the National Revolution—an alliance that he would never explicitly renounce.

When one surveys the course of European social philosophy since the end of the First World War, the cultural prominence of these three intellectual currents, critical theory, existentialism, and poststructuralism, remains indubitable. Yet their vitality and fate have been overdetermined by the needs and requirements of various national cultural contexts. Thus, for example, in France, the Marx-Freud synthesis for which the Frankfurt School had become known was effectuated largely by means of indigenous intellectual traditions, such as surrealism and structuralism.[15] Moreover, France experienced its own renaissance of Marxist philosophy via the phenomenological Marxism of Sartre and Merleau-Ponty; as well as a recrudescence of Marxist orthodoxy under the banner of Althusser's structuralist Marxism. The need for theoretical "imports" from the *outre*-Rhine, therefore, seemed to be relatively superfluous. As a result, to this day, the influence of the Frankfurt School in France has been marginal at best.

In Germany, similarly, the influence of poststructuralism—or, as it has been termed, "French philosophy of the Sixties"[16]—has until very recently been quite modest. In part this was due to the fact that the poststructuralist critique of reason (e.g., Derrida's critique of "logocentrism") was inspired primarily by German philosophical sources (Nietzsche and Heidegger). Why, then, reimport a philosophical standpoint that was of German provenance to begin with? As Habermas has pointed out in *The Philosophical Discourse of Modernity*, the vitalistic overtones of the French critique of reason were also all too reminiscent of the cultural criticism of Germany's own generation of "young conservatives" in the 1920s (the Jünger brothers, Spengler, Moeller van den Bruck, Klages, etc.). In the eyes of Germany's oxymoronic "conservative revolutionaries," the "intellect" or "reason" was viewed as the "antagonist" of the "soul" or "life";[17] a chapter of German intellectual history that, in view of the political consequences that followed, few were anxious to repeat. Only in the last ten years—perhaps dating from the appearance in 1983 of Peter Sloterdijk's influential *Critique of Cynical*

Reason—have the anti-epistemologies of poststructuralism made significant inroads in German intellectual life.[18]

The musings of Alexis de Tocqueville on the idiosyncracies of the American character provide a privileged point of departure for understanding the equally peculiar niche the United States has occupied in the history of modern ideas. According to Tocqueville, the United States was a land that was especially ill-suited to the flourishing of philosophical greatness. Its preoccupations with commerce, exploration, and expansion had given rise to a pragmatic disposition of mind that displayed little patience with the *vita contemplativa* or "theory for theory's sake." In making these arguments, Tocqueville is uncharacteristically blunt. The second volume of *Democracy in America* begins with the observation: "I think that in no country in the civilized world is less attention paid to philosophy than in the United States." He goes on to remark that, though "Americans have no philosophical school of their own, and they care but little for all the schools into which Europe is divided, the very names of which are scarcely known to them," collectively, they stand for a type of *natural Cartesianism*: all feel compelled to make up their own minds, to rely on their own understanding as an ultimate court of appeal; no opinion shall be accepted on the basis of custom or tradition alone. As Tocqueville concludes, although "their social condition deters them from speculative studies," nevertheless, "America is one of the countries where the precepts of Descartes are least studied and are best applied."[19]

As in so many other respects, Tocqueville's reflections have proved prophetic indeed. What he had no way of foreseeing, however, was that, ultimately, Americans would become disillusioned with their own garden-variety Cartesianism and avidly seek out theoretical illumination from exotic, transatlantic shores. As the destinies of North America and Europe became geopolitically intertwined in the aftermath of the Second World War, successive waves of continental theory began their migration westward, leaving the landscape of intellectual life permanently altered.[20] Existentialism, phenomenology, psychoanalysis, structuralism, Hegelian Marxism, and poststructuralism were introduced, discussed, assimilated, and, in various degrees, "Americanized" in the decades following the collapse of European fascism. In the American marketplace of ideas, with its relative dearth of indigenous theoretical traditions (the one significant exception being pragmatism, a recent philosophical "export"), it seemed that all intellectual currents found, at least momentarily, their place in the scholarly limelight.

In the pages that follow, I have not sought to provide yet another introductory account of the intellectual movements in question; nor have I attempted to chronicle the fascinating history of their reception by talented North American interpreters and critics. Instead, my portraits and studies presuppose an initial familiarity with the theoretical currents under scrutiny. Presuming this familiarity, they go on to imply that the initial reception of the thinkers in question has suffered from a certain hesitancy to criticize. To be sure, the three schools of continental thought I undertake to examine have all found their strident detractors. However, currently fashionable slogans concerning "misunderstanding" as the unavoidable basis of "understanding" notwithstanding, willful—and, on occasion, malicious—incomprehension seldom proves a productive basis for criticism. As a rule, if one proceeds from the assumption that the object of study is of little worth, the scholarly results that accrue tend themselves to be of scant value. Instead, I have tried to purvey constructive, immanent criticisms of the various movements of thought at issue; criticisms that I hope might serve as a point of departure for the influential and perhaps decisive histories-of-reception that are destined to follow.

Freud uses the expression "coming to terms with the past" ("aufarbeiten der Vergangenheit") to indicate a process whereby we work or think through an experience or set of experiences that continues to have a latent hold on our present ways of being, thinking, and acting. It seems that those of us who attempt to "come to terms with" or "work through" the influences of inherited intellectual paradigms find ourselves confronted with a scenario that is, *mutatis mutandis*, not at all dissimilar from the analytic situation Freud was describing. Though a tireless advocate of Enlightenment and self-enlightenment, Freud, a Jew living amid the disillusionment of fin-de-siècle *Mitteleuropa*, harbored few illusions about the ultimate prospects for human redemption either on an ontogenetic or a phylogenetic scale. At best, he thought, psychoanalysis could transform "hysterical human misery into normal human unhappiness."[21] The watchword he coined some eighty years ago to describe the analytic method—"where id was, there ego shall be"[22]—has, in a poststructuralist era in which the values of autonomous subjectivity have become intellectually suspect, fallen upon hard times. This is regrettable, since, despite all the unjust scorn that has of late been heaped on Enlightenment, the poststructuralist program itself functions very much in the Enlightenment mold: it, too, seeks to free us from a spate of philosophically conditioned, socially necessary illusions about mind, self, and society. As such, it is very much the legitimate heir of the discourse of unmasking that was initiated by Marx, Nietzsche, and Freud; a discourse that Paul Ricoeur has felicitously labeled a "hermeneutic of suspicion." Even Nietzsche, who, with the zeal of an old testament prophet, rails ceaselessly against "Socratism," Enlightenment, and our modern "superfetation of the intellect," may plausibly be dubbed a modern Socrates: he has become—rightfully—the intellectual gadfly of the modern polis, the bad conscience of an age of enlightenment that has ceased to reflect critically on its own intellectual presuppositions and raison d'être.

The chapters that follow have been written in a spirit of "enlightenment about Enlightenment." Critical Theory, existentialism, and poststructuralism have posed formidable intellectual challenges to the cultural legacies of Enlightenment: political liberalism, instrumental reason, self-positing subjectivity, Eurocentrism, the longing for total revolution, and so forth. The challenges are just. The problems they have raised cannot be preemptively dismissed as "pseudo-problems." Only by sustained reflection on and immanent criticism of the way in which Enlightenment precepts have historically miscarried might the spirit of enlightened criticism—heroically unleashed by moralists, *lumières*, and *Aufklärer* alike—be reunited with its original utopian aspirations. For, as Hegel once described the lacerated ethical totality of modernity, in lieu of utopia, all is merely "the prose of the world": a state of unredeemed particularity and stultifying specialization.

> The immediacy of existence is from this point of view a system of necessary connections between apparently independent individuals and powers, a system in which every individual is used as a means in the service of ends foreign to himself. And since here the Idea as such realizes itself only on the ground of the external, what appears at the same time let loose is the unruly play of caprice and chance, and the whole misery of distress. This is the realm of unfreedom in which the *immediate* individual lives. . . .
>
> [The] individual as he appears in this world of prose and everyday is not active out of the entirety of his own self and his resources, and he is intelligible not from his himself, but from something else. For the individual man stands in dependence on external influences, laws, political institutions, civil relationships, which he just finds confronting him, and he must bow to them whether he has them as his own inner being or not. . . .
>
> This is the prose of the world, as it appears to the consciousness both of the individual himself and of others:—a world of finitude and mutability, of entanglement in the relative, of the pressure of necessity from which the individual is in no position to withdraw. For every isolated living thing remains caught in the contradiction of being itself in its own eyes this shut-in unit and yet of being

> nevertheless dependent on something else, and the struggle to resolve this contradiction does not get beyond an attempt and the continuation of this eternal war.[23]

Hegel's warning must become a warning for us: in effect, a reminder not to make the same error that he made in prematurely celebrating contemporary social conditions—the "actual"—as the apotheosis of reason, as *totality achieved.* The prescriptions of cultural criticism at present may be deduced from insight into Hegel's prophetic misstep.

■ ■ ■ ■ ■ ■

Several of the chapters that follow originally appeared as essays. The "nature and form of the essay" has been the subject of two fascinating mediations in our century by Adorno and the young Lukács. The similarities as well as the differences of their approaches should be briefly highlighted. For both thinkers, the essay qua genre is expressive of the partial character of our knowledge. Proceeding on the basis of this shared insight, their thoughts rapidly diverge, however. For the early Lukács, the essay signifies a transitional form. It is a mere stand-in or placeholder for a more consummate variety of knowledge: the knowledge of totality which is destined to return. For Adorno, conversely, totalities, which are inherently oppressive, are to be avoided under all circumstances. Consequently, in his view, the essay as form maintains a precarious fidelity to those forlorn particulars whose unhappy lot has been one of brutal, involuntary subsumption by the implacable *Weltlauf* or course-of-the-world.[24]

Regardless of whom one agrees with (perhaps, to cite Adorno, the two positions represent "torn halves of an integral freedom to which, however they do not add up"),[25] their meditations on the essay as form have managed to elevate its stature from that of something problematical or "second-best" to a form of knowledge and expression valid in its own right. However much I might disagree with their various material conclusions, the studies that follow are profoundly indebted to the spirit of seriousness with which they approached this genre; a spirit, moreover, that has become increasingly difficult to maintain amid the rampant professionalization of intellectual life and the increasing separation between "academic" and "public" knowledge that has followed in its wake.

Four of the chapters included in the present volume have previously appeared in English: "Critical Theory and the Dialectic of Rationalism," *New German Critique* 41 (1987):23–52; "Mimesis, Utopia, and Reconciliation: A Redemptive Critique of Adorno's *Aesthetic Theory*," *Representations* 32 (1990):33–49; "Carl Schmitt, Political Existentialism, and the Total State," *Theory and Society* 19 (1990):389–416; "Merleau-Ponty and the Birth of Weberian Marxism," *Praxis International* 5 (1985):115–130. A fifth, "Sartre, Heidegger, and the Intelligibility of History," appeared in a special issue of *Les Temps Modernes* (October-December 1990) commemorating the tenth anniversary of Sartre's death. I am grateful to all five publications for permission to reprint.

I'd like to express my sincere thanks to the National Endowment for the Humanities: the Fellowship for University Teachers they were generous enough to bestow upon me made all the difference in my efforts to turn a few inchoate ideas into a fully realized plan. I'd also like to acknowledge the assistance of the Alexander von Humboldt Foundation of Bonn, Germany. For it was in the course of an earlier stay in the Federal Republic which they were generous enough to sponsor that I began to explore many of the concepts and themes that ultimately proved crucial to the successful completion of the volume at hand. Allen Matusow, Dean of Humanities at Rice University, has been terrifically supportive of my research ventures and needs. His characteristic generosity has been an essential precondition for whatever claim I might stake to scholarly achievement.

I am also very grateful for the enthusiastic support and guidance of my editor at Columbia University Press, Ann Miller. I would be hard pressed to imagine a more congenial author-editor rapport than the one that Ann and Columbia have provided.

My enumeration of intellectual debts would not be complete without a special acknowledgment of the invaluable commentaries I received on many chapters of the manuscript from Martin Jay of the University of California, Berkeley. Tirelessly and unselfishly, he proved willing to read countless drafts, chapters, and proto-chapters. The ideal close reader, Marty never shied away from unsparing criticisms when such criticisms were called for. His comments were unfailingly pertinent and incisive. My intellectual gratitude to him is in truth much greater than these few words of thanks are able adequately to convey.

Last, but far from least, I wish to thank my wife, Melissa, for her patience and generosity; but most of all, for simply being the incomparable person she is.

The successful completion of a book-length manuscript is usually a cause for great elation. In this case, joy was tempered with considerable sadness owing to the sudden and unexpected death of my dear friend Ulysses Santamaria. Ulysses personified an uncommon ebullience and warmth—a genuine humanity. As a scholar, too, he was a true rarity, shunning the languorous comforts of academe for the sake of a hard-fought intellectual independence. Like Dostoevsky's Myshkin, he embodied a type of auratic goodness: few persons who knew him remained unmoved by his innate magnanimity and beneficent cast of mind. I dedicate this book to the enduring memory of an unforgettable friend.

A Note on Man Ray's *Imaginary Portrait of D. A. F. de Sade*

Along with Lautréamont, the Marquis de Sade had become a figure of totemic significance for the surrealists. As the novelist Henry Miller recounts: "Complete, absolute liberty—that is what Man Ray waxed fervent and eloquent about in describing Sade's view of life."[1] By chance—or, to be more precise, undoubtedly as a result of *l'hasard objectif*—during the 1930s Man Ray lived in a small hotel in Paris next door to Maurice Heine, the indefatigable compiler of Sade's collected works. Heine once lamented to his neighbor that there was no extant portrait of Sade. Man Ray eagerly pledged his creative talents in order to supply Heine with the missing image to adorn his planned edition.

Man Ray diligently researched his informal commission, traveling to the Vaucluse region to visit the chateau where the marquis was raised. He also managed to procure police and medical records in order to help him reconstruct details of Sade's appearance and physique. Although this was to be an "imaginary portrait," it would be one that was nevertheless faithful to reality.

At the request of his family, Sade had been "institutionalized" in the Bastille since 1784. The historian Simon Schama has observed, in an anti-surrealist spirit, that "if there ever was a justification for the Bastille, it was the Marquis de Sade."[2] As the political crisis of 1789 came to a head, the marquis, like so many of his aristocratic brethren, passed over to the side of the revolutionaries. From the tower parapets he would deliver ceaseless tirades to the Parisian crowds warning that a massacre of the prisoners (all seven of them) was imminent and that the people should rise to their defense before it was too late. Here, to be sure, a good measure of self-interest suffused the marquis' revolutionary zeal. In the end, Sade's rabble-rousing tactics so unnerved the prison's military governor, the Marquis de Launay, that in early July the fortress' most illustrious inhabitant was shipped off to dwell among the lunatics of Charenton—where he might feel more at home.

The result of Man Ray's efforts is one of the most stunning achievements in the entire repertoire of surrealist painting. It has often been read as a celebratory portrait, in keeping with the surrealist glorification of the marquis as a martyr for the cause of untrammeled erotic gratification—Sade as the incarnation of Bataille's "sovereign" individual.[3] Man Ray once described the marquis' quintessential significance for the surrealists in the following terms:

> I admire this man who spent twenty-seven years of his life in prison for his beliefs. In his prison cell, by the light of a candle, using his imagination and a quill, he wrote the most passionate defense of individualism and freedom. And in so doing he revealed a universal trait of our character, a trait that only hypocrisy and puritanism refused to acknowledge. Sade helped us understand ourselves.[4]

Yet if we regard Man Ray's Sade more closely, we see that the imaginary portrait he has left us is far from unequivocally flattering. The Sade we are presented with here—diabolic, one-eyed, literally stone-faced; the impassive voyeur of the horrific panorama unfolding before him—is very much an allegory of political modernity. In point of fact, it may be said that Man Ray's Sade captures something of the dialectic of Enlightenment: the moment in which unchecked revolutionary enthusiasm turns into a licentiousness that knows no bounds; or, to speak with Hegel, the fine line (one we are familiar with from Sade's novels) where absolute freedom turns into unmitigated terror; a correlation that has been immortalized in revolutionary lore by Robespierre's infamous equation of "terror" with "virtue." As the towering fortress burns, the figures in the foreground—minute in their insignificance—seem to melt back into the earth as a result of the intensity of the conflagration that overwhelms them. The storming of the Bastille sounds the death knell of the ancien régime. But it also inaugurates an era of modern political messianism marked by war, revolution, and unlimited ideological zealotry. In his imaginary portrait, does not Man Ray invite us to reflect at length on the sinister origins of political modernity as such?[5]

Introduction: Thrasymachus' Ghost

> I say that the just is nothing else than the advantage of the stronger. . . . Each government makes laws to its own advantage: democracy makes democratic laws, a despotism makes despotic laws, and so with the others, and when they have made these laws they declare this to be just for their subjects, that is, their own advantage, and they punish him who transgresses the laws as lawless and unjust. This then, my good man, is what I say justice is, the same in all cities, the advantage of the established government, and correct reasoning will conclude that the just is the same everywhere, the advantage of the stronger.
>
> —Thrasymachus, Plato's ***Republic***, 338e

I

We live in intellectually contentious times. Yet, were one to compare the predominant matters of intellectual contention today with those of bygone eras—the great battle among religious world-views during the sixteenth and seventeenth centuries; the struggle of "faith" versus "reason" in the century that followed—our disputes would seem to be almost family disagreements, relatively trivial by comparison. For at stake in these earlier debates were not merely individual perspectives or points of view, but often the survival or demise of an entire social formation: the network of traditional social prerogatives that had been perpetuated under the ancien régime. Conversely, today, in those parts of the globe in which a political culture of tolerance has triumphed, those on the losing side of a dispute, while they might be deprived of "tenure," are rarely burned at the stake. Certainly, the few remaining champions of "progress" are correct—*pace* Nietzsche and Foucault—to cite this diminution of gratuitous societal cruelty in support of their position. And in this regard, too, the "end of ideology" theorists

(Daniel Bell, Niklas Luhmann, and, more recently, Francis Fukuyama) have a point. After all, the great romance between twentieth-century intellectuals and communism—perhaps the last, secularized incarnation of an "ethic of ultimate ends"—has, it seems, finally played itself out. In the aftermath of the sudden collapse of bureaucratic socialism, the patrimony of political liberalism (rule of law, civil liberties, and separation of powers) has been dramatically upgraded (for those who had doubts), and we now grope collectively toward a shared, post-totalitarian political ethos.

But, in the absence of a viable public intellectual culture, one wonders whether the "end of ideology" does not mean that today's free-floating intellectuals, largely ghettoized in universities, have been left, in a manner reminiscent of scholasticism, to split hairs among themselves. The *philosophes* of yore—today unfairly maligned as partisans of "modernity"—would sign their letters with an exclamatory, "*Ecrasez l'infâme*!" insofar as there was something truly important at stake. Those of today have been subsumed by the so-called managerial revolution: they have become jobholders, salaried employees, hirelings with tenure. The universalistic vocation of the intellectual, formerly buttressed by a secular devotion to knowledge as "calling" (as in the Weberian ideal of "Wissenschaft als Beruf"), has been superseded by a privatized ethos of vocational success and professional advancement. And in this respect, Agnes Heller's lament concerning contemporary "professional philosophy"—"The real problem lies in the fact that for genuine philosophy it has become a labor of Sisyphus to emancipate itself from the limitation of philosophy as a 'job'"—applies a fortiori to the other intellectual disciplines, in the sciences as well as the humanities.[1]

Max Weber, speaking of the decline of the great "world religions," noted the disappearance of that "prophetic *pneuma*, which in former times swept through the great communities like a firebrand, welding them together."[2] Insofar as that *pneuma*, as manipulated and channeled by charismatic leaders, proved a source of fanaticism, intolerance, and—under the fascist regimes of our century—collective regression, one is certainly relieved to see that it has become, fundamentalist recrudescences notwithstanding, largely a thing of the past. In this respect, too, the "end of ideology" thesis is not without its merits.

On the other hand, in lieu of a vibrant cultural and political life—in modern society, the indispensable loci of both individual and collective self-fulfillment and expression—our modern democratic polities risk succumbing to an *inverse* form of paralysis, one against which Weber also vociferously railed: the "mechanized petrifaction" of an instrumentally rationalist culture, the "iron cage" of disenchanted, bureaucratic capitalism. For the values of instrumental rationalism possess no answer to those so-called ultimate questions posed by Kant in the second and third *Critiques*: "How should I live?" and "What can I hope?" And though they do provide a satisfactory response to the query with which the first *Critique* begins—"What can I know?"—they can give no instructions about how we might genuinely reconcile the scientific quest for pure knowledge with the value orientations through which we find meaning in life. Instead, the two considerations, science and meaning, often prove incompatible. And thus, historically, scientific disenchantment has often led to a disenchantment with science. As far as the naive equation between scientific progress and happiness is concerned, "Who believes in this," asks Weber, "aside from a few big children in university chairs or editorial offices?"[3] Strictly speaking, therefore, science is "meaningless" insofar as it is incapable of providing an answer to Tolstoy's question, the only question that is important to us: "What shall we do and how shall we live?"

This changed attitude toward science, one in which faith has been supplanted by skepticism, and which is mediated by a series of historical catastrophes and near-catastrophes—for our century has been a sad witness to the ease with which scientific techniques can be used indifferently for purposes of mass annihilation as well as human betterment—accounts for what is perhaps the major cultural shift between our age and that of the *philosophes* of two centuries ago.

At the same time, the blurring of the distinction between "science" and "reason," the facile assumption that one might trace the misdeeds of the former back to the sins of the latter, is perhaps one of the most fatal intellectual tendencies of our age. Hence, according to the reigning antimetaphysical spirit, science and reason are, in essence, indistinguishable. On this view, science merely represents the "modern," up-to-date incarnation of metaphysical reason. The "violence of the *logos*" commits the original sin of distinguishing between the true and the untrue, the beautiful and the ugly, essence and appearance. This very act of making "rational" (logocentric) distinctions and judgments, we are told, sanctions unconscionable hierarchies and exclusions. In what is a potentially momentous "transvaluation of values," it is said that the Socratic-metaphysical quest for "justice"—the subject matter of Plato's *Republic*, one of the ur-texts of occidental thought—is the origin (*Ursprung*) of the injustice of Western civilization in general. The credo of this perspective may well be summarized as: *Raison, c'est la torture*.

The critique of metaphysics just described is of Heideggerian provenance. It is a critique of reason that, in its radicality and inattention to nuance, threatens to become a defeatism of thought. Its fundamental tendency is one which, whether one turns to the romantics, to Nietzsche, or, more recently, to the work of Jacques Derrida, has become a central figure of the counter-enlightenment spirit: an attempt to undo the triumph of "Socratism" by reasserting the primacy of *poesis* vis-à-vis the predilection for intellection on which "civilization" has been based.

But as Manfred Frank reminds us: "Postmodernism and antimodernism perfidiously join hands. This is also the case with 'logocentrism': [Ludwig] Klages and the new anti-intellectualism [*Geistfeindlichkeit*] of our day agree in the affect against the achievements of western 'rationality'." Frank fears—not unjustifiably—that the historical precedents for replacing reason with *vitalistic imperatives*—usually based on variants of the Nietzschean "will to power"—are especially ominous: "Let us indeed not forget that from Nietzsche to social Darwinism and National Socialism, struggle [*Kampf*] was viewed as a desirable means of salvation from 'modern ideas,' as was 'the health of the nation in face of the disintegrative influence of modernity.'"[4]

In opposition to the radical critique of reason, one would do better, it seems, to consider the program enunciated by Horkheimer and Adorno in *Dialectic of Enlightenment*: the idea that a "critique of enlightenment [must] prepare the way for a positive notion of enlightenment which will release it from entanglement in blind domination."[5] In other words, whereas the poetical-rhetorical outbidding of reason—in the name of "Being," "sovereignty," or whatever form of hypostasized, precategorial otherness—has become one of the major intellectual temptations of our day, it is a temptation that should be resisted. For as Adorno knew well, only the hand that inflicted the wound can cure the disease. Philosophy has no other choice. "It must strive, by way of the concept, to transcend the concept."[6]

Horkheimer and Adorno's acute sensitivity to the historical excrescences of Enlightenment—a result of the way in which the substantive concept of reason advanced by German idealism had become, with the rise of modern positivism, *instrumentally foreshortened*—may well provide a constructive point of departure for understanding the main task of cultural criticism throughout the modern era: to promote a positive concept of enlightenment via reflection on Enlightenment's historical inadequacies. But when reinterpreted in this way, it becomes clear that the shortcomings of enlightenment must be attributed not, as we are so often told today, to a *surfeit* of reason, but to a *dearth* thereof; a dearth, moreover, that follows from the premature, scientistic curtailment of reason's capacities and horizons.

II

That the critique of reason should today appear convincing to so many is not hard to comprehend. It is historically overdetermined: it corresponds to the apparent collapse, in the aftermath of two devastating world wars, of the European tradition, and the intense anticivilizational mood that followed in the wake of that collapse. In light of the unparalleled historical magnitude of these catastrophes, Enlightenment shibboleths concerning the "infinite perfectibility of man" seemed tantamount indeed to the thinly veiled pretexts and rationalizations that Nietzsche always accused them of being.

At the same time, the tasks of historical understanding demand a finer, more nuanced appraisal of the circumstances responsible for that collapse. It is worth recalling, therefore, that the triumph of totalitarian political forms occurred not from *within* the European democracies, but instead in "belated nations"—Germany, Italy, and Russia—that had failed to make the transition to the modern order of constitutional government. They are, to be sure, *modern* despotisms that represent a hybrid of traditional forms of illiberal, authoritarian rule with advanced technological means of domination and control (above all, a classical Orwellian-demagogic employment of the techniques of mass communication). Their success, however, is less attributable to the triumph of "master thinkers," "logocentrism," or, in Heidegger's lexicon, the "completion of metaphysics" (*Vollendung der Metaphysik*) than to a type of *Logosvergessenheit*: a "forgetting of reason" that betrays a regression behind the civil libertarian thresholds of political modernity.

Given the widespread currency of the critique of reason, one cannot help but wonder: might not the position of Thrasymachus be making a comeback; the view, restated with unmatched brilliance by Nietzsche, that all claims to truth, justice, and right are merely a mask for determinate social interests or considerations of power? As the tradition of political conservatism has always maintained, Thrasymachus' ghost—the prospect of a regression to a Hobbesian condition of nihilistic anarchism, in which power alone holds sway and, ultimately, might makes right—has forever lurked behind conditions of political modernity. For does not modernity's resolute "prejudice against prejudice," its inherent antitraditionalism, militate against the very existence of cultural stability, cohesion, and order? As Burke was quick to point out, the corrosive powers of "naked reason" lead inexorably to a situation in which "all the decent drapery of life is to be rudely torn off," and in which there is nothing left "to cover the defects of our naked, shivering nature."[7] Unlike traditional societies, where "right" is unreflexively based on the sanctity of custom, force of habit, and lineage, modernity is faced with the Munchausenesque requirement of establishing the conditions of its own legitimacy. It finds itself, therefore, in the paradoxical situation of having to provide itself with its own pedigree. Hence, the suspicion of illegitimacy, the taint of parvenu status, can never be far removed. Once the otherworldly, theological ground of premodern societies has been replaced with an immanent, self-generated ground, the very concept of "ground" assumes a new fragility: from now on, all grounds are inherently contestable. And thus, if natural law, which was supposedly suprahuman and thus eternal, has been reduced to the arbitrariness of human convention, is not—as Dostoevsky feared—*everything permitted*? Doesn't this view correspond precisely to the convictions of Sade's heroine, Juliette, who attempts to assuage the guilt of a lecherous accomplice by confiding: "As soon as we no longer believe in God, my dear . . . the desecrations you call for are no more than vain trifles"? In this sense, Juliette is truly a child of her age, a daughter of *Aufklärung*: she believes that Christ is nothing more than "A dead God!"[8]

Such were the conclusions drawn by those "diabolical" heirs to the spirit of Enlightenment radical criticism, Sade and Nietzsche. For in a manner that was fully consistent with Enlightenment materialism, both men heeded, with frightening literalism, the doctrines of eighteenth-century natural law. But instead of finding there God-given "rights of man" or Rousseau's fellow-feeling (*pitié*), they discovered the Hobbesian state of nature, the *bellum omnium contra omnes* in which "might makes right"—*and they liked what they saw*! For it was by virtue of a return to this Hobbesian natural state and the permanent removal of Burke's "decent drapery" that man's animalic self could recapture its lost prerogative: a capacity for untrammeled instinctual expression that had been sublimated and benumbed by a civilizing process based on "mnemotechnics" (Nietzsche): the creation of a domesticated animal, bourgeois man, who will voluntarily and punctually pay back his debts and keep his promises. Or, as one of Sade's heroes observes in a stunning anticipation of Nietzsche:

> Where, I ask you, is the mortal stupid enough to swear against all the evidence to the contrary that men are born equal in justice and in fact? Only such an

enemy of mankind as Rousseau could assert this paradox, because being so very weak himself he wished to draw down to his level those to whose height he could not ascend. . . . How in truth can you require that he who has been endowed by nature with an eminent capacity for crime . . . should have to obey the same law that calls all to virtue or to moderation? Is the law more just when it punishes the two men alike? Is it natural that he whom everything invites to commit evil should be treated exactly as he whom everything drives to behave prudently?[9]

Sade's logic is implacable, seamless, rigorously consistent: "If crime is the spirit of nature, there is no crime against nature, and, consequently, there is no crime possible."[10] Nietzsche is similarly consistent when, upon certifying the rights of birds of prey to devour little lambs ("we don't dislike them at all, these good little lambs; we even love them: nothing is more tasty than a tender lamb"), he observes: "To demand of strength that it should *not* express itself as strength, that it should *not* be a desire to overcome, a desire to throw down, a desire to become master, a thirst for enemies and resistances and triumphs, is just as absurd as to demand of weakness that it should express itself as strength."[11]

One can agree with Bataille when he remarks that "nothing would be more fruitless than to take Sade literally, seriously."[12] The same must be said of Nietzsche, who, as certain translators never tire of pointing out, was anything but a naive proponent of power politics.

But it is also Nietzsche who not infrequently exults in the "profound joy in all destruction, in all the voluptuousness of victory and cruelty" when practiced by certain "noble races"; who, in one of his adumbrations of the "will to power," confesses: "I assess a man by the quantum of power and abundance of his will."[13] Here, Nietzsche shows himself to be in fundamental agreement with Sade in the belief that minor crimes deserve to be punished while those of great magnitude and extent deserve to be celebrated. The Sadean "Société des Amis du Crime"—a response *avant la lettre* to Nietzsche's famous call for a race of "new barbarians"—"is composed primarily of a tiny number of omnipotent men who have had the energy and initiative to raise themselves above the law and place themselves outside the pale of prejudice, men who feel that nature has singled them out and [who] strive to assuage their passions by any and all means."[14] With Sade, there is even tacit acknowledgment of the bourgeois principle of "careers open to talent": the potential for upward social mobility of the truly accomplished miscreant is in no way bounded by the atavisms of class. "The repetition is infinite and extraordinary. It is not unusual for a libertine to torture and massacre four or five hundred victims in a single session; then he starts in again the following day; then again the same evening with a new ceremony."[15] Nietzsche, too, pays homage to the zeitgeist by accepting the convention that would "accept the hanging of a petty thief and elevate imperialistic raids to the level of world-historical missions." By following Nietzsche in "raising the cult of strength to a world-historical doctrine, German fascism carried this position to its absurd extreme."[16]

III

The poststructuralist critique of reason is the heir to the radical experiences of aesthetic modernism: the experiences of an unbounded self, decentered subjectivity, shock effects, and the autonomization of poetic language. Like Nietzsche, poststructuralism must defend itself against the charge of nihilism: of promoting a condition of the "loss of meaning" (*Sinnverlust*) that was, according to Weber, one of the main perils of modern, posttraditional society. By endorsing Nietzsche's "genealogy of morals," by searching for alternative structures of experience in the archaic, the heterogeneous, the qualitatively Other, poststructuralism has succeeded admirably in overturning inherited structures of belief and convention. Such impulses of radical contestation, moreover, are central to the ethos of modern cultural criticism. In this sense, it may be deceptive to exaggerate the differences between the modern and the postmodern. For in many respects, postmodernism has merely carried forth the legacy of modernism qua "adversary culture" (Daniel Bell). Thus, Jean-François Lyotard, a tireless advocate of the "unpresentable" or "sublime," has correctly insisted on the essential elements of continuity between modern and postmodern. According to Lyotard, the postmodern is already contained in the modern; it is the spirit of modernity when it remains true to itself: true, that is, to the demands of nonpresence or absence vis-à-vis the (obsolete, metaphysical) longing for "presence"—the nostalgia for which Lyotard views as the sign of a dangerous "slackening" in the contemporary period. As Lyotard explains: "The postmodern would be that which, *in the modern*, puts forward the unpresentable in presentation itself; that which denies itself the solace of good forms, the consensus of a taste which would make it possible to share collectively the nostalgia for the unattainable; that which searches for new presentations, not in order to enjoy them but in order to impart a stronger sense of the unpresentable."[17] Postmodernism would thus signify a nonsentimental adieu—a farewell without tears—to the traditional metaphysical longing for totality, holism, and presence. Poststructuralism would correspondingly become the epistemological—or better: anti-epistemological—corollary of this epochal cultural transvaluation.

Nevertheless, the ethico-political lineage of poststructuralism—which may be traced to the influences of Nietzsche, Heidegger, and Bataille—is far from unproblematical and has increasingly become an object of concern. As an antimetaphysical movement of unmasking, de-definition, and provocation, poststructuralism has excelled at challenging inherited epistemological positions and hierarchies. However, when it has come time to set forth its own determinate ethico-political persuasions and convictions, both supporters and detractors alike have felt its acute limitations. The commonplace equation of "totality" with "terror" (cf. Lyotard, "Answering the Question: What is Postmodernism?") threatens to turn into a ritual incantation with very little empirical explanatory power. The ironies here are profound. What began as a protest against metaphysical thinking risks, in its patented recourse to quasi-metaphysical explanations based on the omnipresence of "metanarratives," "consensus," and "totalities," becoming a full-blown idealism. When the values of conceptual coherence themselves fall under suspicion of coercive practice or "terror," how does one avoid succumbing to an anti-intellectual posture in which, ultimately, conceptual rigor as such gives cause for alarm?

As far as the theme of poststructuralism and morality itself is concerned, we are left in a situation of relative paralysis: viz., with a flaccid ethic of "negative autonomy" which "accords well with [poststructuralism's] general defense of heterogeneity, difference, marginality and nonidentity against the coercive power of totalization and closure."[18] It is, ironically, a situation highly reminiscent of the pitfalls of Sartrian "bad faith." We must take a position or "choose," though any choice we make risks congealing into a reification by virtue of which we renounce our essential nature as infinitely negative consciousness or Being-for-Self. Yet can a viable ethical stance result from an epistemological program in which all fixed positions and determinate positivities are a priori suspect of having "always already" relapsed into a dreaded "metaphysics of presence"; a program whose thoroughgoing rejection of the demands of human agency or selfhood—concepts redolent of the antiquated values of coherence, norm, and self-presence—leaves "subjects" potentially at the mercy of reigning social powers? And thus, "Throughout much of poststructuralist thought one finds the disjunction between endless, objectified process, whether theorized in terms of a 'play of the text,' or of a metaphysics of power or desire, and a subjectivism which is paradoxically subjectless, since it abolishes the relation to the other which is constitutive of subjectivity."[19] As Martin Jay has remarked in an important essay on the theme of poststructuralism and ethics:

> Of all the aspects of the loose and heterogeneous body of thought that has come to be called poststructuralism, none seems to engender as much unease and resistance as its assumed debunking of ethics. The charge of nihilism, so often leveled by its critics against its epistemological implications, is even more frequently directed at its moral ones as well. A variety of lineages has been adduced to account for poststructuralism's putative moral deficit: its freely acknowledged debt to Nietzsche's attempt to go "beyond good and evil," its fascination for scenarios of violence, mutilation, and sacrifice from de Sade to Bataille, its attraction to politically tainted figures like Heidegger and the early Blanchot (a weakness only magnified by the de Man scandal), and its inheritance of the aesthetic modernist gesture of forgetting the victim so long as the gesture is beautiful.[20]

According to Jay, the ethical stance of poststructuralism remains valuable insofar as it "compels us to reflect on the costs of moral absolutism, the violence latent in trying to construct fully realized ethical forms of life." Ultimately, though, it does not provide "any help with the thorny question of how to adjudicate in the present different, often conflicting ethical claims." By elevating aesthetics over reason, by rejecting the empirically based social sciences as still "metaphysical," "logocentric,"[21] by valorizing "undecidability" over intersubjective agreement and the hermeneutics of meaning, in the end, it seems, "we are left with little beyond assertions and evocative rhetoric."[22]

The rejection of social scientific empiricism seems to be an especially debilitating feature of the poststructuralist approach to cultural criticism. According to Derrida, the methods of social science are intrinsically conformist. For insofar as they remain indebted to an intellectual paradigm that privileges rationality and reason, they buy into an entire train of exclusions, prejudices, and hierarchies associated with metaphysical thought: a preference for the one over the many, essence over appearance, sense rather than non-sense. Hence, they "never touch upon that which, in themselves, continues to be based on the principle of reason and thus on the essential foundation of the modern university. They never question scientific normativity, beginning with the value of objectivity or of objectivation, which governs and authorizes their discourse."[23]

But, here, two objections seem to be pertinent. First, the discourse of the social sciences has been rife with significant internal challenges to the primacy of methodological objectivism: for example, the criticisms posed by Dilthey and Weber in the course of the "understanding vs. explanation" controversy in the first two decades of our century;[24] or, more recently, the extensive debates over the concept of "rationality" in social scientific explanation that were triggered in the 1960s by Peter Winch's essay "Understanding a Primitive Society," a controversy which precipitated the celebrated "interpretive turn" in the human sciences.[25] To claim, therefore, that the social sciences have been methodologically unreflective is simply untenable; although one can agree with Derrida that further demystification of their "objectivating attitude" is needed.

But, more seriously, this steadfast avoidance of the discourse of the human sciences has allowed poststructuralist criticism to languish in a state of extreme empirical impoverishment. And thus, despite its critique of the idealistic assumptions of the "hermeneutics of meaning" (inasmuch as it is claimed that all "understanding" is predicated on "misunderstanding"), poststructuralism, in its aversion to empirical claims and, more generally, to "reference," shares with hermeneutics a certain "linguistic idealism": a naive privileging of the concepts of language, text, and signification in general; a position that has been carried to its extreme in the assertion that "every human act whatsoever" is a variant of "Reading."[26] To be sure, the accusation of "pan-textualism" (following Derrida's by now infamous bon mot, "il n'y a pas de hors texte") is probably *the* criticism that has been most frequently raised against poststructuralism. Even Foucault, the most "worldly" among the poststructuralists, never fully clarifies the relationship between "discursive regimes" and social institutions. It is merely assumed that the workings of the latter are fully subsumed by the prescriptions of such "regimes" qua transcendental-empirical behavioral codes.[27]

The important point here is that the dynamics of power are not exclusively semiotic in nature. Only an empirically informed approach to the analysis of power relations can meet the object of study—historically conditioned social practices and institutions—halfway. In lieu of such an approach our understanding of the actual historical functioning of power threatens to become idealistically skewed.

The poststructuralist ethos of "negative autonomy" has come into vogue as an alternative to the post-Cartesian ideal of self-positing subjectivity or the "liberal self." The French Heideggerians have argued that when it is transferred from the plane of the individual self to the community, this classical western model of self-realizing subjectivity represents the "origin" of the modern totalitarian impulsion. Thus, following Heidegger, Philippe Lacoue-Labarthe argues that with National Socialism, it is "the ontology of subjectivity (of the will to will) that finds its fulfillment. Nazism is the Nazi myth, i.e., the Aryan type, as absolute subject, pure will (of the self) willing itself." Lacoue-Labarthe goes on to claim that inasmuch as it derives from the myth of self-totalizing subjectivity, "Nazism is a humanism [!] insofar as it rests upon a determination of *humanitas* which is, in its view, more powerful—i.e., more effective—than any other."[28]

But do such arguments—which derive from Heidegger's critique of Western reason qua onto-theology—possess genuine explanatory value? Can Nazism really be explained as a result of the "completion of metaphysics" and the "forgetting of Being"—as Heidegger contends—or are there a series of more proximate, concrete, historico-empirical causes that better account for its success in Germany during the interwar years? If, as Lacoue-Labarthe suggests, National Socialism is indeed ultimately the product of a determinate philosophical paradigm—*humanitas*, the "ontology of subjectivity," the "will to will"—how then can one account for its flourishing in Germany as opposed to so many other nations where that paradigm has also been predominant? Finally, isn't a more telling characteristic of those nations that did voluntarily succumb to the lure of fascism (e.g., Italy, Spain) their concerted *rejection* of the values of "enlightened modernity"—above all, the political values of the tradition of civic humanism—rather than the perverse apotheosis of such values suggested by Lacoue-Labarthe?

The poststructuralist critique of the modern ideal of self-fashioning subjectivity has, it seems, two possible outcomes.[29] The first has been determined by Bataille and has exerted a profound influence on the political self-understanding of the French Heideggerians. In opposition to the Western ideal of the self-realizing community—the model of onto-theology—it sets forth the image of an *ecstatic community*, or, in the words of Jean-Luc Nancy, the "communauté désoeuvrée." This would be a community that no longer strives teleologically after the goals of organic totality, self-transparency, or *immanentism*—which is defined by Nancy as "the aim of the community of beings in essence to produce their own essence as their work (oeuvre), and moreover to produce precisely this essence *as community*."[30] Instead of being self-infinitizing, its content and composition would be fully mediated by the claims of otherness, heterogeneity, and finitude. It would be akin to the community of *nonproductive expenditure* described by Bataille in works such as *La Part maudite* and "Théorie de la dépense." In such a community, the utilitarian mentality of equivalent exchange would be renounced in favor of a capacity to give selflessly, joyously, without return. Or, as Bataille remarks: society has "an *interest* in considerable losses, in catastrophes that, *while conforming to well-defined needs*, provoke tumultuous depressions, crises of dread, and, in the final analysis, a certain orgiastic state." In other words, it has an interest in "nonproductive expenditure": "luxury, mourning, war, cults, the construction of sumptuary monuments, games, spectacles, arts, perverse sexual activity (i.e., deflected from genital finality)—all these represent activities which, at least in primitive circumstances, have no end beyond themselves."[31]

Nietzsche's youthful reconstruction of the Dionysian-communal self-oblivion ritualistically induced by Greek tragedy serves as an important precedent for Bataille and his successors. But could such an ecstatic community, which threatens to consume itself in a grandiose, albeit beautiful, gesture of self-immolation, be realized at a price other than that of extreme historical regression? Don't all the dangers of an *aestheticized politics*, which, for Walter Benjamin, represented the historical essence of fascism—in which, according to Benjamin (in a description strikingly reminiscent of Bataille), society experiences "its own destruction *as an aesthetic pleasure of the first order*"—return here to haunt the postmodern ideal of a "communauté désoeuvrée."[32] Later in life Bataille himself realized that his fascination with the aesthetics of violence and a politics of transgression exhibited a "paradoxical fascist tendency."[33] In "The Psychological Structure of Fascism," he had, after all, invoked the fascist experience as a paradigmatic instance of "sovereignty":

> Opposed to the democratic politicians, who represent in different countries the platitude inherent to homogeneous society, Mussolini and Hitler immediately stand out as something *other*. . . . Heterogeneous fascist action belongs to the entire set of higher forms. It makes an appeal to sentiments traditionally defined as *exalted* and *noble* and tends to constitute authority as an unconditional principle, situated above any utilitarian judgment.[34]

The second direction in which poststructuralist ethics proceeds is an anticommunitarian embrace of "an-archic" subjectivity. Here, "anarchy" is intended in the etymological sense of living without law or first principles. This model forms a striking contrast with the Greco-liberal ideal of moral autonomy, where the end of action is not law-lessness, but "giving oneself one's own law." In an important sense, with the model of an-archy, the virtues of autonomy have been exchanged for those of a-nomie, or living without law.

The politics of anarchic subjectivity is a distinct legatee of the critique of metaphysics and the antifoundationalist spirit that this critique has bequeathed. As such, it is of Heideggerian provenance, though it has divested itself of Heidegger's characteristic nostalgia for home, origin, and place. Instead, in its dominant version, it has been thoroughly imbued with a French modernist sensibility emphasizing the rather un-Heideggerian themes of play, *jouissance*, and free signification. Its uncompromising antifoundationalism is deemed the basis of thoroughgoing anti-authoritarianism. In this respect, it is fully consistent with the "ethic of negative autonomy" alluded to above. Yet, as the phrase "negative autonomy" itself suggests, there is a strange convergence between this ethic—despite its apparent radicality—and the philosophy of liberalism conceived of as a defense of the sanctity of the individual or "private sphere" vis-à-vis the heteronomous prescriptions of state authority (though, of course, the vocabulary of modern natural law is quite foreign to it; and it is usually a decentered, disunified "self" that is privileged).

In its most radical, Foucauldian articulation, the politics of anarchic subjectivity is not only anti-authoritarian, it is also rigorously *anti–institutional*: it perpetually seeks to dissolve the grounds, principles, and conventions by virtue of which we find ourselves constituted as social selves. The critique of order "is directed not against some particular order (such as late capitalist order) but against order *as* order, i.e., as a system of exclusions as such." Yet, "when the attack on order *as* order becomes universal, it is no longer directed at any particular; i.e., the targets of the attack become indifferent and interchangeable."[35] Freedom is thus comprehended after the model of Heidegger's groundless ground (*Ab-grund*), Derridean *différance*, Lacanian dehiscence, or Foucauldian resistance. It "is something asocial which cannot be instituted or guaranteed. . . . Our real freedom is found in dissolving or changing the polities that embody our nature, and as such it is *asocial* or *anarchical*."[36] Or, as a like-minded thinker, writing in a more Derridean vein, has phrased it: the politics of anarchic subjectivity implies that "power has no intrinsic purpose, that playfully reaching ever new social constellations is an end in itself; that its essence is boundless interplay without a direction imposed by central authority."[37] Hence, if one focuses on the anti-authoritarian disposition of an-archic subjectivity, its paradoxical affinities with the liberal ideal of "negative freedom" or "freedom from" are profound.

But, then, too the limitations of the idea of "freedom as anarchy" would be similar to those of the liberal view of freedom as "negative freedom." For this conception of freedom would seem to preclude—or, at the very least, it would significantly minimize—the values of human solidarity: forging and maintaining the goals of an intersubjective human community. Instead, when the strictures of negative or anarchic freedom are doggedly pursued, then political decisions or goals that have been collectively mandated will be perceived not as the true realization of my freedom (as in Rousseau's nonliberal, protocommunitarian conception), but as a heteronomously imposed fetter on my capacity for self-expression. It seems that in both the liberal and anarchic models, an a priori antagonism is established between the values of the individual and those of society: the latter can never serve as a vehicle and means for my self-fulfillment or self-realization. The resultant notion of politics would be curiously nonparticipatory. Civic virtue would cease to be "virtuous." Instead, there is a profound risk that the political sphere, as an arena of collective action, law, and institutions, would appear as a sphere of "inauthenticity"—as it was qua "publicness" for the early Heidegger.

Moreover, the question arises as to whether an image of freedom that is purely negative or anarchic could be truly meaningful. In this respect, it would be essential to distinguish freedom from mere willfulness or arbitrariness. For it seems that what makes our freedom intrinsically valuable is a certain *lack* of arbitrariness; that is, the fact that it is based on a quasi-coherent, nonrandom set of self-chosen principles, values, and norms. Such principles, values, and norms must be perceived not as the antithesis of our capacity for free action but as its subject matter or content. Thus, in a fundamental sense, we would consider a life that is characterized by nonteleological randomness—though it might nominally be "free"—as ethically impoverished. For as directionless, as a species of "boundless interplay without direction," it would be devoid of those elements of continuity, solidarity, and substance that first make freedom—and human life itself—meaningful. In the context at hand, therefore, everything depends on our capacity to distinguish freedom from anomie or gratuitous social deviance.

Lyotard has attempted to address the dilemma of poststructuralism and ethics in his theory of "language games," which is in part taken over from the work of the later Wittgenstein. The logic of the "differend" suggests that the differences among language games are so extreme that, in the last analysis, their various claims to "right" are incommensurable, undecidable. For Lyotard, justice is attained by allowing the multiplicity of language games to subsist in their various states of difference, that is, by our refusal to totalize them according to a repressive logic of consensus. In this way, argues Lyotard, the values of pluralism are best served. So are the agonistic ends that Lyotard views as being intrinsic to language qua expression. "To speak is to fight," argues Lyotard, but "this does not necessarily mean that one plays in order to win. A move can be made for the sheer pleasure of invention. . . . Great joy is had in the endless invention of turns of phrase."[38] Here, as well as in Lyotard's partisanship for the sublime, the poststructuralist predilection for basing ethics on aesthetics is evident.

Among poststructuralist thinkers, it is undoubtedly Lyotard who has been most conscientious and thorough regarding questions of ethical grounding. Since the late 1970s the theme of a viable post-totalitarian ethic has occupied center stage in his work. Yet, there remain many problematical aspects of his quasi-Wittgensteinian attempt to base ethics on the incommensurability of language games. The de facto avowal that all language games are equally valid represents a potential abnegation of the demands of moral judgment. By virtue of our historical experiences and considered convictions, aren't we driven to say that certain language games or "forms of life"—e.g., those that systematically violate the rights and dignity of human beings—are, in a far from trivial sense, immoral and unjust? Lyotard is concerned about the dangers of backsliding in the direction of the "metanarrative" of modern natural law or human rights. Yet, for want of a more developed set of ethical criteria or principles, aren't we potentially left with a flabby egalitarianism, an impotent pluralism? For if all standpoints are deemed equally valid, we seem bereft of a basis for making significant moral and intellectual judgments; the specter of incommensurability threatens, as it were, to paralyze our judgmental capacity.

Lyotard's error derives from his inability—or unwillingness—to differentiate between *warranted* standards or criteria and ones that are unwarranted. As a result, he proceeds according to the mistaken conviction that *all* standards or criteria are potentially terroristic, totalitarian. In the last analysis, his attempt to salvage a workable criterion of justice in terms of the equality of all language games falls victim to a performative contradiction: if all language games are indeed equal, on what basis can we make *justice* stand out as the privileged arbiter among them? Why follow *its* presumptions and dictates if it is, in truth, merely one more language game among others? Lyotard cannot have it both ways: he cannot privilege "justice" without in fact endowing it with a certain quasi-foundational, metalinguistic status; that is, without turning it into precisely the ground or "metanarrative" he is seeking at all costs to avoid. (The same criticism would hold true for Lyotard's discussion of "paralogy," or "the endless invention of new turns of phrase," as a metalinguistic precept that should ideally govern all language games. Aside from its problematical vitalist implications—which flirt with the aforementioned "aesthetic modernist gesture of forgetting the victim so long as the gesture is beautiful"—here, too, Lyotard's argument ends up clashing with his own cherished premises, insofar as he seeks to provide a criterion for adjudicating the "health" or "vitality" of language games that is context-transcendent.)

Finally, despite Lyotard's partisanship for the values of play and paralogy, there is a potentially conservative dimension to his emphasis on the entirely discrete character of linguistic context or forms of life. For if all language games are ultimately self-referential, if validity claims are exclusively contextual (now that the demise of metanarratives has been proclaimed), doesn't the important distinction between "power" and "validity" threaten to evaporate? When the meta-ethical centrality of adjudicating validity claims—that is, the vocabulary of normative rightness or legitimacy—is discounted, contexts become "contexts of domination" and thus potentially self-perpetuating. Were one to cede such inordinate power to context, then the moment of validity would become irretrievably subsumed by the claims of power: that is, with the meanings that are dominant in a given context. This problem merely points to one of the more general dilemmas of poststructuralist ethics. For once it is denied that ethics should be understood primarily in *cognitive* terms—that is, in terms of the discursive redemption of validity claims—one has no other choice than to fall back upon a "view that regards language as an *evocative* medium, in which validity and force, reasoned belief and manipulated opinion, can no longer be distinguished."[39] This is essentially the (cynical) conclusion that Lyotard himself reaches when he observes: "We judge without criteria. We are in the position of Aristotle's prudent individual, who makes judgments about the just and unjust without the least criterion. . . . [The ability to judge] bears a name within a certain philosophical tradition, namely, Nietzsche's: the will to power."[40]

But here we find ourselves on the precarious terrain of an ethical transvaluation that must be forsworn. For according to this recommendation—and following Nietzsche—it is no longer the discourse of moral legitimacy that determines the scope and prerogatives of power, but power itself that determines the scope and prerogatives of legitimacy. The relation between might and right has been reversed, morality and expediency become indistinguishable. The context-shattering power of validity claims is broken. Instead of being tied to the force of the better argument, justice is reduced to "agonistics" (or rhetoric); force (or paralogy) is all there is. The power to convince is, in a Nietzschean spirit, deemed an instance of *sheer power*; agreement based on validity is merely a subterfuge for vested social interests. And thus, "It is not the supposed truth, but the powerfulness (understood completely in a vital, life-conserving and life-intensifying sense), the *force* of an argument that determines its possible truth."[41] As a salutary contrast to the new contextualism (Lyotard characterizes his standpoint as that of a "local determinism"),[42] one might invoke the "transcendent moment of universal validity [which] bursts every provinciality asunder."[43]

In an early essay, Walter Benjamin observes that "there is a sphere of human agreement that is nonviolent to the extent that it is wholly inaccessible to violence: the proper sphere of 'understanding,' language."[44] However, as Benjamin knew, the realization of this nonviolent linguistic utopia, this "kingdom of ends," is barred to us in the here and now insofar as we simultaneously inhabit the sphere of empirical contingency, the "phenomenal realm." Still, the avowal of such a sphere as a type of regulative ideal alone prevents social interaction in the immediate present from succumbing to an irredeemable, self-perpetuating cycle of power and violence, in which *force* becomes the sole guarantor of *right*. Thus, according to Benjamin, in the realm of human affairs, "a gaze directed only at what is close at hand can at most perceive a dialectical rising and falling in the lawmaking and law-preserving formations of violence."[45] This dialectic corresponds to a cycle of mythical violence qua fate. It exemplifies the rule of *mere life* over the *just life*. For Benjamin, it is a cycle that must be broken. Only in this way can humanity be redeemed from the arbitrary injustice of myth qua fate. The breach occurs when the ideal, purifying powers of justice intervene amid the benumbing, fatalistic routine of mere life.

As a philosopher of redemption, the early Benjamin still interprets this intervention theologically. For him, it is tantamount to divine intervention, which manifests itself in the form of an expiatory "divine violence." Divine violence can even serve to underwrite (Sorelian) revolutionary violence, which—although it is "not visible [i.e., comprehensible] to men"—is "the highest manifestation of unalloyed violence by man."[46]

Today, however, we know this route is blocked to us. The "sovereign" expiatory violence on which Benjamin placed his hopes constitutes a regression to an "ethic of ultimate ends." We know that the interventions of justice can neither emanate from an otherworldly source nor from the privileged standpoint of a nonfalsifiable philosophy of history. Instead, they must be legitimated immanently and democratically in a process of discursive will formation: by the mutual approbation and consent of those potentially affected by a given norm. Such ends are achieved via language as a medium of human intersubjectivity. Yet, far from being a-historical and disembodied, "processes of mutual understanding" are always rooted in determinate forms of life, cultural contexts, and diachronic sequences. They are, as it were, *saturated with historicity*. Only the strictest attention to the historical determinacy of these processes can determine the point of departure for cultural criticism as *immanent criticism*. In this way, societal norms that have congealed into immovable and unreflected *faits sociaux*—repositories of socially superfluous domination—stand a chance of being linguistically, intersubjectively redeemed. Language is not only, or even primarily, a mechanism of semiological slippage and semantic subterfuge (although it is certainly that too). It is also that sphere in which unconscious human experiences that have come to assume the repressive force of a blind and unmastered "second nature" can first be brought to conscious articulation. In this sense, the idea of the linguistic redemption of validity claims and the "transcendent moment of universal validity" that underlies it—harbors a modest utopian vision according to which illegitimate relations of authority, domination, and force will be replaced by those of human mutuality. To acknowledge our lot in these terms means to credit the profane illuminations of language with the power to defetishize a reified social world and to reforge relations of solidarity and trust among women and men.

PART I

The Legacy of the Frankfurt School

ONE

Critical Theory and the Dialectic of Rationalism

I

The problem of a viable normative foundation for Critical Theory has been at the heart of contemporary debates concerning the legacy of the Frankfurt School. No one has explored this problematic with more tenacity than Jürgen Habermas. First in *Knowledge and Human Interests* (1968) and then in *The Theory of Communicative Action* (1981), the ethical basis of the Marxist tradition has been analyzed with meticulous precision. While acknowledging the significance of Habermas' achievements in this regard, it would be duplicitous not to recognize the idiosyncrasies of his own account of Critical Theory's attempts to grapple with the problems of normative grounding. Unlike Marx, whom Habermas correctly identifies as having objectivistically falsified epistemological problems by collapsing the types of human action under the category of labor, the Critical Theorists showed themselves to be methodologically self-conscious. They were well aware of the contemporary lack of self-evidence when it came to resolving epistemological questions. Although the bulk of their writings could not be described as metatheoretical, all phases of their theoretical development display an implicit awareness of and concern for questions of methodological foundations.

In *Knowledge and Human Interests*, explicit references to the Critical Theory tradition are remarkably scant. In *The Theory of Communicative Action* I, Habermas apparently remedies this injustice by including a chapter entitled "From Lukács to Adorno: Rationalization as Reification." However, the results are somewhat disappointing. We are left with more of an abstract dismissal of Critical Theory than a dialectical *Aufhebung*. The legacy of the Frankfurt School appears to be cursorily rejected for remaining imprisoned within the epistemological paradigm of the philosophy of consciousness; that is, a philosophical tradition inaugurated by Descartes that conceives of human action primarily in terms of individual speaking and acting subjects. Missing in this approach, according to Habermas, is the dimension of intersubjectivity, a realm that comes to the fore only when it is recognized that social identities are first constituted by shared linguistic paradigms, their intersubjective fundament, as it were.

Yet his assimilation of the first generation of Critical Theorists to the aforementioned Cartesian frame of reference—that of a philosophy of consciousness—is potentially misleading. Instead, it is clear that their approach has its origins in a Hegelian-Marxist framework emphasizing the methodological primacy of "objective spirit" rather than that of a purportedly free-floating, subjective, individual consciousness. In truth, much of the early work of Critical Theory consisted of laying bare the pseudo-independence of bourgeois thought by showing its rootedness in social being. All of the critical theorists were resolute critics of the illusory purity and autonomy of "bourgeois interiority" (the "model" study in this regard was undoubtedly Adorno's 1931 Kierkegaard book).[1] Consequently, whatever the independent merits of Habermas' own communicative approach to ethics (a question to which we shall turn in conclusion), when it is brought abstractly to bear on the efforts of his Frankfurt School progenitors, the result risks obscuring the thematic richness and complexity of their various theoretical projects. We turn now to a more precise consideration of their attempts to address the question of a normative basis for theory—a reappraisal of the merits of their approach, but also of its inadequacies.

II

Both early and recent commentators on Critical Theory have identified the central problem of the Institute for Social Research in the 1930s as the attempt to come to grips with the nonrevolutionary nature of the European proletariat. Thus, in Germany, the working classes seemed to carry the

Marxian notion of false consciousness to a new extreme by supporting the fascist right in numbers that were far from insignificant.[2] Already with Horkheimer's accession to the directorship in 1930, the precedent was set for a more theoretical, less narrowly empirical course of research.[3] This was a trend that would only be accentuated by the inclusion of two philosophically trained intellectuals—Herbert Marcuse and Theodor Adorno—who, along with sociologist of literature Leo Lowenthal and political economist Friedrich Pollock, came to constitute the "inner circle" of the Institute during the 1930s. Yet the "philosophical turn" of the Institute in the 1930s (especially in comparison to the *ouvrièriste* orientation during the Grünberg years) was itself a product of objective conditions. For it was the eclipse of the proletariat as a revolutionary class—a notion that served as the linchpin for the first generation of Western Marxists, Lukács, Korsch, and Gramsci—that compelled the Institute for Social Research to seek a normative basis for theory elsewhere. It had become clear that vastly altered sociohistorical and political conditions—well summarized by Horkheimer in his seminal 1940 essay on the "Authoritarian State"—had rendered the Lukácsian distinction between "empirical" and "ascribed" class consciousness obsolete. Consequently, the twofold task of Critical Theory since the inception of the *Zeitschrift für Sozialforschung* in 1932 became: 1) to account for the psychological/cultural integration of the proletariat under changed historical circumstances, an effort which resulted in a revision, profoundly indebted to Freud, of the reification thesis of *History and Class Consciousness*; and 2) the attempt to salvage a normative foundation for theory, critique, and the praxis of an "imaginary future witness," in light of the obsolescence of Marx's theory of the proletariat as a "universal class."

The ensuing discussion will concentrate on the latter of these two strategies. Certainly, the preceding description of Critical Theory's basic developmental tendencies in the 1930s contains little that is startling or unique. Similar accounts been suggested both by Martin Jay in his classical history of the Frankfurt School[4] and by Michael Löwy in an essay on "Le Marxisme rationaliste de l'école Frankfort."[5] Yet what seems lacking in the foregoing and other accounts of Critical Theory's "rationalist turn" is: 1) a sense of the commitment of certain Institute members to philosophical reason as a new normative ideal (in the case of Marcuse, such tendencies persist through the 1960s); and 2) the degree to which this partisanship conflicts with another major tendency of Critical Theory: a predisposition to view the tradition of western rationalism itself as having sown the seeds of modern political despotism.

One may date the "rationalist turn" in Critical Theory circa 1937—an auspicious year, in which both Horkheimer's programmatic essay "Traditional and Critical Theory" appeared along with an essay by Marcuse titled "Philosophy and Critical Theory." Previously, the attitude of the Institute toward metaphysics, as well as toward "bourgeois philosophy" as a whole, had been critical in a dialectical/Lukácsian vein: metaphysical problems—the Kantian thing-in-itself, the mind/body dichotomy, and so forth—raised a host of fascinating questions concerning the fundamental contradictions of bourgeois society, though they typically masked the social origins of these contradictions, either by portraying them as immutable aspects of the "human condition" (e.g., Kant and *Existenzphilosophie*), or by reconciling them via illusory, speculative philosophical harmonies (Hegel, Husserl). In the last analysis, both philosophical practices were viewed as detracting from the concrete, immanent prospects of rectifying ongoing social antagonisms. Hence, Critical Theory's relation to the philosophical tradition, though far from purely dismissive, was heavily indebted to the Marxist notion of ideology-critique, in which the autonomous contents of philosophical reflection are minimized in view of the moment of their historical determination. Only in this sense, as a type of false consciousness from which one can nevertheless learn, did metaphysics remain of interest.

Typical of such attitudes are the following insights from Horkheimer's essay, "The Latest Attack on Metaphysics" (1937):

> Metaphysics claims to apprehend being, to grasp totality, and to lay bare by means of cognitive methods available to every man a meaning of the world independent of man. From the inner structure of reality, it derives precepts for the conduct of life; for example, the dictum that man's most fitting and worthy activity is to occupy himself with supreme ideas, the transcendental or the primary cause. As a rule, metaphysical theories harmonize with the belief that hardship is an eternal necessity for the great majority of men and that the individual must always surrender himself to the designs of the powers that be. Metaphysics bases this belief not on the Bible, but on allegedly indubitable insights.[6]

Yet, already in "Traditional and Critical Theory," signs of a transformed relation to the Western philosophical tradition were apparent. This change in perspective was attributable not only to the retrograde character of the current political situation, but also to the fact that reason itself seemed increasingly jeopardized given the prevalence of a positivist intellectual methodologies that reduced theory to a process of registering and classifying "facts." Hence, the autonomous capacity of theoretical insight that had been emphasized in Lukács' profoundly Hegelian reading of Marx—that is, theory's capacity to conceptually mediate the given, rather than to adapt passively to it—had been all but occluded by new forms of knowledge ("traditional theory") that cheerfully accepted their own integration within the reigning social division of labor.

To be sure, "Traditional and Critical Theory" stopped short of drawing the conclusion that Western rationalism had become a new touchstone of progressive theoretical insight. Instead, one finds there the more or less standard Frankfurt School criticisms of bourgeois idealism: criticisms of its merely contemplative character, its ready acceptance of philosophical dualism, and, perhaps most importantly, its hypostatization of the highest value ideals—freedom, justice, and beauty—as residing in the sphere of *Innerlichkeit* or "bourgeois inwardness," values that were deemed matters of private consolation, never to be realized in society writ large. Yet, in many respects, "Traditional and Critical Theory" serves as a crucial anticipation of the subsequent claim that philosophical rationalism might serve as basis for the renewal of critique.

The argument proceeds roughly as follows. Under no circumstances can theory present itself as the direct and unmediated expression of the consciousness of the oppressed. On the contrary, its tasks are always anticipatory and projective. Yet, in the late 1930s, the lack of objective possibilities for social emancipation affected Critical Theory's very raison d'être. The question that Horkheimer et al. were forced to address was: whither Critical Theory in an era where objective prospects for radical change had become all but chimerical? The Frankfurt School thus represented the first generation of critical theorists who were forced to grapple with the problem of not merely a temporary setback for "class struggle," but, in effect, the prospect of its permanent eclipse. This eclipse was understood as a logical consequence of the emergence of three historically new social formations: 1) bureaucratic socialism, 2) authoritarian statism (fascism), and 3) New Deal state capitalism; all of which combined to seal off all imminent (and immanent) prospects of social emancipation.[7]

In "Traditional and Critical Theory," therefore, one detects the onset of the *Flaschenpost* ("message in a bottle") mentality that would become the signature of Critical Theory's labors in ensuing decades. In the absence of contemporary historical addressees, the insights of Critical Theory were destined to be received, if at all, by an "imaginary future witness." Horkheimer explicitly differentiates critical from traditional theory on the basis of the former's partisanship for a "rational organization of society" now that "the situation of the proletariat is no guarantee of correct knowledge."[8] Since the critical theorists could no longer sustain a claim to being "organic intellectuals," they needed not only to find a different normative basis for critique; they also needed to legitimate this new standard in terms that were sufficiently distinct from those subjective "bourgeois ideals" that had previously been little more than a privileged target of criticism. Certainly, the recourse to the category of Reason—with all its manifest Hegelian resonances—represented for Critical Theory a significant reevaluation of the legacy and import of Western philosophy. Yet Engels had (however crudely) once described the proletariat as the "heir of classical German philosophy"; and in the wake of *History and Class Consciousness*—whose seminal influence on the first generation of Frankfurt School theorists is a matter of record—the essential links between Marx and the Hegelian tradition need hardly be emphasized. Consequently, there is some justification in suggesting that the renewed emphasis on the philosophical antecedents of the materialist tradition was in many ways already implicit in that tradition itself. After all, it was the young Marx who spoke vigorously of the need to "realize philosophy." Even the later Marx still talked about the "rational kernel" of the Hegelian dialectic and its continued methodological importance to him.[9]

The "Flaschenpost" motif became increasingly prominent once the necessary link between theory and praxis had dissolved, and the goal of "changing the world" had itself been postponed until an unforeseeable future date. Horkheimer claims that

> under the conditions of late capitalism and the impotence of the workers before the authoritarian state's apparatus of oppression, truth has sought refuge among small groups of admirable men. . . . History teaches us that such groups, hardly noticed even by those opposed to the status quo, outlawed but imperturbable, may at the decisive moment become the leaders because of their deeper insight.[10]

The wager on Critical Theory's future as a potential revolutionary avant-garde seems both self-serving and grandiose. But it is this conception of Critical Theory as a refuge of truth in an era in which the objective social situation had repulsed the "true" by failing to "realize philosophy" that increasingly defined its self-understanding.

A more systematic attempt to define Critical Theory's relation to the western philosophical tradition was made later the same year by Marcuse in "Philosophy and Critical Theory." Marcuse, too, was cautious about a precipitate identification of Critical Theory with philosophy. And thus, no matter how much the two might be alleged to have in common, he was equally interested in pointing out their differences. To begin with, it was still assumed that ultimately philosophy would have to be surpassed in the direction of "Critical Theory"—a term that in the 1930s had become a euphemism for critical Marxism. The transcendence of philosophy was to be modeled upon Marx's own transformation in the 1840s from young Hegelian to historical materialist. Insofar as pure philosophy failed to understand the role of "material factors" in the history of human development—the division of labor, the dialectic of forces and relations of production, capital, etc.—its attempts at social analysis (such as Hegel's idealistically skewed attempt in the *Philosophy of Right* to understand the relationship between "civil society" and the "state") were bound to fly wide of the mark.

But Marcuse did not wish to imply that Critical Theory and orthodox Marxism were equivalents. Instead, he was quick to suggest that, when viewed from a materialist standpoint, economic concepts possessed a different status than they would from the perspective of political economy: to this extent, they were also philosophical categories.[11] In this way Marcuse sought to reemphasize a crucial aspect of the original historical relationship between Marxism and philosophy: the task of materialist praxis was to facilitate the *realization* of the ideals that had been established by the philosophical tradition; that is, to bring about the reconciliation between the "real" and the "rational," a reconciliation that idealism (Hegel) could only invoke abstractly insofar as it habitually conflated "objectification" (praxis) with "alienation"—and on this basis shunned praxis. As Marcuse observes: "When reason has been realized as the rational organization of mankind, philosophy is left without an object. For philosophy, to the extent that it has been, up to the present, more than an occupation or a discipline within the given division of labor, has drawn its life from reason's not yet being reality."[12]

This renewed emphasis on the essential relationship between Critical Theory and philosophy—which had already been rethematized by Horkheimer, following the lead of the early Marx—suggests a need to reexamine Critical Theory's relationship to "identity theory" or the subject-object nexus. For it has often been said that the crucial difference between Critical Theory and its Hegelian Marxist forebears (such as Lukács and Korsch) pertains to the Frankfurt School's putative renunciation of identity theory. Perhaps this point has been stated most forcefully by Martin Jay, who observes:

> In repudiating identity-theory, Horkheimer was also implicitly criticizing its reappearance in Lukács' *History and Class Consciousness*. To Lukács the proletariat functioned as both the subject and object of history, thus fulfilling the classical German idealist goal of uniting freedom as an objective reality and as something produced by man himself. . . . To Horkheimer all absolutes, all identity theories were suspect.[13]

Now there was certainly one aspect of identity theory that was rejected by Horkheimer—the Hegelian idea that nature was merely "spirit" in the guise of "otherness." But this was a position that had also been vigorously rejected by Lukács, who proceeded on the basis of Vico's verum-factum principle (we can know history and not nature insofar as we have created the former but not the latter). In this respect Western Marxism was at odds with Marx, who, in phrases such as "the humanization of nature and the naturalization of man," in his discussion of nature as man's "inorganic body," and in his celebration of the elevating powers of human labor vis-à-vis unformed, brute nature, maintained greater allegiances to the Hegelian conception of identity (and in this respect Marx was very much influenced by the romantic tradition).[14] Yet, since both Lukács and early Critical Theory espoused varieties of praxis-philosophy, their theories suggested that the "realization of reason," which would facilitate an identity or congruence between the ideal and the real, was a desirable historical goal. It became the responsibility of praxis to transpose philosophical ideals to the domain of human practical life, thereby facilitating a reconciliation—or identity—between these two terms, which had heretofore been opposed. This reconciliation would yield a situation—and on this score, none of the Western Marxists seemed to be in disagreement—in which, as Marcuse suggests, philosophy would be left "without an object."

When viewed from this perspective, philosophy is conceived of as a type of ersatz, sublimated gratification for the fulfillment that is denied in life itself. As Novalis expressed it: "philosophy is a longing to be at home in the world"—which implies that, for want of reconciliation (between philosophy and the world), philosophy is perennially *at odds with the world*. In Western Marxism, therefore, philosophy needs to be taken seriously, for it is only once philosophical ideals are actualized, once their ideal contents are rendered immanent or concrete, that humanity may be released from its present antagonistic condition. At the same time, there seems to be a fear that, in keeping with the motif of sublimation, if philosophy is taken *too* seriously—were it to become an end in itself—valuable human practical energies would be diverted from their ultimate aim. In this respect Paul Ricoeur has correctly identified a growing distrust of philosophical ideals in the second half of the nineteenth century in terms of the emergence of a "hermeneutic of suspicion"—a position he attributes to Nietzsche and Freud as well as Marx.[15]

A mistrust vis-à-vis self-referential philosophical ideals was a stance that Critical Theory would never relinquish. At the same time, the difficulties of breaking through the impasse of contemporary authoritarian social formations led to an important reevaluation of the meaning of such ideals for Critical Theory. Marcuse offered one of the most striking articulations of the value of autonomous philosophical principle in the opening pages of "Philosophy and Critical Theory." His thoughts are worth quoting at length:

> Reason is the fundamental category of philosophical thought, the only one by means of which it has bound itself to human destiny. Philosophy wanted to discover the ultimate and most general grounds of Being. Under the name of reason it conceived the idea of an authentic Being in which all significant antitheses (of subject and object, essence and appearance, thought and being) were reconciled. Connected with this idea was the conviction that what exists is not immediately and already rational but must rather be brought to reason. Reason represents the highest potentiality of man and of existence; the two belong together. For when reason is accorded the status of substance, this means that at its highest level, as authentic reality, the world no longer stands opposed to the rational thought of men as mere material objectivity. Rather, it is now comprehended by thought and defined as a concept [*Begriff*]. That is, the external, antithetical character of material objectivity is overcome in a process through which the identity of subject and object is established as the rational, conceptual structure that is common to both. In its structure the world is considered accessible to reason, dependent on it, and dominated by it. In this form philosophy is idealism; it subsumes being under thought. But through this first thesis that made philosophy into rationalism and idealism it became critical philosophy as well. As the given world was bound up with rational thought and, indeed, ontologically dependent on it, all that contradicted reason or was not rational was posited as something that had to be overcome.[16]

It would be difficult to find a more enthusiastic endorsement of Western rationalism in the writings of Critical Theory. Yet, in the passage just cited, it is a specific branch of philosophical rationalism that Marcuse singles out for praise: the "continental rationalism" of the seventeenth and eighteenth centuries. This tradition would encompass the doctrine of moral autonomy as elaborated in theories of modern natural right (in Rousseau and Kant;

not, however, Locke, who bases his conception of natural law on the right to property ownership); a tradition that in Marcuse's eyes culminates in Hegel's apotheosis of philosophical rationalism. Thus, for all his misgivings concerning Enlightenment, Hegel's credentials as *Aufklärer* remain secure insofar as he makes *reason* the alpha and omega of philosophical judgment. For Marcuse, Hegel—the archfoe of all positivist encroachments upon the autonomy of spirit—is the true heir of Enlightenment, inasmuch as his philosophical idealism proves the ultimate bulwark against eighteenth-century empiricism and vulgar materialism. Moreover, it is Hegel who, in the spirit of Rousseau and Kant, unfailingly associates reason with the ethical category of freedom; a rapport that culminates in his celebrated characterization of history as "progress in the consciousness of freedom."[17] In all these respects it is far from coincidental that Marcuse's major philosophical project of the 1930s was the felicitously titled Hegel study, *Reason and Revolution* (1941).

Marcuse believed that in conceptualizing the necessary relationship between reason and freedom, philosophy had advanced matters as far as they could be advanced on the plane of pure thought. The next step would be to drive these philosophical ideals from the sphere of bourgeois *Innerlichkeit* into the domain of material life itself. In Marx's words, "the weapons of criticism must become the criticism of weapons."[18] More seriously, however (and this is the foremost danger of all idealist philosophy, Hegel being a primary offender), by prematurely proclaiming the reconciliation of the "ideal" and the "real," philosophical idealism runs the risk of glorifying the historical present in its current unredeemed state. Still, insofar as it continues to take seriously the category of reason and all it entails, idealism will always remain irreducible to ideology per se. For qua idealism, philosophy contains an irreducible moment of transcendence in light of which the immediate historical present cannot help but seem wanting. As Marcuse observes: "If reason means shaping life according to men's free decision on the basis of their knowledge, the demand for reason henceforth means the creation of a social organization in which individuals collectively regulate their lives in accordance with their needs."[19]

The idealist tenor of philosophy has always seemed a mixed virtue. On the one hand, philosophy's separation from the sphere of material life endows it with an otherworldly character. Yet it is that very otherworldliness which, by surpassing the given, promotes a utopian dimension that has historically always gone hand in hand with authentic philosophizing.[20] Since Critical Theory seeks to indict the established social order on the basis of latent possibilities and tendencies that are often imperceptible from the vantage point of the average socially integrated consciousness, its standpoint betrays a certain quixotic character. Especially in "dark times" when authoritarian social formations have the upper hand, all truth that surmounts the socially dominant consensus will inevitably seem out of synch vis-à-vis reigning societal norms. In such historical periods, it could turn out that a social theory that is "abstract" and out of step with the times will also be the most "true." "This abstractness, this radical withdrawal from the given, at least clears a path along which the individual in bourgeois society can seek the truth and adhere to what is known," remarks Marcuse.[21] "Critical Theory's interest in the liberation of mankind binds it with certain ancient truths," he comments elsewhere. "It is at one with philosophy in maintaining that man can be more than a manipulable subject in the production process of class society."[22]

At the end of "Philosophy and Critical Theory," Marcuse invokes a concept that would play a paramount role in his work of the 1950s and 1960s, one which provides indispensable theoretical leverage for the purposes of critique: the *imagination*. He argues that under present historical circumstances the imagination plays a role that is akin to that of philosophy: it contravenes the narrow dictates of the reigning reality principle and thereby holds out prospects for a qualitatively different future. By virtue of its capacity to take the materials with which it is provided in the here and now and refashion them according to the autonomous demands of spirit, the imagination serves as a harbinger of an emancipated sensibility. Insofar as it is able to represent for the intellect an object that is not physically present, the imagination displays an anticipatory capacity, a fierce independence vis-à-vis the empirical given in its prosaic immediacy. In the context of an inverted social world in which *social* relations exist between objects and *material* relations exist between persons (Marx's definition of commodity fetishism), the imagination's partisanship for "appearance" over "reality" functions on behalf of humanity's need for a form of truth that transcends the contemporary universe of discourse. Marcuse's spirited endorsement of the reality-negating force of the imagination presages the inordinate emphasis that Critical Theory would place in later years on the "aesthetic dimension" as an indispensable locus of critical transcendence. Marcuse insisted repeatedly that the faculty of the imagination is central to the tasks of authentic philosophy: "Without the imagination, all philosophical knowledge remains in the grip of the present or the past, severed from the future, which is the only link between philosophy and the real history of mankind."[23]

III

In two texts from the 1940s, "The Social Function of Philosophy" and *The Eclipse of Reason*, Horkheimer forcefully reiterates the thesis that, in lieu of any immanent prospects of social transformation, preserving the critical potentials of philosophy has become an essential goal of Critical Theory. It is of more than passing interest to note that Horkheimer, in seeking to vindicate metaphysics, relies primarily on ancient Greek philosophy in order make his case. The philosophy of the Socratic school that occupies pride of place in his argument, insofar as in its doctrines metaphysical questions are always interwoven with ethico-political concerns. Thus, questions of truth are integrally related to the question of "the good life"; a connection that manifests itself most vividly in the Socratic dictum that "virtue is knowledge."[24] Given Critical Theory's interest in a "rational organization of society," the Greek conception of the relationship between philosophy and life-practice seemed a natural point of reference.

One of first philosophy's virtues is a consistent generality of perspective. Its perennial search for universals or "archai" proves fundamentally at odds with the modern principle of scientific specialization, by virtue of which thought relinquishes its capacity to reflect on the whole and instead compliantly occupies a preestablished niche in the social division of labor. This problem becomes especially grave in the context of a bourgeois society in which utility seems to be the raison d'être of all phenomena, thought included. In our century, speculative thought must endure pressure from two opposed camps: on the part of the philosophical vitalism or *Lebensphilosophie*; and on the part of a logical empiricist approach, whose scientistic self-understanding finds itself fully at home in the Weberian iron cage of "specialists without spirit, sensualists without heart."

Horkheimer turns to the Socratic school insofar as "ever since the trial of Socrates, it has been clear that [philosophers] have a strained relationship with reality as it is, and especially with the community in which they live."[25] Because of its inherently antitraditional, reflexive tenor, philosophy often finds itself at odds with the reigning powers. It refuses to accept societal norms and decrees merely because "custom" (*nomos*) says that they must be accepted. It is impelled to legitimate all received truths before the tribunal of principle or what is right "by nature" (*physis*). Hence the principle of conscience has become indissociable from the notion of the philosophical life, from Socrates' *daimonion* to Kant's doctrine of moral autonomy.[26] Philosophy sets the claims of rationally grounded individual insight in opposition to the stifling drive toward social conformity characteristic of regimes of unfreedom. To this end, philosophers have founded academies and lycea as enclaves of free thought in the midst heteronomous social milieus—an institutional parallel with which the Institute for Social Research clearly identified. This situation has changed radically in the contemporary period, where links between the academy and outside material interests have become increasingly prevalent.[27] Following Horkheimer, one might say that the social function of philosophy has always been an ideological-critical one: it has always called attention to the hiatus between the proclamations of the established order and the underlying truth of *die Sache selbst* or the matter at hand. Its intellectual mission has been to identify "rationality deficits" of the reigning sociopolitical order. Or, as Horkheimer phrases it, in what might be taken as the watchword of a critical theory of society: "The real social function of philosophy lies in its criticism of what is prevalent" with an eye toward the goal of a "rational organization of human existence."[28]

It thus falls due to philosophy to stake claims of greater generality vis-à-vis the sheer particularism of reigning social interests; even though, in doing so, its claims often appear as outlandish and idiosyncratic. Here, the Parmenidean origins of the Socratic school prove exemplary. Socrates' search for the universal principle that alone will allow an individual definition to cohere, his disdain of the one-sidedness and partiality of particularistic definitions (e.g., Laches' definition of courage as "never running away in battle"), is a Parmenidean inheritance which in turn becomes the hallmark of the Platonic dialectic in its search for the "one," the unity in diversity, by virtue of which the "many" properties of a thing become comprehensible.

In view of the seriousness with which Critical Theory took Marx's dictum concerning the need to realize philosophy, it will perhaps come as little surprise that Horkheimer expresses sympathy for one of Plato's more tendentious doctrines, the theory of philosopher-kings. "For Plato, philosophy meant the tendency to bring and maintain the various energies and branches of knowledge in a unity which would transform these partially destructive elements into productive ones in the fullest sense," observes Horkheimer.[29] Thus, when understood metaphorically, the maxim concerning philosopher-kings implies that reality will only be fully rational when it is informed and guided by the spirit of philosophical insight: "Philosophy is the methodical and steadfast attempt to bring reason into the world," remarks Horkheimer.[30] It is this spirit that motivates the Socratic quest for morality, the Platonic inquiry concerning justice, and the Aristotelian search for the good life. Consequently, Socrates' momentous confrontation with the Sophists must be understood as an intercession against self-interest and on behalf of rational principle as an appropriate basis for ethical conduct.

Horkheimer concludes "The Social Function of Philosophy" in a more contemporary spirit by invoking the Enlightenment as a model instance of the successful alliance between philosophy and politics. In the struggle of the bourgeois class vis-à-vis the ancien régime, philosophy was actually realized, argues Horkheimer. To be sure, it has often been said with the *philosophes* in mind that the French Revolution was accomplished in thought before it was accomplished in reality (e.g., disapprovingly by Tocqueville in *The Old Regime and the Revolution*); a claim, of course, that should not be misconstrued as implying that once the revolution in thought was made, the Revolution itself was a forgone conclusion. What is perhaps most striking about Horkheimer's conclusion, however, is its unqualified endorsement of Enlightenment—an endorsement well-nigh inconceivable from the standpoint of *Dialectic of the Enlightenment*, composed jointly with Adorno over the ensuing three years (1941–1944).

As we have already suggested, Critical Theory's attempt to resuscitate the legacy of philosophical rationalism can only be explained in terms of a more fundamental realignment of the Frankfurt School's theoretical energies, viz., a move away from the critique of political economy and toward a critique of instrumental reason. In the midst of an era in which authoritarian states predominated, the "stakes" for Critical Theory no longer concerned imminent prospects for progressive social change, but centered instead on the very capacity of thought itself to preserve a measure of autonomy or critical vigilance in face of a new array of heteronomous political imperatives. Since the realization of the "realm of freedom" was integrally tied to the actualization of certain traditional philosophical principles, Critical Theory's theoretical self-understanding was increasingly tied to the goal of preserving endangered universal ideals.

However, recourse to Greek philosophy, instructive as it might be, is far from unproblematical. The standard of reason established in ancient Greece cannot be reappropriated verbatim as a panacea for the failings of modernity. The Platonic ideal of divine *nous* displays an aura of unapproachability, a lack of responsiveness vis-à-vis merely human ends, that calls into question its overall value as a model. Were Horkheimer to have singled out for praise the reflexivity of the Socratic *elenchos*—a method of questioning that is the direct forebear of dialectics as "immanent critique"—or the Aristotelian view of democracy—defined as "ruling and being ruled in turn"—then perhaps the determinate affinities between the Greek beginning and the emancipatory impulses of the modern age could be viewed as logical corollaries. Horkheimer was interested in redeeming a version of metaphysics—Plato's—that was intended to provide a normative basis for the indictment of a post-Periclean Athenian society that was perceived to be in an advanced state of decline. However, what also needs to be explained is how the foremost utopia of Greek metaphysical thought—the *Republic*—could assume a character that was so radically *dystopic*. Are the more loathsome excesses of the ideal Platonic community—the banishment of the poets, the noble lie concerning the myth of the metals, the network of social castes, "eugenics"—mere excrescences, or are they necessary correlatives of Plato's metaphysics in general? Does Plato's obsessional concern with the "one" or unity to the exclusion of plurality and difference suggest a more fatal and fundamental flaw with the Parmenidean origins of his worldview?

Horkheimer himself provides an implicit answer to several of these questions in *Eclipse of Reason*:

> Great philosophical systems, such as those of Plato and Aristotle, scholasticism, and German idealism were founded on an objective theory of reason. It aimed at evolving a comprehensive system, or hierarchy, of all beings, including man and his aims. The degree of reasonableness of a man's life could be determined according to its harmony with this totality. . . . [In Plato's philosophy, the soul] reveals itself as the vision of truth or the individual subject's faculty to perceive the eternal order of things and consequently the line of action that must be followed in the temporal order. The term objective reason thus on the one hand denotes as its essence a structure inherent in reality that by itself calls for a specific mode of behavior in each specific case be it a practical or theoretical attitude.[31]

These views are representative of Horkheimer's desire, in *Eclipse of Reason* and elsewhere, to counterpose the "objective reason" of the Western metaphysical tradition to the "subjective reason" of modern scientific-technical thinking. In his view, the momentous cultural transformation that is brought about in the wake of this shift in rationality paradigms simultaneously entails a significant setback for the interests of a free humanity. Yet the shortcomings of this critical strategy must also be highlighted; for example, those evident in Horkheimer's description of the primacy of "ontological structures" in metaphysical reasoning. According to Horkheimer, such reasoning aims at "a hierarchy of all beings," and it falls due to human actors to be in "harmony with this totality." The highest vocation of the soul in Platonism is to "perceive the eternal order of things"—to which the soul must passively adapt or conform. Hence, objective reason refers to structures "inherent in reality" with which the knowing subject must simply align him or herself. Fundamentally, then, qua ontology, metaphysics promotes the primacy of a preexisting, harmonious natural order. It thus invites an attitude of compliant adaptation on the part of those individuals who have internalized that order as a behavioral code. As a species of first philosophy, ontology posits an immutable order of being. Far from there being anything intrinsically "emancipatory" about this ideal, it is a conception fully compatible with the most authoritarian and rigid forms of political life. Thus, in addition to the Parmenidean prejudices alluded to above ("unity" stifling plurality and multiplicity), Horkheimer voluntarily numbers "scholasticism"—a doctrine hardly noted for its valorization of human freedom—among the occluded and forgotten representatives of the tradition of objective reason. The Enlightenment suspicion that there exist telling affinities between systematic philosophy, intellectual dogmatism, and political unfreedom is a critique that merits further examination in this context.

The "rationalist turn" undertaken by Horkheimer and Marcuse in the 1930s and 1940s suffers from an insufficiently differentiated concept of reason. Once "objective reason," "metaphysics," and so forth are abstractly invoked as models of critical discourse, the crucial distinctions between the various different, and at times competing, conceptions of rationality are blurred. For example, with the transition from an "ontology" to "epistemology" inaugurated by Descartes, "reason" and "truth" need no longer be accepted on the basis of a spurious, supramundane claim to ontological primacy—for example, the claim that the "good" would be somehow a priori lodged in the "order of Being"; a claim to which human agents must simply submit. Instead, all truth claims and claims to right must be legitimated through the mediating agency of individual insight. The seventeenth-century shift from ontology to epistemology, therefore, displays profound affinities with the foundational values of political modernity: freedom, autonomy, and self-legislation.

Via the primacy of "spirit," Hegel tried unsuccessfully to reconcile the two philosophical traditions. With the empiricist epistemologies of Locke, Berkeley, and Hume, the autonomy of mind threatened to disintegrate amid a concatenation of sensations received from a (hypothetical) external world. Perhaps only in the ethical writings of Rousseau and Kant are the precepts of subjective autonomy preserved in a way that avoids the pitfalls of dogmatism and sensualism. In their view the conflicts of ethical life can only be resolved by an appeal to an ideal *sensus communis*—in Kant's lexicon, the community of all "rational natures." Only such approaches, which point toward the principles of intersubjectively validated agreement, might surmount the dogmatic prejudice that norms are superordinate or logically prior vis-à-vis the community of individuals immediately affected by such norms.

Horkheimer is unable to accede to such conclusions on intraconceptual grounds. In his eyes a consensus theory of truth would, in essence, be indistinguishable from the other manifestations of "subjective reason." Thus, the critique of subjective reason remains incapable of distinguishing, for example, between Kant's Copernican turn and theories of instrumental reason from Bacon to positivism. This suspicion is borne out by the Kant-critique of *Dialectic of Enlightenment*, in which the first *Critique* is interpreted as little more than as a glorification of Newtonian physics.

Ultimately, Horkheimer and Marcuse's recourse to "metaphysical reason" proves unserviceable for the role it was intended to play—that of a new "normative foundation" for a critical theory of society. To be sure, their approach manages to highlight in a highly effective way what Weber referred to as the "paradox of rationalization"—the fact that our increasing degree of instrumental mastery over the natural and social world is purchased at the cost of a "loss of freedom" and a "loss of meaning." As such, it remains a theoretical turn that is far from devoid of heuristic value. Moreover, it provides a necessary critical perspective on the history of philosophy. Via the concept of "objective reason," Horkheimer sought to hold on to a category in whose absence Critical Theory as an emancipatory enterprise seemed doomed to extinction, or, worse still, to irrelevance: the category of "totality."[32] Totality symbolized theory's capacity to view the whole. When shorn of this capacity, theory—and the praxis that supposedly followed from it—risked degenerating to the level of merely one more partial and specialized form of knowledge amid the all-encompassing social division of labor. It seemed that once the category of totality was surrendered, Critical Theory risked becoming indistinguishable from traditional theory.

In his later work, Horkheimer downplayed the normative significance of philosophical rationalism and instead attempted to view religion as a repository of repressed alternatives and possibilities.[33] Conversely, in works such as *One-Dimensional Man* (1964), Marcuse continued to emphasize the affinities between metaphysical thought and utopian politics. Thus, in a compelling discussion of "The Historical Commitment of Philosophy," he stalwartly defends the merits of "philosophical universals" in opposition to their neutralization on the part of contemporary analytical philosophy. For whereas universals—the Nation, the Party, the University are among the ones he mentions—permit insight into the social whole or totality, philosophical nominalism, which may be analytically correct in arguing that no real entities actually correspond to such inflated linguistic constructs, forswears a view of the whole. Marcuse goes on to claim that the fact that such categories actually *do* function in society as autonomous, self-actualizing wholes is indicative of the historical level of reification of existing social institutions—their unresponsiveness vis-à-vis the individuals and groups that comprise them. Or as he remarks at one point: "The real ghost is a very forcible reality."[34] But at least as important are traditional philosophical categories—Beauty, Justice, Happiness—which, although they remain uninstantiated, nevertheless testify to "a divided world, in which 'that which is' falls short of, and even denies, 'that which can be.'"[35] Here, as well as in the ensuing discussion of the Aristotelian distinction between "actuality" and "potentiality," Marcuse once again seeks to promote the utopian suggestiveness of abstract philosophical concepts: their capacity both to resist the discursive closure of the prevailing social order and to indict the latter on the basis of utopian philosophical contents. Similarly, in *Eros and Civilization* (1955), Marcuse had praised Hegel's *Phenomenology of Spirit*—"the self-interpretation of Western Civilization"—for concluding with the "Idea" and thereby remaining faithful to the emancipatory *telos* of the philosophical spirit in general:

> Western philosophy ends with the idea with which it began. At the beginning and at the end, in Aristotle and in Hegel, the supreme mode of being, the ultimate form of reason and freedom, appear as *nous*, spirit, *Geist*. . . . The repressed liberation is upheld: in the idea and in the ideal.[36]

Thus, at least in the case of Marcuse's work—and despite the shortcomings that we have already glossed—the persistence of "rationalist motifs" in Critical Theory remained keen even in the 1950s and 1960s.

IV

Our chronicle of Critical Theory's rationalist turn suggests a number of significant intellectual tensions within the inner circle of the Frankfurt School itself. Moreover, it implies that in light of the various competing epistemological conceptions embraced by the School's individual members, an attitude of healthy skepticism toward the idea of a "unified" Critical Theory would be very much in order.

The one name that has been conspicuous by its absence from the foregoing account has been that of Theodor Adorno. For among the members of the Institute's inner circle Adorno, a relative latecomer (he officially joined the Institute in 1938), alone failed to share the others' enthusiasm for the utopian kernel of philosophical rationalism. Adorno's characteristic distaste for the fundamental problems of philosophy is already unmistakable from one of his earliest philosophical writings, "The Actuality of Philosophy" (1931).[37] Walter Benjamin's influence fed his suspicions of general philosophical concepts, which tended to mask the concrete specificity of the things themselves.[38] Like Benjamin, Adorno pursued a methodological tack that might be referred to as *philosophical micrology*: a self-described "logic of disintegration" that compelled the "universal" to step forth only after thoroughgoing immersion in the particular. The saying of Aby Warburg, "Der lieber Gott wohnt in die Einzelheiten" ("Dear God dwells in details"), might have served as the motto for the lifework of both thinkers.

Though *Dialectic of Enlightenment* was allegedly jointly dictated by Horkheimer and Adorno, the work's basic theoretical inclinations seem to be overwhelmingly indebted to Adorno's influences and proclivities. In fact, its fundamental argument tended to contradict not only the Institute's previous positions on Western philosophy, metaphysics, and so forth, but also its philosophy of history, which had been, in the Marxist tradition, basically progressivist. Instead, according to the new philosophy of history proposed by *Dialectic of Enlightenment*, "progress" became tantamount to *progress in domination*: mastery of the self, extended to mastery over other persons, and then, ultimately, to the realm of "inner nature" with the "culture industry" of late capitalism. Here, too, Benjamin's notion of history as incessant process of ruination and decline, a *Verfallsgeschichte* (dramatized most vividly perhaps in his account of Paul Klee's watercolor, *Angelus Novus*, in the "Theses on the Philosophy of History") appears to have exerted a determinant influence on the thinking of Adorno and Horkheimer.[39]

The critique of the "domination of the concept" in *Dialectic of Enlightenment* evolves from the following considerations:

> Abstraction, the tool of enlightenment, treats its objects as it did fate, the notion of which it rejects: it liquidates them. . . . The universality of ideas as developed by discursive logic, domination in the conceptual sphere, is raised up on the basis of actual domination. The dissolution of the magical heritage, of the old diffuse ideas, by conceptual unity, expresses the hierarchical constitution of life determined by those who are free. The individuality that learned order and subordi-

> nation in the subjection of the world, soon wholly equated truth with the regulative thought without whose fixed distinctions universal truth cannot exist.[40]

The explanation offered by Horkheimer and Adorno for the emergence of rational thought is thoroughly disenchanted—in both the literal and figurative senses of the word. It is more suggestive of a radicalized ideology-critique of Nietzschean provenance—a "genealogy of the rational concept"—than of the Marxist tradition with which Critical Theory was earlier associated. It would be safe to say that the putative utopian potentials of the rational concept could only emerge with great difficulty from this perspective. The faculty of rational thought would appear to have more determinate links with the history of domination—over human and nonhuman nature—than with prospects for emancipation. In his later work Horkheimer seemed to retain this "negative" historico-philosophical orientation (that is, history conceived of as a history of decline), though he never attempted to work out fully the epistemological implications of the critique of reason adumbrated in *Dialectic of Enlightenment*. Instead, this task was left to Adorno, who, one might say, carried it out with a vengeance in *Negative Dialectics* and other works, where it seems that the central task of conceptual thought would be to reflect on its own inadequacies. As Adorno observes: "Reflection upon its own meaning is the way out of the concept's seeming being-in-itself as a unit of meaning. . . . Disenchantment of the concept is the antidote of philosophy. It keeps it from growing rampant and becoming an absolute unto itself."[41] But the main risk of a thought that understands its primary task as perpetual self-criticism is that it will become only further ensconced in ideational prisms of its own manufacture.

The foregoing critical reconstruction suggests that the Frankfurt School's ambivalences concerning the legacy of Western rationalism need to be taken into account to a much greater extent than has been the case heretofore. One possible interpretive strategy would be to emphasize the exceptional character of Adorno's philosophical inclinations vis-à-vis the other members of the Frankfurt School. Yet this strategy could also prove misleading. Horkheimer, after all, was co-author of *Dialectic of Enlightenment*. And if one examines Marcuse's texts more closely (for example, the masterful "Philosophical Interlude" in *Eros and Civilization*), one discovers not only praise for the "rationalist utopia" of Hegelian idealism, but also an emphatic endorsement of Nietzsche's dismantling of Western metaphysics—a Nietzsche whose "total affirmation of the life instincts . . . is the will and vision of an erotic attitude toward being for which fulfillment and necessity coincide."

As a philosopher of life, Nietzsche facilitates this erotic vision by exposing "the gigantic fallacy on which Western philosophy and morality were built—namely, the transformation of facts into essences, of historical into metaphysical conditions."[42] Here, Marcuse criticizes the mystificatory influences of "first philosophy" in a way that is virtually indistinguishable from similar criticisms to be found in Adorno's work. By echoing Nietzsche's call for a "total affirmation of the life-instincts" and an "erotic attitude toward being," Marcuse endorses an aesthetic attitude toward life, a motif that would figure prominently in many of his later writings (for example, his enthusiasm for the reconciling powers of Schiller's "play-impulse" in *An Essay on Liberation*). It also brings him into immediate proximity with the aestheticist tendencies in Adorno's work, where, similarly, the aesthetic dimension is invoked as a remedy for the pan-logistic biases of philosophical thought. But whereas Adorno's position remained relatively consistent over the years, it is unclear how Marcuse intended to reconcile his occasional flirtation with a quasi-Dionysian aesthetic vitalism and his otherwise stalwart defense of the emancipatory potential of speculative philosophy.

Habermas, the rightful heir to the Frankfurt School tradition, has of course devoted the greater part of his theoretical labors to addressing precisely the question with which our inquiry began—the question of an adequate normative foundation for Critical Theory. The original formulation of the "ideal speech situation," based on a theory of universal pragmatics, ran the risk of neglecting the objective and historical bases of communicative action in the life-process of society.[43] In response to this problem, and in perhaps his most significant reformulation of the paradigm to date, Habermas has attempted to ground this theory in the process of socialization itself.[44] Its new locus is the life-world, where, unlike the strategically oriented spheres of economy and state administration, social integration proceeds primarily via intersubjective agreement (*verständigungsorientierte Handlung*). Since social action in the life-world must be predominantly meaning- rather than goal-oriented—at issue is the formation of cohesive, meaningful social identities—one might logically look toward the sphere of the life-world as a "concrete" repository of communicative ethics, that is, a sphere where the ideal of action oriented toward mutual understanding very much serves as a type of counterfactual norm.

The shift, following the lead of Durkheim, Schütz, and Mead, in the direction of a theory of socialization in order to provide a concrete historical basis for the theory of communicative action is a promising step. However, the utopian *telos* behind the discourse ethic—the hyper-rationalist ideal of virtual communicative transparency—remains an extremely disenchanted, intellectualist utopia: one that recognizes men and women primarily in their capacities as "rational animals." Their natures as impassioned, sentient, desiring beings, who also long to satisfy a variety of eudaemonistic concerns, falls out of account in this approach.[45] In sum, the rationalist ideal of "communication free from domination" has very little to tell us about the prospects of human happiness—which, as the first generation of critical theorists realized, have long nourished the nobler utopian impulses of humankind.[46]

Habermas himself would be the first to acknowledge the limitations of a philosophical approach that exclusively aims at adjudicating the formal prerequisites of *justice*, with little interest in substantive questions concerning eudaemonia or "the good life." He realizes that the limitations of his own theory raise the very real specter of a "meaningless emancipation." Thus, in an essay on Walter Benjamin, he pertinently inquires:

> Can we preclude the possibility of a meaningless emancipation? In complex societies, emancipation means the participatory transformation of administrative decision structures. Is it possible that one day an emancipated human race could encounter itself within an expanded space of discursive formation of will and yet be robbed of the light in which it is capable of interpreting its life as something good? The revenge of a culture exploited over millennia for the legitimation of domination would then take this form: Right at the moment of overcoming age-old repressions, it would harbor no violence but it would have no content either. Without the influx of those semantic energies with which Benjamin's rescuing criticism was concerned, the structures of practical discourse—finally well established—would necessarily become desolate. . . . Benjamin's conservative-revolutionary hermeneutics, which deciphers the history of culture with a view to rescuing it for the revolutionary upheaval [*Umsturz*], may point out one path to take.[47]

With these words, Habermas provides us with an essential methodological directive for bridging the generation gap among the Frankfurt School theorists. For a utopia that is not grounded in reason would be empty, just as a reason divested of utopian longing would be joyless.

TWO

The Frankfurt School: From Interdisciplinary Materialism to Philosophy of History

> The group spoken of here was formed during the German Republic, around the Frankfurt Institute for Social Research. It cannot be said that they all had the same academic background. The director of the Institute, Max Horkheimer, is a philosopher, and his closest co-worker, Friedrich Pollock, an economist. They are joined by the psychoanalyst Fromm, the economist Grossmann, the philosopher Rottweiler [Adorno's pseudonym], who is equally a music aesthetician, the historian of literature Lowenthal, and several others. The idea in terms of which this grouping took place is that "the study of society can be developed today only in the closest possible cooperation with a number of disciplines, above all, economics, psychology, history, and philosophy."
>
> —Walter Benjamin, "An Independent German Research Institute" (1937)

The Institute for Social Research in Frankfurt was founded in 1923 by Felix Weil, whose father, Hermann, had made his fortune in the Argentinian wheat trade. It was the younger Weil's hope that the Institute's contributions to an understanding of the German workers' movement would assist in the ultimate triumph of progressive political forces in Germany. Although in its early years the Institute had many informal contacts with the as yet non-Stalinized KPD (German Communist Party), for Weil, it was equally important that the Institute, in its capacity of as a research center, maintain its independence from the vortex of contemporary Weimar politics. Its initial director, Carl Grünberg, vacated a professorship in law and political science at the University of Vienna to come to Frankfurt.[1]

Of course, what has become known to us over the years as the Institute for Social Research—the organizational seedbed of the Critical Theory of the Frankfurt School—was not the Institute of Carl Grünberg, but that of Max Horkheimer, who would succeed Grünberg as director in 1930. Nevertheless, the propitious circumstances surrounding the Institute's founding in the early 1920s is crucial for understanding the nature of the institution that Horkheimer would inherit in the early 1930s and subsequently transform into a model center of interdisciplinary research.

It is unlikely that the Institute envisioned by Felix Weil in the early 1920s could have survived, let alone prospered, in any other German city at the time, despite the generally tolerant climate of the Weimar Republic. Frankfurt, a cosmopolitan city with a long-standing reputation for liberal sympathies, thus proved the ideal site. For the sake of professional respectability and scholarly productivity, Weil wished to establish an official connection between the Institute and Frankfurt's Goethe University. Here, too, the prospects were unusually favorable. Unlike most German universities, whose charters were under direct control of the state, and thus highly restrictive, Goethe University had been privately endowed by local benefactors. This factor, coupled with the university's uniquely "modern" outlook—it was, after all, the newest of Germany's universities, having been founded in 1914—made Goethe University a bastion of progressivism amid the traditional, mandarin-conservative tenor of German university life.[2] Finally, the uninhibited atmosphere of both university and city resulted in an intellectual climate that was comparatively free of the virulent anti-Semitism that was otherwise so prominent at German universities. (To take only one example: the sociologist Georg Simmel was denied a full professorship until the age of sixty, only four years before his death in 1918). This motif takes on added importance when we realize that the Institute's so-called inner circle consisted entirely of persons of Jewish descent.[3]

If the historical conditions surrounding the Institute's founding were propitious, by the time Horkheimer took over the directorship in the early 1930s, the situation had changed drastically. In the Reichstag election of May 1928, the Nazis, with twelve seats, were the smallest party represented. In the elections of September 1929, they captured 107 seats to become the second largest party. The Great Crash in October and the world economic depression that followed seemed to all but seal the fate of the fledgling Weimar democracy. As early as 1931, the Institute prudently transferred its endowment to Holland. Shortly thereafter, it began researching possibilities for relocating abroad. After considering Paris and London, and after a brief interim period in Geneva during 1933, the Institute ultimately moved to New York where it maintained a loose affiliation with Columbia University.

On the very day of Hitler's accession to the Chancellorship—January 30, 1933—the house that Horkheimer and the Institute's administrative director, Friedrich Pollock, shared in a Frankfurt suburb was seized by Hitler's Storm Troopers. Six weeks later, the Institute itself was closed down by the Gestapo and its library confiscated.[4] Inevitably, the research program of the Institute, as formulated under Horkheimer's directorship in the early 1930s, bore the marks of Germany's transition from a democratic to a totalitarian state.

The methodological gist of this program was sketched by Horkheimer in his inaugural lecture as director, "The Present State of Social Philosophy and the Tasks of an Institute for Social Research."[5] The inaugural address represents as much a polemical confrontation with the dominant intellectual tendencies of Weimar Germany as it does an autonomous statement of methodological intention. The reasons for this strategy, however, are clear. In Horkheimer's opinion, the "schismatic" nature of contemporary German scholarship effectively militated against the possibility of fruitful interdisciplinary work. This situation needed to be overcome if philosophy and social scientific research were to be brought into a mutually beneficial symbiosis.

According to Horkheimer, German intellectual life had long been stymied by a profound mutual antagonism between the fields of philosophy and social science. For its part, philosophy was dominated by *Lebensphilosophie*, a philosophical vitalism that displayed an innate distrust of all empirical or scientifically verifiable data. *Lebensphilosophie* dismisses empiricism out of hand for being essentially "hostile to life": life is fluid, pulsating, and forever changing; "science," conversely, seeks to freeze and reduce the vitality of lived experience by accepting as "true" only that which is statistically verifiable. For Horkheimer, Martin Heidegger's fundamental ontology became the prototype of this irrationalist, antiscientific philosophical standpoint.

The social sciences, on the other hand, were dominated by a positivism that proved constitutionally blind to the central normative questions of human existence. Since all such questions defied formulation in terms of the reigning empiricist methodologies, they were in effect banished to the nonserious realm of "prescientific" speculation. Moreover, the logical positivists of the Vienna Circle had succeeded in incorporating this narrowly scientistic worldview into the discipline of philosophy itself.

To the mutual shortcomings of both approaches Horkheimer in effect replies with Immanuel Kant's well known caveat from the *Critique of Pure*

Reason: "Thoughts without content are empty, intuitions without concepts are blind."[6] That is, in Horkheimer's view, the two disciplines, philosophy and social science, are necessary mutual complements. Empirical research that proceeds without the guidance of general concepts tends to churn out a mass of disunified and meaningless data—data for data's sake. In place of a coherent and systematic account of the dominant social trends, it merely presents the increasingly unrelated results of the individual special disciplines; a practice which elevates the current state of social fragmentation to the second power, as it were. Moreover, when raised to the status of a methodological absolute, empiricism, with its uncritical reverence for the "facts," represents a de facto confirmation of the given social order in its sheer immediacy. In consequence of its asceticism regarding evaluative or normative questions, as well as its steadfast neglect of the larger trends and dynamics of social development, it ends up, like the later Hegel (albeit for different reasons) indentifying the Real with the Rational. And thus, in order to combat the self-canceling nominalism of positivist social science, Horkheimer has recourse to a category that Lukács, following the lead of Hegel and Marx, tried to reintroduce into the discourse of twentieth-century social philosophy: the category of *totality*.[7] For in Horkheimer's view, by neglecting this concept, conventional social science, which is governed by a restrictive copy theory of knowledge, remains condemned to mirror the fragmentation and crisis-ridden nature of contemporary social life. Only by virtue of being integrated into a theoretical program that keeps the standpoint of the social order *as a qualitative whole* foremost in mind can the results of empirical research be preserved from a fate of triviality and meaninglessness. In this way, Horkheimer's address articulates a critical perspective concerning the social scientific "aimless accumulation of facts" that presages the arguments of Robert Lynd's influential 1939 study, *Knowledge for What?*[8] But, at least implicitly, he is also gesturing in the direction of Max Weber's interpretive sociology (*verstehende Soziologie*), in contrast to the causal-empirical model of explanation that was so widespread in the initial decades of the twentieth century.[9]

Conversely, autonomous philosophical reflection will prove solipsistic and barren once it systematically shuns contact with the lived reality of social practice. Only when measured against the concreteness of empirical social findings will its abstract musings about the essence of "man," "society," "the individual," "human freedom," and so forth assume a meaningful cast. The *materialist* approach to knowledge that figures so prominently in almost all of Horkheimer's programmatic writings of the 1930s aims at setting limits—in the Kantian sense of dialectical criticism—to unwarranted flights of philosophical speculation. In this respect, Horkheimer attempts to reconstitute a new ideal of "social philosophy": one which, without succumbing to the methodological illusions of positivism—which threatens to turn into a new variety of "metaphysical materialism"—would be appropriate to a postmetaphysical era. Thus, both ends of the intellectual spectrum, philosophy and empirical research, must mutually inform one another if socially meaningful conclusions are to result. The predominant atmosphere of mutual distrust between these two spheres of intellectual endeavor is merely another manifestation of the present "crisis," which Horkheimer defines in terms of the vast disjuncture between society's immense technological-scientific capacity and the failure to implement this capacity in humane and benevolent terms. Or, as Horkheimer observes in 1932:

> In the general economic crisis, science proves to be one of the numerous elements within a social wealth which is not fulfilling its function. This wealth is immensely greater today than in previous eras. The world now has more raw materials, machines, and skilled workers, and better methods of production than ever before, but they are not profiting mankind as they ought. . . . Scientific knowledge in this respect shares the fate of other productive forces and means of production: its application is sharply disproportionate to its high level of development and to the real needs of mankind.[10]

In contrast, the notion of interdisciplinary materialism advanced by Horkheimer emphasized the methodological reconstruction of reality as a "concrete totality." Social facts should no longer be viewed as unalterable things-in-themselves, but in relation to the normative *telos* of a self-conscious and free humanity. In this way, the potential for social enlightenment that lay untapped in the individual sciences as currently practiced could be revivified.

The type of knowledge that fulfills such desiderata is best defined, Horkheimer explains, by the term "social philosophy." By this locution, he is not attempting to define a new academic discipline, but, instead, suggesting a potentially more productive and general approach to the understanding of advanced industrial societies with their complexities and contradictions. "Social philosophy" would thus be a type of "substantive sociology" ("*materiale Soziologie*"). On the basis of these methodological recommendations, Horkheimer seeks to foster not a new series of intellectual hierarchies, but "a constant, dialectical interpenetration and development of philosophical theory and the praxis of the individual sciences." Success will only be achieved if two conditions are satisfied: if "philosophy, whose theoretical intentions are directed toward the universal and the 'essential,' can become the animating impulse for specialized research projects; in order that [philosophy] itself might be influenced and transformed by the advances made in concrete studies."[11] On at least one crucial point, Horkheimer's program for an interdisciplinary materialism shows marked affinities with the standpoint of the early Marx: both theorists remain convinced that philosophy can only fulfill its traditional goals and promise by becoming *worldly* or *practical*. In this regard, Horkheimer would no doubt be in accord with Marx's claim in the "Theses on Feuerbach" (1845) that: "The question whether objective truth can be attributed to human thinking is not a question of theory but is a *practical* question. Man must prove the truth, that is, the reality and power, the this-sidedness of his thinking in practice. The dispute over the reality or non-reality of thinking which is isolated from practice is a purely *scholastic* question."[12] Thus, only by being reconceptualized as "social philosophy"—that is, as a critical *theory of society*—could philosophy escape the fate of becoming sheer ideology: the intellectual masking of an indigent social reality.[13]

Although Horkheimer's criticisms of the dominant intellectual paradigms are directed primarily against the failings of so-called bourgeois philosophy and social science, his remarks may be equally interpreted as an indictment of contemporary Marxist approaches to understanding society: as a critique of the "diamat" Marxism of Engels and Kautsky, according to which the economy is the ultimate instance in light of which all other social phenomena must be understood; a fully mechanistic approach to social analysis that had been recently canonized by the Marxism of the Third International. In Horkheimer's view, scientistic, unreflective Marxism was merely the poor cousin of its bourgeois counterpart, positivist social science.

It would be potentially misleading to endow Horkheimer's 1931 inaugural address—his appeal for a revamped "interdisciplinary materialism"—with too much theoretical significance. Moreover, the success of the research program advocated can of course only be judged in terms of the Institute's practical achievements during the 1930s: as exemplified by the individual studies in the *Zeitschrift für Sozialforschung* (1932–1940), as well as by its larger, collective research efforts, such as *Studies on Authority and the Family* (1936). Nevertheless, it is worthy of note that "The Present State of Social Philosophy" already contains *in nuce* the analytical distinction between "traditional and critical theory" which Horkheimer's 1937 programmatic essay of that title would make famous. As Horkheimer will contend, whereas traditional theory, based on a passive, dualistic theory of knowledge, remains content to mirror the contemporary state of social decline, Critical Theory, conversely, seeks to *actively intervene* in the process of social reproduction, for the sake of a more rational and just organization of social life. In Horkheimer's words:

> The inability to grasp in thought the unity of theory and practice [on the part of traditional theory] . . . [is] due to the Cartesian dualism of thought and being. That dualism is congenial both to nature and to bourgeois society insofar as the latter resembles a natural mechanism. The idea of a theory which becomes a genuine force, consisting in the self-awareness of the subjects of a great historical revolution, is beyond the grasp of a mentality typified by such dualism.[14]

Horkheimer's claim that the superiority of Critical Theory over traditional theory lay in its capacity to lend theoretical clarity to ongoing social struggles raises a number of important questions. Above all, one is led to inquire: *in whose name* is this process of theoretical self-clarification undertaken? Or again: what social group or groups constitute the *addressee* of Critical Theory?

For Horkheimer's precursors in the realm of socialist political theory—Lenin, Rosa Luxemburg, and even Georg Lukács—the basis of theoretical truth was unambiguous: it was the class consciousness of the proletariat. Horkheimer breaks with this tradition. Under the weight of historical circumstances, which attested to the far-reaching integration of the working classes under conditions of advanced capitalism, the criterion of truth for Critical Theory became increasingly *transcendental*—that is, it was no longer immediately identifiable with the interests or standpoint of a determinate social class or group. Despite this fact, however, the theoretical self-understanding of the Institute's inner circle in the early 1930s remained tied to the expectation of progressive historical change. Or, as Horkheimer would remark in a 1934 essay: "The value of a theory is decided by its relation to the tasks taken up at a certain point in history by society's most progressive forces. It is not immediately valuable for all humanity but in the first instance only for that group interested in these tasks."[15]

However, the residual optimism embodied in such remarks would give way circa 1935 before the realities of a triumphant European fascism. It was this eventuality, above all, that deprived Horkheimer's original program of an interdisciplinary materialism of its raison d'être and forced a fundamental reevaluation of the basic historico-philosophical premises of Critical Theory. The rigors of intellectual exile, therefore, took their toll on the theoretical standpoint of the critical theorists: in effect, they rendered obsolete the theory-practice nexus upon which the entire enterprise of early Critical Theory had been predicated.

■ ■ ■ ■ ■ ■ ■

It was in response to the triumph of fascism that the interdisciplinary research program of the Institute in the 1930s was formulated. Thus, the primary question its members sought to address in their empirical studies of this period was: what are the social conditions and forces responsible for the social integration of the German working classes and the triumph of an authoritarian social order. This question was pursued from every conceivable angle: Marcuse addressed it from the standpoint of ideological factors, e.g., the triumph of irrationalist values and theories as exemplified in thinkers such as Heidegger and Carl Schmitt ("The Struggle Against Liberalism and the Totalitarian State"); Pollock in light of the collapse of the laissez-faire economic order ("Remarks on the Economic Crisis"); Fromm in terms of the social psychology of the authoritarian character structure ("The Method and Function of Analytic Social Psychology"); Lowenthal in view of the way such developments were reflected in contemporary literary tastes and trends ("Knut Hamsun: On the Prehistory of Authoritarian Ideology"); Neumann in terms of the political sociology of the National Socialist state (*Behemoth*); Kirchheimer in light of the National Socialist legal system ("The Legal Order of National Socialism"); and Adorno in terms of the regressive cultural traits of the fascist order ("Fragments on Wagner"). In his own essays, Horkheimer often attempted to systematize and integrate the findings of the various individual studies. In this way, he sought to realize in practice the concept of an empirically grounded "social philosophy" originally outlined in his 1931 inaugural address.[16]

All of the articles referred to above (with the exception of Neumann's *Behemoth*) appeared in the Institute's literary organ, the *Zeitschrift für Sozialforschung*. Every essay published in the journal was the subject of lengthy discussions by the entire inner circle of the Institute and often underwent substantial revisions. As Martin Jay has observed, "Exhaustively evaluated and criticized by the other members of the Insitute before they appeared, many articles were almost as much collective productions as individual works."[17] Even so, many of the decisions were ultimately made by Horkheimer, who, in his 1931 address, had endorsed Grünberg's idea of "the dictatorship of the director." The Institute held regular seminars in which the individual members would present their work for criticism and discussion. As of 1936, they also held public lectures in the Extension Division of Columbia University. Until 1939, Horkheimer et al. continued to publish in German, hoping thereby to offer a counterweight—however limited in scope—to the Nazi cooptation of the German intellectual heritage. But as a result of this decision, they remained fairly isolated from their American colleagues.

A closer look at the Institute's major collective research project of the 1930s—*Studies on Authority and the Family*—will perhaps yield a more insightful picture of the way in which Horkheimer's vision of an "interdisciplinary materialism" was realized in actual practice. This volume, published in Paris in 1936, may well be viewed as an archetype of that delicate interlacing of philosophical acumen and empirical detail which the Institute strove to realize in the 1930s.

Studies on Authority and the Family was divided into three parts: "Theoretical Sketches," "Surveys," and "Individual Studies," with Horkheimer, Fromm, and Lowenthal respectively assuming editorial responsibility for each division. The general political problem the work sought to address was the increasingly important role played by the family as a conduit for the transmission of authority structures in modern Western societies, with special emphasis on the contemporary German situation.

In retrospect it is quite clear that it was the concept of "analytical social psychology" advanced by Fromm that served as the inspiration and model for the project as a whole. Fromm's theory of social psychology was developed in polemical opposition to the deterministic conception of the relationship between consciousness and society that was currently advanced by both Marxism and bourgeois social science. Economy and society never affect individual consciousness in direct and unmediated fashion, argued Fromm. Instead there exists a crucial mediating element, a *tertium quid*, through which societal influences must first pass. This mediating agency is the family. As Fromm explains in his important 1932 essay, "The Method and Function of Analytic Social Psychology":

> The first critical influences on the growing child come from the family. But the family itself, all its typical internal emotional relationships and the educational ideals it embodies, are in turn conditioned by the social and class background of the family; in short, they are conditioned by the social structure in which it is rooted. (For example, the emotional relationships between father and son are quite different in the family that is part of a bourgeois, patriarchal society than they

> are in the family that is part of a matriarchal society.) The family is the medium through which the society or the social class stamps its specific structure on the child, and hence on the adult. *The family is the psychological agency of society.*[18]

In this way, Fromm proposed a *materialist re-reading of Freud* that would prove crucial for Critical Theory's understanding of the way domination is transmitted in advanced industrial societies.[19] Despite their later differences, Marcuse's great work of the 1950s, *Eros and Civilization*, is unthinkable without the historical reinterpretation of Freud's *Trieblehre* or theory of the instincts that was initiated by Fromm. Hence, as the foregoing citation suggests, Fromm's important methodological correction of Freudian theory showed how the instincts, far from being static, biological constants, are variously realized and fulfilled under varying historical circumstances. Following the lead of Fromm's 1932 essay, much of the Institute's empirical work in the 1930s came to view the family as a type of "social cement" in terms of which the authority relations of society as a whole are solidified.

The methodology for the empirical portions of the *Studies on Authority and the Family* was originally developed by Fromm in one of the first Institute studies commissioned by Horkheimer, *The Working Class in Weimar Germany*.[20] There, Fromm contributed a major innovative advance over the traditional, static methods of social scientific data gathering. Answers by the respondents were transcribed verbatim by the interviewers and subsequently subjected to a complex interpretative analysis based on the psychoanalytic model. Thus, "certain key words or recurrent patterns of expression were interpreted as clues to the underlying psychological reality beneath the manifest content of the answers."[21]

Of the three introductory theoretical essays by Horkheimer, Fromm, and Marcuse, Fromm's was undoubtedly the linchpin and pacesetter. In it he attempts to show the importance of understanding drive theory—as elaborated by Freud in works such as *The Ego and the Id* and *Group Psychology and the Analysis of the Ego*—and thus character structure in general, as *historically conditioned.* His essay therefore embodied a type of frontal assault on Freud's theory of the Oedipus complex. In opposition to Freud's view of "biology as destiny," Fromm argues for the primacy of the social. He sets forth his main thesis in the following observations:

> The degree of fear and intimidation that small children experience is for the most part conditional upon the measure of fear that adults have vis-à-vis society. It is not primarily the biological helplessness of the small child that engenders a strong need for a super-ego and inflexible authority; the needs that are the result of

> biological helplessness can be satisfied by a non-intimidating authority-figure who is kindly disposed toward the child. Instead, it is the social helplessness of the adult that leaves its mark on the biological helplessness of the child and that allows the super-ego and authority to attain such importance in ontogenesis.[22]

With this insight, Fromm develops his theory of the sadomasochistic character type that becomes prototypical for the authoritarian personality. According to Fromm, the era of monopoly capitalism represents especially fertile soil for the proliferation of this personality type. For it promotes a social order in which the mass of men and women become increasingly dependent upon a small clique of economically powerful individuals. The result is a widespread feeling of social helplessness and the creation of nonautonomous ego identities—in essence, a social situation that is conducive to regression to a state of *Un-mündigkeit* or im-maturity. Under these circumstances, the social superego exercises a direct and unmediated influence upon the process of character formation. For the buffer of the rational ego—the "reality-testing" principle, the Socratic precept of individual moral responsibility or conscience—has essentially been done away with. This situation stands in stark contrast to the dynamics of ego formation in the laissez-faire era, where the predominance of the entrepreneurial type allowed for a significant measure of individual self-affirmation—at least for those who were fortunate enough to belong to the entrepreneurial class.

The consequences of these economic developments for family life under conditions of advanced capitalism are, according to Fromm, extremely negative. For in essence, rational paternal authority can no longer serve to deflect heteronomous social influences.[23] Consequently, the entire nature of socialization in advanced industrial societies undergoes an enormous transformation. Socialization is, with increasing frequency, accomplished by the direct and unmediated influence of predominant social institutions, resulting in the emergence of character types that are correspondingly compliant and uncritical vis-à-vis the reigning patterns of social authority.

The sadomasochistic personality dispositions forged under the socioeconomic conditions described by Fromm represent the ideal characterological building blocks for a totalitarian society. The characteristic social comportment assumed by this personality type is: *deference to superiors, contempt for inferiors*. The end result is a rigidly structured social system in which the individual members are seamlessly inserted in an all-encompassing network of hierarchical dependencies. As Fromm himself expresses this idea at one point in his contribution: "We have attempted to show that an authoritarian social structure produces and satisfies those needs which develop on the basis of sado-masochism."[24]

In face of this rather bleak portrayal of the social psychological predicament of the individual in advanced industrial societies, the only hopeful prospects gleaned by Fromm pertain to the reservoir of compassion and humanity embodied in the female character structure—what one might refer to as the "matriarchal ethos."[25] However, here, too, "character" must not be interpreted biologically. Instead, the point the Critical Theorists seek to make is that the discriminatory and prejudicial exclusion of women from the sphere of professional life simultaneously contains an unexpected benefit: they remain exempt from the prevailing logic of industrial socialization and, therefore, in a certain measure remain free of the reified personality traits of their male counterparts.

A critical glance at *Studies on Authority and the Family*, however, shows that the project was far from an unqualified success. Its shortcomings, moreover, are extremely revealing concerning the limitations of the Institute's overall efforts to realize Horkheimer's program of an interdisciplinary materialism.

The failings of the project suggest both internal and external grounds. To begin with, the empirical part of the study remained incomplete owing to the Institute's hasty departure from Germany under conditions of extreme duress. For example, only 700 of the 3,000 questionnaires distributed for Fromm's study of workers and clerical employees were ever returned. Similar problems affected other parts of the *Studies*, which were nothing if not ambitious. In addition to the study supervised by Fromm just mentioned, there were to be surveys with German doctors on contemporary sexual mores, one pertaining to authority patterns among European youth, as well as a survey of the attitudes of the German unemployed toward authority. In consequence of the serious problems with data collection, the study's title page appeared with the caveat emptor: "work in progress." Moreover, in his introductory remarks to the volume, Horkheimer was careful to specify that, owing to the deficiencies of the empirical part, no direct generalizations could be produced on the basis of the partial results obtained.

Yet, as Martin Jay has remarked, "fragmentary and inconclusive as the empirical studies were, they provided valuable methodological experience, which aided the Institute in all its subsequent investigations of authority."[26] Fromm, for example, in opposition to Horkheimer, was more sanguine about the possibilities of salvaging meaningful results from the deficient data. On the basis of the questionnaires returned from his survey, he sought to distinguish three predominant character types: authoritarian (supporters of the German National People's Party), revolutionary (KPD sympathizers), and ambivalent (Social Democratic backers). Given the predominance of the authoritarian and ambivalent scores, the prospects for a democratic German future looked exceedingly dim. In addition, it was on the basis of this trichotomous typology discerned by Fromm that an analogous tripartite schema of character classification was decided upon for the *The Authoritarian Personality* (1950)—albeit, with one important emendation that reflected a significant shift in the political thinking of the institute members: the "revolutionary" personality type that had served as normative ideal for the *Studies* subsequently became the "democratic" personality type.

But there is no circumventing the fact that the project, originally conceived of as the definitive realization of "interdisciplinary materialism," fell drastically short of its goals. This was true insofar as, with the important exception of Fromm's contributions, the theoretical and empirical parts of the study remained thoroughly unintegrated, rather than serving as the "mutual correctives" envisaged by Horkheimer. Moreover, it is clear that the reasons for this failure cannot be solely attributed to the problem of numerous unreturned questionnaires. Instead, despite the refreshing boldness of Horkheimer's 1931 program, one cannot help but conclude that the philosophically inclined inner circle of the Institute—Horkheimer, Marcuse, and Adorno—retained, despite all protestations to the contrary, a strong mistrust of empiricist methodologies.[27] It is perhaps only a slight exaggeration to say that in this respect their attitudes may be situated squarely in line with the German Idealist tradition, which took to heart Fichte's infamous dictum that "if the facts fail to correspond to the Idea, so much the worse for the facts." As a sympathetic, yet disillusioned critic has remarked of the *Studies*:

> The fact that the theoretical sketches are in no way related to the surveys, research, and literature-report demonstrates to an extreme how little one may speak of an "interpenetration of constructive and empirical procedures." As the correspondence between Fromm and Horkheimer demonstrates, empirical research and disciplinary expertise provided the two main theorists of the Institute with a type of protective shield behind which a theory was promoted that wished to distinguish itself from pure philosophy, but which behaved in a skeptical fashion toward the individual sciences and was therefore uncertain as to its own status.[28]

Wiggershaus' verdict may strike some as overly severe. Yet the *mutual indifference* between theory and empirical research that colored *Studies on*

Authority and the Family would also characterize much of the Institute's subsequent work.

Earlier I sought to distinguish between the "internal" and "external" reasons for the collapse of the Institute's research program. The latter, in all fairness, were far from trivial. The theoretical self-understanding of Horkheimer and his colleagues was based on the transcendence of the traditional, contemplative view of the role of theory. They were partisans neither of "theory for theory's sake" nor of empirical research as an end in itself. The critical theorists understood their work as standing in an essential relation to a more general program of social enlightenment. In their capacity as intellectuals, they believed all thought that ignored questions of social emancipation, that shied away from a commitment to the realization of an authentically democratic society, remained partial and flawed. The disintegrating fabric of social life during the final years of the Weimar Republic seemed to lend a special urgency to this program. As such, Critical Theory actively sought out a potential agent of progressive social change. They tentatively placed their hopes in the enlightened strata of the German working classes.

But their expectations concerning the ultimate triumph of a just society were rudely crushed. Within two years of Horkheimer's compelling inaugural lecture, the Institute members were forced to flee for their lives. If the success of Horkheimer's program of an interdisciplinary materialism was in an important sense contingent on the idea of social philosophy as "practical enlightenment," then with the triumph of Nazism and the pains of forced emigration, the Institute's raison d'être seemed to disappear.

It is clear, moreover, that its members, once expulsed from their native land, had difficulties in transferring a framework of social analysis that had been developed under Weimar conditions to their adoptive home. Their Weimar experiences had taught them a lesson that in many respects proved inapplicable to the majority of Western democratic societies: behind the democratic normalcy of liberalism there lurked the specter of a fascist, authoritarian state. In this respect, their initial diagnosis of the relationship between liberalism, capitalism, and fascism proved deficient; a diagnosis whose essence was captured by Marcuse's 1934 observation that "the turn from the liberal to the total authoritarian state occurs on the basis of one and the same economic order"—viz., capitalism.[29] But as the examples of Spain and Italy show, the existence of a highly advanced, capitalist economic order is neither a necessary nor sufficient condition for fascism. Conversely, in nations with relatively stabile democratic traditions, fascist ideologies manifested little staying power.[30] For their analysis of fascism to have been successful, they would have had to have paid much closer attention to those specifically *German* historical and social conditions that proved especially conducive to the triumph of National Socialism—which should not necessarily be confused with "normal fascism."

Thus, the ease with which Weimar democracy passed over into a fascist social order was turned by the Frankfurt School into a parable concerning the foibles of liberal democracy in general. Under the influence of this misleading historical paradigm, the Institute's later treatment of American society tended to elide too many of the essential differences between these two fundamentally different political systems. Herein lie the historical origins of the concept of a "totally administered world" advanced by Adorno and that of a "one-dimensional society" embraced by Marcuse. In truth, the lessons of Weimar proved much more historically and geographically limited than the Critical Theorists were willing to acknowledge. As a result, their postwar analyses of Western democratic societies were prone to summary and undifferentiated judgments.

The Institute as a functional entity died in the early forties—not with a bang but a whimper. Horkheimer's decision to cease formal operations (publication of the *Zeitschrift für Sozialforschung*, abandonment of the New York collective) was in part conditioned by the Institute's rapidly dwindling endowment, which would have required harsh cutbacks in any event. Late in 1941, he came to the conclusion that according to the charter of the foundation established by Felix Weil, the maintenance of the Institute was not really necessary. Instead, he decided the funds should be made available for four or five "private" research projects. The Institute, with Horkheimer at its helm, was forced into practicing lifeboat ethics. Beginning in 1939, "notice" was in effect given in succession to Benjamin, Fromm, the economist Julian Gumperz, and Neumann.

Despite the very real economic difficulties facing the Institute, the decision to disband cannot be separated from the personality of the director. Horkheimer's decision to dissolve the Institute seems in no small measure to have been motivated out of a concern for personal survival. Put bluntly, he was not about to place his own financial security at risk because of the plight of others.

It seems that Horkheimer was motivated by a type of theoretical selfishness as well, which reflects poorly on his overall commitment to the program of an interdisciplinary materialism. Since the mid-1930s he had been planning to write his own magnum opus on "dialectical logic." As Wiggershaus has shown, he increasingly perceived his duties and responsibilities as director as a bureaucratic encumbrance which interfered with his own intellectual work.[31] By dissolving the Institute he disengaged himself from these responsibilities and was thus free to devote all his energies to the book on dialectics. And this is precisely what happened. In late 1941, Horkheimer and Adorno moved to Pacific Palisades, California; *Dialectic of Enlightenment* was the result of their three-year collaboration.

The entire tale of the Institute's dissolution in the early 1940s—above all, the callous way in which the welfare of the other Institute members was dealt with—suggests that for Horkheimer the continuation of the intellectual enterprise of Critical Theory became narrowly equated with the survival of his own personal theoretical interests and pursuits.

In the drama of Critical Theory that has been reenacted thus far, Adorno's name has once again been conspicuous by its omission. Although he was a frequent contributor to the *Zeitschrift* in the 1930s, he only became a member of the Institute's inner circle in 1938. But from that time on, the orientation of the Institute as a whole changed decisively. In Adorno, Horkheimer found the gifted philosophical spirit he had long been seeking as a collaborator for his book on "dialectical logic." It is not hard to see that Adorno, whose interests were exclusively philosophical and aesthetic, weaned Horkheimer further away from the empirical side of his 1931 program and in the direction of a social philosophy unencumbered by empirical moorings.

With *Dialectic of Enlightenment* (written 1941–1944) we enter an entirely new phase in the development of Critical Theory. It represents the Frankfurt School's decisive shift away from interdisciplinary materialism and toward a philosophy of history. Unfortunately, the loss in sociohistorical concretion is not repaid by the gains in historico-philosophical breadth and speculative richness. That the book—in truth, a self-professed collection of "Philosophical Fragments"—is loaded with provocative and stimulating insights is unarguable. Equally incontestable, however, is the fact that as a philosophically grounded theory of social evolution, the conclusions purveyed are faulty to an extreme. Here, too, the firsthand experience of the Critical Theorists with a totalitarian regime is improperly generalized: the entirety of Western cultural development, from the *Odyssey* onward, is reductively viewed as a prelude to the modern authoritarian state. According to this explanatory approach, the factor chiefly responsible for the advent of totalitarianism is not a *deficit* of human rationality, but instead a *hypertrophy* of human reason: the reduction of the other to what is equivalent and familiar that characterizes formal logic, so-called identitarian thinking. This is an argument that bespeaks not only the primacy of Adorno's influence (and ultimately, that of Walter Benjamin's conception of history as a *Verfallsgeschichte*—a history of decline), but a fundamental change in intellectual orientation from Marx to Nietzsche: above all, Nietzsche the critic of a nihilistic and despiritualized bourgeois *Zivilisation*. Instead of a revamped "materialist theory of society," one is left with, in essence, a *negative philosophy of history*; one, moreover, that seems theoretically impervious to empirical revision. However, as a result of this simplistic, antirationalist maneuver—which, in its equation of reason with domination, bears superficial affinities with the poststructuralist critique of reason—Horkheimer and Adorno proceed to undercut the very basis of their critical project. When "enlightenment" becomes equated with "myth" and "domination" *simpliciter*, the project of human emancipation renounces its most essential means: rational reflection and critical thinking. These were the tools that served Critical Theory so well in its early years. Without them, the entire project of an interdisciplinary materialism must be abandoned in favor of philosophical esoterics—as proves to be the case in Adorno's later works, *Negative Dialectics* and *Aesthetic Theory*, as well as Horkheimer's late *Notizen*.[32] Once an integral and irrevocable relationship between reason and domination has been proclaimed, the only means we have at our disposal to remedy our condition of affliction—the means of the rational concept—are preemptorily dismissed as being inherently coercive and prejudicial. Whereas Adorno's philosophy seeks refuge in the remembrance of fallen nature in works of art—to be sure, an authentically Benjaminian motif—Horkheimer views religion as one of the last repositories of hope and truth beyond a society dominated by considerations of instrumental reason. But since the negative philosophy of history of *Dialectic of Enlightenment* had seemingly ruled out in advance the prospect of discovering fissures in the reigning continuum of domination that would be immanent and this-worldly, Horkheimer's qualified reliance on a theological frame of reference is perhaps not the absolute break it may appear to be on first view.[33]

THREE

Mimesis, Utopia, and Reconciliation: A Redemptive Critique of Adorno's *Aesthetic Theory*

In 1980, Leo Lowenthal formulated a set of prescient insights about the future of Critical Theory in an interview entitled "The Utopian Motif is Suspended."[1] By "utopian motif," Lowenthal was referring to the eschatological hopes for a better life in the here and now that inspired not only the enterprise of Critical Theory, but an entire generation of Central European Jewish thinkers who, like himself, came of age around the time of World War I and drew on utopian aspects of the Jewish tradition as a source of messianic inspiration.[2] Among this generation, a decisive influence on the "inner circle" of Critical Theorists was exercised by the thought of Ernst Bloch, Georg Lukács, and Walter Benjamin.[3]

Prima facie, the claim epitomized in the title of the Lowenthal interview cannot help but seem a startling admission. For if we try to imagine the work of Horkheimer, Adorno, and Marcuse stripped of this dimension of utopian longing, it seems divested of its most fundamental impulses. Moreover, Lowenthal's contention seems a striking concession in the direction of Jürgen Habermas, who has made a point of trying to integrate Critical Theory with contemporary developments in social science and philosophy of language at the expense of its speculative-utopian tendencies. "Maybe [Habermas] is right," Lowenthal observes. "Perhaps [the speculative-utopian moment] is ballast. When I speak of such things, I feel a bit old and obsolete. After all, one cannot just live from utopian hopes based in never-never land, whose realization seems scarcely in the realm of the possible. Maybe this is a cause of the sadness I spoke of at the outset. But perhaps the theoretical realism I sense in Habermas is the only means of salvaging the motifs present in Critical Theory and thereby of protecting them from a complete disintegration into an empty, melancholy pessimism."[4]

Of course, Lowenthal's comments must in no way be construed as an abandonment of the critical intellectual legacy he helped found. Instead, in keeping with the nobler aspects of the dialectical tradition, they represent a constructive modification of what seem to be, from the vantage point of the current historical hour, extraneous preoccupations. As Lowenthal explains, Critical Theory's own revolutionary ardor was decisively cooled in the aftermath of the twin catastrophes of Nazism and Stalinism. For him, however, the loss of concrete utopian prospects in fact signifies the need for a redoubling of original critical energies. "It would be criminal to bury ideology critique now," Lowenthal remarks. "What has not been lost is, of course, the critical approach: the process of analysis, retaining the good and rejecting the bad, the need to accuse, the indictment of all that exists, . . . but without explicit hopes. What has occurred is not a retreat into skepticism or cynicism but sadness. The utopian motif has been suspended."

Lowenthal's sober appraisal of the utopian side of Critical Theory represents a valuable point of departure for examining Adorno's *Aesthetic Theory*. For it is in *Aesthetic Theory* that we find Adorno at his most utopian. In the later Adorno, philosophy is assigned the "negative" role of ruthlessly criticizing itself in order, against all odds, to undo its manifold past failings. This is the message of *Negative Dialectics*, a work which, in eminently quixotic fashion, fights against the domination of the concept through the use of concepts. Only as aesthetics does philosophy for the first time truly come into its own. It thus relinquishes its traditional position of privilege as *prima philosophia* and instead becomes a handmaiden to the arts as their faithful interpreter. Its new mission is to give voice to the speechless particularity of aesthetic objectivations, which, as "art," are nonconceptual, and thus devoid of the capacity for theoretical expression. It is precisely at this intersection of art and philosophy, that the utopian dimension of Adorno's work manifests itself. For this intersection is also the locus of *aesthetic theory*.

The stakes in this debate over the continued relevance of the utopian dimension of Critical Theory are high: an answer to this question will go far toward determining one's receptivity to the "linguistic turn" in Critical

Theory spurred by the work of Habermas. To be sure, Habermas' oeuvre is far from devoid of utopian potential: the theory of communicative competence sets forth an ideal speech situation in which generalized and unconstrained participation in decisionmaking becomes the counterfactual normative touchstone. Yet, unlike his predecessors, Habermas is someone who is fully at home with the ethical presuppositions of the modern world. He is for the most part interested in bringing these preconditions to consummation; or, as he once phrased it, the project of the modern age must be brought to completion. It is in this spirit that he has felicitously characterized the political implications of his theories as a "radical reformism." Absent from his perspective is the "romantic anti-capitalist" impulse that pervaded the worldview of the first generation of Frankfurt theorists. It was precisely this impulse that impelled their program of a "ruthless critique of everything existing" (Marx), which took the form of an unmitigated existential antipathy toward capitalist modernity as a whole. In eminently dialectical fashion, it was precisely this existential antipathy that spurred the profound utopian longings of Adorno, Horkheimer, Lowenthal, Marcuse, etc.

While Habermas has not hesitated to criticize vigorously the various "social pathologies" engendered by late capitalism, the sentiment of anticapitalist, "existential antipathy" is fundamentally foreign to his way of thinking. Correspondingly, he has often attacked the romantic anticapitalist utopianism of Critical Theory as one of its weakest aspects. The Critical Theorists' rejection of the notion of "immanent critique" is seen as essentially Nietzschean: they accept Nietzsche's *Zeitdiagnose* of bourgeois modernity by concurring with him that its cultural ideals are wholly bankrupt; and this conclusion forces them, like Nietzsche, to abandon the concept of immanent critique for that of "total critique." In both cases, the equation of modernity with a prosaic logic of "rationalization" ("instrumental reason"), where the unexalted mentality of the Weberian "Fachmensch" reigns triumphant, leads to a search for *aestheticist* alternatives. For Habermas, conversely, the ideals of bourgeois modernity (embodied in the differentiated spheres of science, morality, and art) remain serviceable as a basis for the immanent criticism of its various "social pathologies." The authors of *Dialectic of Enlightenment* have abandoned too much by succumbing to Nietzsche's heady, totalizing critique of the bourgeois world—for example, the potentials for communicative reason embodied in modern bourgeois law and morality.

We may summarize Habermas' objections by saying that as a result of a totalistic and undialectical understanding of the significance of modernity,

Horkheimer and Adorno remained incapable of comprehending future sources of social change: from a "totally administered world" no good can conceivably emerge. And in consequence of this diagnostic incapacity, emancipatory prognoses of necessity took on an unrealistic, utopian hue. Unable to locate progressive emancipatory tendencies in the concrete historical present, the Critical Theorists were constrained to identify ersatz repositories of negation deriving from the aesthetic sphere. But in the last analysis, art was unable to bear the heavy burden accorded it in their framework. Instead, one is left with the conceptual aporia of a "totally administered world" side by side with historically unrealizable utopian projections. Both Lowenthal's observations and Habermas' critique, therefore, cast serious doubt on the utopian aspirations of Adorno's aesthetics.

One cannot help but be struck by the indebtedness of Adorno's aesthetic theory to insights first expressed by Max Weber in the famous "Zwischenbetrachtung" to his great work on the *Sociology of World Religions*.[5] Certainly, Adorno the musicologist learned much from Weber's essay on the *Rational and Social Foundations of Music*. The fundamental concept of that work—the "rationalization" of musical techniques in the modern West—plays a major role in Adorno's analysis of aesthetic modernity *tout court*. As Adorno emphasizes repeatedly, the imperatives of aesthetic modernity dictate that only those works of art which rely on the most advanced techniques historically available become worthy of serious consideration. In this context, he approvingly quotes Rimbaud's dictum, "Il faut être absolument moderne."

But it is Weber the theorist of the "Aesthetic Sphere" in modern life who establishes the parameters for Adorno's theory of aesthetic modernism. Following Kant's discussion of art in the third *Critique* as "purposiveness without purpose," Weber points out that in traditional or premodern art, art's inner logic remained stultified, insofar as *form* was always subordinated to *content*: the independent development of artistic technique was perennially subservient to the ends of salvation. In fact, these two aspects, form and content, stood in grave conflict, since aesthetic means inherently threatened to outstrip the demands of the religious message per se. (The annals of art history are replete with such tensions. For the sake of illustration, I mention three: Augustine's concern about the enticement to pleasure for pleasure's sake in musical liturgy; Tarkovsky's conflicted icon painter in *Andrei Rublov*; and the threat posed to the worldview of the Church by the "new realism" of Renaissance painting.)

All this changes, according to Weber, with the differentiation of the spheres of science, morality, and art that follows from the thoroughgoing rationalization of life in the modern age. For the first time, art (and the same claims can also be made for the spheres of morality and science) need no longer legitimate itself in terms of a logically prior, all-encompassing worldview. Instead, it is free to develop its own intrinsic formal potentialities to an unprecedented extent. The result, for Weber, is the creation of the "Aesthetic Sphere" in the modern sense, a historically unique network of artists and persons of taste, whose interactions are mediated by a new series of public institutions: theaters, galleries, feuilletons, critics, public libraries, museums, and so forth. Weber encapusulates this development—with characteristic pith and discernment—as follows: "[Under] the development of intellectualism and the rationalization of life . . . art becomes a cosmos of more and more consciously grasped independent values, which exist in their own right. Art takes over the function of this-worldly salvation, no matter how this may be interpreted. It provides *salvation* from the routines of everyday life, and especially form the pressures of theoretical and practical rationalism."[6]

I think there could be no better lead-in to the basic intentions of Adorno's aesthetic theory than the remarks of Weber just cited; above all, his characterization of aesthetic modernism as a type of inner-worldly salvation. To be sure, Adorno, following the lead of Walter Benjamin, is primarily concerned with de-auraticized (or postauratic) art; that is, with forms of modernism that have relinquished the immediacy of the Stendhalian *promesse de bonheur*, the "beautiful illusion" that happiness might be attainable in the here and now. Nevertheless, Weber attributes a special *redemptory function* to art in the modern world, which, for men and women of culture, surpasses religion to become a unique locus of ultimate meaning and value in life.

Art performs an analogous *redemptory* function in Adorno's aesthetics. For him, too, art represents a form of salvation vis-à-vis the pressures of "theoretical and practical rationalism" that predominate in daily life. Moreover, in Adorno's aesthetics, art becomes a vehicle of salvation in an even stronger sense. It takes on a compelling utopian function as a *prefiguration of reconciled life*. If Adorno stands Hegel on his head by claiming that "the whole is the untrue," it is art alone that offers the prospect of reversing this condition, of redirecting a lacerated social totality along the path of reconciliation (*Versöhnung*).

It is important to recognize that *Aesthetic Theory*, Adorno's magnum opus, fulfills an important systematic function in his oeuvre as a whole, addressing a concern originally posed jointly with Max Horkheimer in *Dialectic of Enlightenment*.[7] There, social evolution is comprehended, in a manner reminiscent of both Nietzsche and Freud, in terms of the progressive mastery of unsublimated impulse. The latter must be perpetually subordinated to the "organizational imperatives" of civilization. *Individuation* thus means *domination*: increasing control of human drives on the part of the superego, the internalized agent of social authority. Ultimately, this dual process of self-renunciation and the extirpation of "otherness"—of those spheres of life that remain nonidentical with the subject qua *res cogitans*—leads to the horror of Auschwitz: the Jew, with his pre-Christian rites and physiognomy, represents the ultimate incarnation of otherness at the heart of European modernity. So pervasive is this dilemma that *conceptualization itself*—the very process of making the nonidentical intellectually comprehensible to the subject—is fully implicated in this world-historical march of unreason. As Horkheimer and Adorno observe, "The universality of ideas, as developed by discursive logic, domination in the conceptual sphere, is raised up on the actual basis of domination. The dissolution of the old magical heritage, of the old diffuse ideas, by conceptual unity, expresses the hierarchical constitution of life by those who are free. The individuality that learned order and subordination in the subjection of the world, soon wholly equated truth with the regulative thought without whose fixed distinctions truth cannot exist." And further: "Enlightenment behaves toward things as a dictator behaves toward men. He knows them insofar as he can manipulate them."[8] *Dialectic of Enlightenment* may thus be read as a type of cautionary tale concerning the fate of civilization once it has succumbed to the identitarian spell of formal logic.

In the context at hand, it is not so much the accuracy of the *Zeitdiagnose* set forth by Horkheimer and Adorno that concerns us, as the fact that an analogous preoccupation with "domination in the conceptual sphere" pervades Adorno's epistemological musings some years later in *Negative Dialectics*. To be sure, the historico-philosophical framework of the latter work is very much of a piece with *Dialectic of Enlightenment*. As Adorno remarks at one point: "No universal history leads from savagery to humanitarianism, but there is one that leads from the slingshot to the megaton bomb."[9] But of greater relevance for our purposes is the fact that the theme of the "domination of the concept" occupies pride of place in the work, which may thus be understood as an elaborate meditation on a specific *epistemological* problem that had been inherited from the philosophy of history of the 1940s. For Adorno, "the original sin of all philosophy is that it tries to grasp the non-conceptual through conceptual means." It is the tacit alliance between society and ratiocination, which manifests itself in their mutual hostility to the nonidentical, that Adorno seeks to undo via negative dialectics—which, paradoxically, "strives by way of the concept, to transcend the concept."[10] Adorno has drunk deeply from Nietzschean waters: his critique of conceptualization derives from the latter's characterization of philosophy as a manifestation of the "will to power."

Adorno offers a succinct rendering of his philosophical program—an intransigent defense of nonidentity—in the following statement: "To change [the] direction of conceptualization, to give it a turn toward the non-identical, is the linchpin of negative dialectics. Insight into the constitutive character of the nonconceptual in the concept would end the compulsive identification which the concept brings unless halted by such reflection. Reflection on its own meaning is the way out of the concept's seeming being-in-itself as a unit of meaning. . . . Disenchantment of the concept is the antidote of philosophy. It keeps it from growing rampant and becoming an absolute unto itself."[11]

A prior account of Adorno's stance on the philosophy of history and theory of knowledge is crucial for an informed appreciation of the stakes of his *Aesthetic Theory*, which is the direct philosophical heir of these earlier works. More importantly, in *Aesthetic Theory*, Adorno explicitly attempts to posit "solutions" to the dilemmas of abstract conceptualization—"domination in the conceptual sphere"—targeted in his previous work. And these solutions are integrally related to the redemptory or utopian function he assigns to works of art as ciphers of reconciled life.

Adorno fully accepts the Hegelian turn in aesthetics whereby art is deemed a serious vehicle of knowledge and truth. Thus, for Adorno, like Hegel, art remains an embodiment of Spirit; however, in opposition to Hegel, art is no longer deemed a subaltern manifestation of the latter insofar as it represents the Idea merely in the realm of sensuous appearance. Instead, he in effect reverses the terms on his idealist predecessor. The truth claims of the aesthetic sphere are potentially superior to those of philosophical truth precisely because of their greater affinities with the realm of sensuous appearance.

Philosophical truth is by definition disembodied. Whereas for Hegel, this high degree of "spiritualization" accounted for its distinct superiority vis-à-vis, for example, the pictorial representation of the absolute in religious lore, for Adorno, the reverse is true: the sensuous nature of works of art means that they display a greater affinity with objectivity as such. In his eyes, therefore, philosophical thought, which seeks to represent the nature of things by use of abstract concepts, operates at a more distant remove from the reality it seeks to grasp.

The greater concretion of works of art, their inherent affinities with the realm of "sensuous externality," is not, however, an unequivocal gain. Instead, the increase in material concretion simultaneously signifies a diminution in intelligibility. For unlike philosophy, the language of art is sensuous. Its mode of articulation relies on images, sounds, and colors rather than the clarity of discursive argument. Consequently, as vehicles of truth, works of art are inherently enigmatic, *rätselhaft*. And it is precisely this enigmatic quality that beseeches, implores, and requires the *philosophical interpretation* of art. This dynamic alone mandates the necessity of *aesthetic theory*.

Similarly, it is only in light of the epistemological problematic inherited from *Dialectic of Enlightenment* and *Negative Dialectics* that one of Adorno's more controversial theoretical strategies in *Aesthetic Theory* becomes comprehensible: a rehabilitation of the category of natural beauty. Here, too, a comparison with Hegelian aesthetics is instructive. For Hegel, natural beauty was indisputably inferior to the humanmade variety, insofar as nature is inherently de-spiritualized. At best, it represents spirit in the mode of "otherness." There is no mistaking the fact that *Aesthetic Theory* is in the main a theory of aesthetic modernism. But this fact only makes the elaborate justification of natural beauty contained therein all the more surprising. To be sure, if various artistic movements throughout history have emphasized "naturalism" as a paramount criterion of aesthetic value, such a mind-set is completely foreign to the sensibility of modernism, for which all residues of naturalist sentiment must be ruthlessly expulsed (otherwise one ceases to be "absolument moderne"). Adorno's concerted efforts to rehabilitate this category from the legacy of pre-Hegelian aesthetics can only be understood in light of the ulterior epistemological agenda of his aesthetics.

Thus, just as Adorno criticizes the pan-logism of Hegelian metaphysics for its perpetual willingness to sacrifice the nonidentical to the imperatives of systematic unity, he similarly attempts to overturn Hegel's dismissal of natural beauty as part and parcel of a process of "spiritualization" (*Vergeistigung*) that must be combated. "Spiritualization" bespeaks an imperious anthropocentrism, in which all that is alien to and other than the subject must be rendered equivalent to the latter at the expense of its own intrinsic contents. Consequently, in the framework of Adorno's nonidentitarian theory of knowledge—a theory that takes issue with the main epistemological desideratum of German idealism: the *identity of subject and object*—the category of natural beauty is endowed with immense metaphorical significance: it represents the irreducible Other, a pristine condition beyond the reach of subjective self-assertion that is for this reason to be cherished and emulated. Adorno expresses this view forcefully when he opines, "The beautiful in nature is *the residue of non-identity in things* in an age in which they are spellbound by universal identity." As a "residue of non-identity," natural beauty is at the same time a utopian cipher of "reconciliation": utopia would be a state of "reconciliation," i.e., a condition in which the nonidentical could freely articulate itself, rather than function—as is the case at present—solely under the aegis of the concept. "The beautiful in nature," observes Adorno, "is different from both the notion of a ruling principle and the denial of any principle whatsoever. It is like a state of reconciliation."[12]

It is the conceptual triad nonidentity-reconciliation-utopia that assumes central significance in *Aesthetic Theory*; though for Adorno, unlike Hegel, in the *Aufhebung* of reconciliation, nonidentity is not effaced but first truly comes into its own. For Hegel, it is the very existence of nonidentity that accounts for an antagonistic (or unreconciled) state; and this condition must be overcome via the moment of synthesis. Conversely, for Adorno, it is the *suppression* of nonidentity by its other, the concept, that is the root of all injustice in the theoretical sphere; thus, reconciliation signifies the elimination of the identitarian urge, rather than, as with Hegel, its consummation.

But on the whole, the utopian potential of natural beauty is of minor moment in *Aesthetic Theory* in comparison to that of works of art—and especially modern works. Works of art are utopian constructs of necessity, according to Adorno. Social life exists in an unredeemed, "fallen" state. Its elements are subject to the rule of heteronomous and alien principles such as the law of universal equivalence characteristic of a commodity economy. Amid the omnipresent degradation of the phenomenal world, works of art possess a unique *saving power*: they incorporate these phenomena within the context of a freely articulated, noncoercive totality, thereby redeeming them from their deficient everyday state. According to Adorno, in a capitalist society dominated by considerations of utility, phenomena are allowed to subsist only in an inferior state of universal Being-for-Other, which militates against the prospects of authentic Being-for-Self. In a flash, works of art dramatically reverse this state of affairs: "Whereas in the real world all particulars are fungible, art protests against fungibility by holding up images of what reality might be like if it were emancipated from the patterns of identification that are imposed on it."[13] Works of art for the first time allow the Being-in-Itself of things to emerge by virtue of the redeeming capacities of aesthetic form: "The utopia anticipated by artistic form is the idea that things at long last ought to come into their own. Another way of putting this is to call for the abolition of the spell of selfhood hitherto promoted by the subject."[14]

For Adorno, art is intrinsically utopian by virtue of the nonutilitarian principle of construction that is peculiar to it. Art emancipates by virtue of its formal principle, which is that of "free articulation" rather than "instrumental reason." And this emancipatory aesthetic practice is actually *enhanced* in the case of *modern* works of art, in which the principle of montage becomes predominant, such that the individual parts attain independence, and are thereby no longer mechanically subjugated to the whole. Art redeems the material elements of everyday life by absorbing them within the liberating contours of an aesthetic constellation. This inherently emancipatory effect of aesthetic form contrasts starkly with the coercive nature of contemporary social organization. According to Adorno, at the present stage of historical development, aesthetic form signifies a unique refuge in which things are temporarily freed of the constraints of Being-for-Other and their Being-for-Self is allowed to flourish. In this way alone can one break the "spell" of the subject as well as the principle of social organization that follows therefrom—instrumental reason.

In the discussion of the utopian function of art in *Aesthetic Theory*, Adorno comes close to violating the Judeo-Marxian *Bilderverbot* (the taboo against graven images), insofar as utopia is well-nigh concretely depicted. He explicitly recommends aesthetic form as a positive alternative to the reigning principle of social organization. His aestheticist solution to the dominant pressures of "theoretical and practical rationalism" is wholly consistent with Weber's discussion of the aesthetic sphere. In this respect, Adorno's approach is at one with a tradition beginning with romanticism and continuing through *l'art pour l'art*, whereby the nonutilitarian logic of the aesthetic realm is viewed as the only alternative to an increasingly rationalized and prosaic bourgeois social order. In accord with both the romantics as well as the proponents of art for art's sake, Adorno seeks to redeem the vaunted *promesse de bonheur* that art counterposes to an antagonistic social totality. Art comes to represent a world of happiness and fulfillment that is denied in the workaday world of bourgeois material life. It embodies claims to sensuousness and affective solidarity that are repulsed in a social world in which formal rationality is the dominant principle. For Adorno, "Art is a refuge of mimetic behavior" and thus signifies a "response to the evils and irrationality of a rational bureaucratic world. . . . The memory trace of mimesis unearthed by works of art . . . anticipates a condition of reconciliation between the individual and the collectivity." As such, art becomes a form of "remembrance," joining "the present to the past." As Adorno phrases it, "Remembrance alone is able to give flesh and blood to the notion of utopia, without betraying it to empirical life." That Adorno interprets works of art as *concrete utopian projections* in more than a metaphorical sense is indicated by his contention that one must "reverse the copy theory of realist aesthetics: in a sublimated sense, reality ought to imitate works of art, rather than the other way around."[15]

That Adorno makes a concerted effort to emphasize the relation between mimesis, reconciliation, and utopia in the passages just cited is far from accidental. For the utopian program of *Aesthetic Theory*—and the link between "mimesis" and "remembrance" which is its linchpin—bears a profound resemblance to the one adumbrated jointly with Horkheimer some twenty-five years earlier in *Dialectic of Enlightenment*. There, too, ruthless domination over external nature becomes the central theoretical problematic. What has been lost in the species' inexorable drive toward rational self-assertion is the capacity to view nature *mimetically* or *fraternally*. The solution to this dilemma hinges upon the capacity for remembrance of nature in the subject: "By virtue of the remembrance of nature in the subject, in whose fulfillment the unacknowledged truth of all culture lies hidden, enlightenment is universally opposed to domination."[16] The subject must remember that it, too, is part of nature; and that consequently all violence perpetrated against the latter will in the last analysis redound implacably against subjectivity itself. The program of enlightenment is thus fulfilled only in a distorted and one-sided sense when it is equated simply with the advance of the rational concept. Equally important is the "natural" or "sensuous" substratum of subjectivity—the subject as a medium of desires, drives, and somatic impulses—which comes into its own only via a conscious act of remembrance: an act that recaptures the "natural" dimension of subjectivity which remains ever-present, though dormant, in our mimetic faculty.[17]

The mimesis-reconciliation-utopia triad plays a key role in Adorno's response to the epistemological problem of the "domination of the concept." For in his eyes, works of art possess the singular advantage of greater immediacy over against the abstract mediations of the conceptual sphere. It is this enhanced immediacy that accounts for their greater affinities with the sensuous dimension of objectivity as such, unlike pure concepts, which exist at a studied remove from the objective world they seek to grasp intellectually.

Art, therefore, may be said to possess a certain epistemological superiority vis-à-vis philosophical truth. Philosophical cognition is suspect insofar as it is inherently implicated in the dialectic of enlightenment: since concepts know phenomena only insofar as they can manipulate them, they are a priori part and parcel of the historical unfolding of domination. As Adorno remarks: "The derivation of thought from logic ratifies in the lecture room the reification of man in the factory and office."[18]

Since theoretical reason is untrustworthy, the aestheticist solution Adorno posits in response is far from surprising. It is of a piece with the standard critique of a rationalized, bourgeois cosmos by the elevated *Kulturmensch*. It is precisely because of this inordinate distrust of formal rationality that the wager on the aesthetic dimension in Critical Theory is so pronounced: art alone, it would seem, can undo the damage wrought by a logic of unrestrained subjective rationality gone awry.

Adorno emphasizes the superior representational capacities of the aesthetic faculty, as opposed to philosophy, when the depiction of truth is at issue. In art the mimetic faculty, long repressed, is emancipated: one no longer need suppress the desire to be like the Other. The realm of aesthetic illusion or *Schein* thus frees the subject from his or her otherwise natural compulsion to objectify the Other for purposes of enhanced control. "Works of art represent self-sameness that has been freed of the compulsion to identify," remarks Adorno.[19] Only works of art are exempt from the Kantian proscription against depicting the "intelligible realm"—a ban that must be upheld in the case of theoretical reason. They alone possess the capacity to express the ineffable, to represent the unrepresentable, by virtue of the magical, transformative capacities of aesthetic *Schein*. Works of art represent a secular redemption of myth: they alone are capable of depicting a superior, transcendent world order in which—unlike the world at present—good, evil, and beauty are assigned their rightful niches. Yet, unlike traditional myth, aesthetic cosmologies no longer stand in the service of alien powers, but in that of a potentially redeemed humanity. At the same time works of art, in contrast to philosophy, never attempt to serve up the absolute as something immediately accessible. Instead, it always appears enigmatically, via the embellishment and indirection of aesthetic form. As Adorno himself expresses this point: "Works of art speak like fairies in tales: if you want the absolute, you shall have it, but only in disguise." They are enigmatic "images of Being-in-itself."[20] Art restores the element of wonder or *thaumazein* to the everyday phenomenal world; a power, according to Aristotle, once possessed by philosophy, but which the latter has surrendered in recent times in favor of protocol statements and analytical truths. Art is the utopian reenchantment of radically disenchanted social totality. It serves as irrefutable proof of the fact that the existing universe of facts is not all there is. It is a constant reminder of a state of not-yet-Being (Bloch) that eludes our concrete grasp at the moment, but which for that reason remains nonetheless "real." As Adorno remarks, "Aesthetic experience is the experience of something which spirit per se does not provide, either in the world or in itself. It is the possible, as promised by its impossibility. Art is the promise of happiness, a promise that is constantly being broken."[21]

■ ■ ■ ■ ■ ■

Can the utopian potential of Adorno's aesthetics be redeemed? This is only another way of responding to the Lowenthal query with which we began: to what extent has the utopian motif in Critical Theory been suspended? The case of Adorno's aesthetics is paradigmatic, since the utopian wager of Critical Theory was so often couched in aesthetic terms.

In order to be redeemed, Adorno's aesthetics must be refunctioned. To be sure, few theorists have probed the fundamental parameters of aesthetic experience in the modern world more deeply than Adorno. Yet it seems that the true import of Adorno's aesthetic utopianism remains limited by certain fundamental shortcomings of his metatheoretical framework. Adorno's aesthetics are therefore in need of a redemptive critique so that they may be freed from the prejudicial constraints of his own theoretical presuppositions.

The conceptual deficiencies alluded to emanate primarily from two quarters: Adorno's theory of knowledge and his philosophy of history. Both components of his theoretical framework were originally articulated in *Dialectic of Enlightenment*.[22] It is these two aspects of the Adornian worldview that prevent his aesthetic doctrines from receiving the fully exoteric redemption they merit.

We turn first to his theory of knowledge, having already indicated that *Aesthetic Theory* is very much concerned with resolving certain epistemological problems inherited from German Idealism.

In this respect, it is in no way accidental that one of the book's central categories is the eminently Hegelian concept of the "truth-content" or *Wahrheitsgehalt* of art. It was unquestionably an advance on the part of Hegel over the aesthetic doctrines of the eighteenth century to have valorized the cognitive dimension of aesthetic objectivations, to have viewed them as legitimate incarnations of the "Idea" or truth. And in this regard, Adorno's aesthetics are eminently Hegelian, even if he values the sensuous side of works of art to an incomparably greater extent.

Nevertheless, once works of art are viewed primarily as "epistemological vehicles" (and in this fundamental respect there is really very little difference between Hegel and Adorno), another crucial component of aesthetic experience tends to fall out of account: the *pragmatic dimension*, on which the essence of aesthetic experience depends. Because Adorno tries to conceive of works of art primarily as vehicles of philosophical truth, in his approach the entire pragmatic side of works of art—their role in shaping, informing, and transforming the lives of historically existing individuals—falls by the wayside.

That Adorno succumbs to this error in judgment is due to an eminently Hegelian preconception: a belief in an "emphatic concept of truth," whereby truth is viewed as something transcendent and noncontingent, which escapes the fallibility of the human condition. Adorno's thought—despite the conceptual pyrotechnics of negative dialectics—still very much moves within the horizon of traditional metaphysical theories of truth. One might go so far as to say that his entire philosophical program is motivated by a nostalgia for the lost prelapsarian unity of subject and object, concept and thing. It is this nostalgia that accounts for the prominence of *mimesis* in his thinking—the importance of a fraternal, nonobjectivating relationship to the external world—as well as the category of *reconciliation*, the explicit hope for a future condition *beyond* the subject-object split.

As a result of this tendentious preoccupation with works of art as vehicles of truth, the richness of aesthetic experience—i.e., art's status as a pragmatic phenomenon capable of altering the existential parameters of human life—is significantly downplayed. Interpreting art becomes primarily an *esoteric philosophical excercise* in deciphering the work's "enigmatic character" (*Rätselcharakter*); with the result that Walter Benjamin's question concerning the exoteric value of aesthetic experience—the capacity of art to produce "profane illuminations"—is lost sight of.

This deficiency of Adorno's framework is, moreover, systematic rather than accidental in nature. Since his debate with Benjamin in the 1930s over the status of mechanically reproduced works of art, Adorno—who was very likely correct in terms of the particulars of the debate itself—remained undialectically wedded to the concept of an esotericized, autonomous art as an absolute model of aesthetic value. In the debate with Benjamin, he pointed out, in the cases of both film and surrealism, that the act of bursting the vessels of aesthetic autonomy does not automatically produce an emancipatory effect. Instead, one runs the risk of a false sublation of autonomous art, whereby a crucial refuge of negativity and critique would be prematurely integrated with facticity as such. Adorno's cautionary remarks concerning the dangers of a premature integration of art in life-praxis remain valuable to this day. The problem, however, is that his own stance in this debate became rigidified, and thus possible countervailing tendencies in the postwar period were ruled out a priori. The "culture industry" thesis from *Dialectic of Enlightenment* ossified into a monolithic, self-fulfilling prophecy—a mere mirror image of that undifferentiated continuum of the always-the-same that Adorno himself had projected onto social life under advanced capitalism.

In the present context, we can only fleetingly touch on the second systematic deficiency of Adorno's approach: a philosophy of history that was formulated during one of the darkest hours of recent memory: the era of Nazism, Stalinism, and the ensuing Cold War period, when international politics was reduced to the avoidance of successive, imminent catastrophes. However, his theory of a "*totale Verblendungszusammenhang*"—a context of total delusion—formulated during these years cannot withstand transposition to very different historical conditions without undergoing extensive modification. Consequently, Adorno's historico-philosophical thinking became similarly ossified, reinforcing his unreceptiveness to oppositional cultural forms with genuinely exoteric, generalizable potential.

The utopian moment of Critical Theory is redeemable; but one must specify very carefully what type of utopia one intends to redeem. What is *not* meant by utopia in the present context is the variety of utopianism criticized by Marx throughout his writings of the 1840s: a utopian future which is in essence a secularized version of eschatological religious longing. This strong version of utopianism resurfaces in the secular messianism of Bloch, Benjamin, the early Lukács, and Marcuse. In Adorno's work, it appears in the guise of a "negative theology": utopia would be the obverse of the present state of things.[23] This *strong version of utopianism*, whose *telos* is a state of reconciliation—of humanity with nature, existence and essence, thought and being—beyond the split between subject and object, is the type that Lowenthal has rightly consigned to an outmoded theoretical paradigm.

The weak version of utopianism that is recuperable from Adorno's *Aesthetic Theory* pertains to his advocacy of "aesthetic alienation": art presents the familiar and everyday to us in a new and unexpected light, such that we are impelled to modify our habitual modes of thought and perception.

Authentic works of art are the archfoes of all intellectual complacency and positivist affirmation. Adorno is essentially correct in his claim that works of art exist in a state of constant polemical tension vis-à-vis the given universe of facts. Genuine works of art are intrinsically utopian insofar as they both highlight the indigent state of reality at present and seek to illuminate a path toward what has never-yet-been. The profane illuminations of aesthetic experience seek to unseat the predominant tendencies toward "theoretical and practical rationalism"; and as such they give expression to an affective dimension of life that is routinely tabooed by bourgeois subjectivity and its unceasing will toward rational self-preservation: they are powerful repositories of a mimetic, noninstrumental relation to nature, of human fraternity, of nonutilitarian playfulness.

Habermas has expressed a similar insight: aesthetic experiences "are possible only to the extent that the categories of the patterned expectations of organized daily experience collapse, that the routines of daily action and conventions of ordinary life are destroyed, and the normality of foreseeable and unaccountable certainties are suspended." By being "incorporated into the context of individual life-histories" art "belongs to everyday communicative practice. It then . . . reaches into our cognitive interpretations and normative expectations and transforms the totality in which these moments are related to each another. In this respect, modern art harbors a utopia that becomes a reality to the degree that the mimetic powers sublimated in the work of art find resonance in the mimetic relations of a balanced and undistorted intersubjectivity of everyday life."[24]

A precondition for redeeming Adorno's theory of aesthetic modernity would be its transposition to an exoteric context: aesthetic illumination is not just the province of critics, aesthetes, artists, and experts, but a general phenomenon of daily life that concretely alters the life-histories of individuals. The "truth-content" of art is in principle accessible to a plurality of recipients.

There are, moreover, several structural features of contemporary aesthetic experience that suggest that Adorno's argument for the esoteric redemption of artistic truth-content is being undercut from below. For example, in an essay on "The Decline of the Modern Age," Peter Bürger points to the obsolescence of modernist high art in favor of a new series of hybrid genres and forms that are loosely identified as "postmodern."[25] Bürger correctly questions the descriptive cogency of the latter term, observing that many so-called postmodern art forms (e.g., neo-dada, neo-expressionism, etc.) are in fact continuous with the modern. The important point is that the conception of modernism on which Adorno's aesthetic theory was predicated—the idea of a select canon of hermetic, self-referential, autonomous works—has burst asunder. Any attempt to preserve the contemporary relevance of his theories must of necessity incorporate this manifestly new "state of the arts" into the total picture.

The changed configuration of contemporary aesthetic experience, the dissolution of traditional genre distinctions that has been described by Bürger and others, suggests the prospect of redeeming Adorno's aesthetics on a truly generalizable scale. And although this new aesthetic constellation is fraught with contradictions and tensions whose ultimate outcome remains difficult to foresee, it seems to indicate a potentially new sphere of operation for an aesthetics of negativity such as Adorno's. For the contemporary fusion of genres and levels of aesthetic experience suggests the real possibility that the profane illuminations Adorno sought to cull from esoteric art may now be *exoterically available*—in a way Adorno himself may have been incapable of anticipating. The apparent dissolution of the traditional European "aesthetics of autonomy" seems to indicate that the types of critical aesthetic experiences Adorno confined to hermetic works have now taken root in the life-world of late capitalism in general. That the aesthetic sensibility of modernism seems to have been *democratized*—and this is certainly one prominent aspect of the various strands of cultural experience commonly referred to as "postmodern"—is a phenomenon to be welcomed. For it means that an aesthetics of rupture, discontinuity, de-familiarization, and disenchantment—in sum, the "ideology-critical" function Adorno attributes to authentic works of art—has shifted to the plane of everyday artistic endeavor. An entire series of "popular" genres and cultural forms that as a rule fell beneath the threshold of Adorno's theoretical purview—popular music, cinema, even television in certain respects—have over the course of the last two decades displayed a new pluralism and inventiveness. To subsume them immediately under the "culture industry" thesis as originally formulated in the 1940s would be rash. It is, moreover, hardly surprising that this assault on the tenets of high modernism originated in the U.S., where (European) cultural elitism has always been at odds with a fundamentally democratic cultural self-understanding.

Nevertheless, the tendencies we have just described are far from unambiguous. The two most salient features of the much vaunted postmodern turn in the arts are 1) random historical borrowing of artistic styles; and 2) a collapse of the distinction between high and low culture, art and entertainment. The first trend poses the specter of a historicist loss of historical consciousness; if "all ages are equally close to God" (Ranke), then the course of history itself is trivialized, and all epochs are simultaneously equally meaningful and equally meaningless. And an absolute effacement of the distinction between high and low culture would be a far from untroubling development: for it harbors the prospect of a false sublation of art in the domain of life praxis, whereby art would to all intents and purposes become *fused* with the phenomenal sphere of daily life. The last-named tendency represents a real danger for the various artistic currents commonly referred to as postmodern. And thus, from the bursting of the vessels of aesthetic autonomy, an emancipatory effect does not necessarily follow. Here, the main risk is a slackening of the critical tension between art and life that proved the linchpin of modernist aesthetics. Consequently, the danger arises that once the boundaries between art and life become blurred, the critical potentials of art decay, and art itself is transformed into a *vehicle of affirmation*: i.e., the uncritical mirror-image of the "happy consciousness" of late capitalism. Adorno's "aesthetics of determinate negation" provide an important safeguard against this eventuality.

PART II

Political Existentialism

FOUR

Carl Schmitt, Political Existentialism, and the Total State

> [Racial] homogeneity of the united German Volk is the most indispensable presupposition and foundation for the concept of political leadership of the German Volk. The thought of race . . . is no theoretically idle postulate. Without a basis in homogeneity the National Socialist state could not exist and its legal life would be unthinkable. . . . All questions and answers intersect with the demand for homogeneity, without which a total *Führerstaat* could not subsist for a day.
>
> —Carl Schmitt, *State, Movement, Volk* (1933)

> It would be worthwhile to study in detail the careers of those comparatively few German scholars who went beyond mere cooperation and volunteered their services because they were convinced Nazis. . . . Most interesting is the example of the jurist Carl Schmitt, whose very ingenious theories about the end of democracy and legal government still make arresting reading.
>
> —Hannah Arendt, *The Origins of Totalitarianism*

The foregoing citations raise a number of fascinating interpretive questions concerning the political philosophy of Carl Schmitt—one of the leading German legal theorists of the Weimar years, whose wholehearted support for Hitler's dictatorship remained a scandal that followed him to his grave in 1985 at the advanced age of ninety-six. On the one hand, there is Arendt's characterization of Schmitt as a "convinced Nazi"; a statement certainly borne out by the facts of the years 1933–1936, when Schmitt, inspired to new heights of prolificness, authored no fewer than five books and thirty-five tracts in support of the new Reich. During this phase, there were few depths to which Schmitt would not sink: he penned an essay in support of the bloody SA purge of June 30, 1934—the famous "Night of the Long Knives"—with the ominous title, "The Führer Protects the Law." The following year he authored an article vigorously endorsing the Nuremberg anti-Semitic legislation of 1935 with an equally disingenuous title, "The Constitution of Freedom."[1] These facts, coupled with the ringing defense of "racial homogeneity" in *State, Movement, Volk* cited above would seem to confirm the first part of Arendt's description.

On the other hand, to do justice to Schmitt's work in its entirety, one must equally confront the second part of Arendt's portrayal, i.e., his "ingenious theories about the end of democracy and legal government"—a reference to Schmitt's conviction, developed in numerous books and articles during the Weimar years, that democracy had lost its legitimacy as a form of government in the twentieth century owing to the continued strength, rather than the demise of, liberal institutions.

Arendt's remark implicitly raises what has become the essential question for Schmitt scholarship over the years: is there a direct connection between his political and legal writings in the 1920s—which are largely concerned with justifying the notion of political dictatorship–and his avid involvement in the Nazi regime in the following decade? As Arendt suggests, the answer to this question is by no means straightforward. Schmitt, unlike the majority of the intellectual adherents of Nazism, was in no way a hack. Instead, he is generally recognized as perhaps the most gifted political and legal theorist of his generation. The controversial link between these two phases of Schmitt's career—Nazi and pre-Nazi—will serve as the focal point of the investigation that follows.

There are two main reasons that compel a fresh reconsideration of Schmitt's legacy at this time. First, MIT Press has recently published translations of three of Schmitt's major texts from the Weimar period.[2] This fact, coupled with a 1976 translation of what was perhaps Schmitt's most influential (and controversial) book of these years, *The Concept of the Political* (1927),[3] means that the most significant of his extensive pre-Nazi writings are now available to an English-speaking readership for the first time.

Second, the majority of secondary commentaries on Schmitt in English to date have been of a strangely apologetic character; a fact that stands in marked contrast to the postwar German reception of Schmitt's work, in which he has certainly found disciples, but also strident detractors.[4] To be sure, in contrast with the Federal Republic, an Anglo-American political context would seem to have little to fear with respect to the more authoritarian overtones of Schmitt's political philosophy. Yet the English language commentary on Schmitt, much of it very recent, has bordered on whitewash: a concerted effort has been made either to downplay Schmitt's Nazism or explain it away by reference to the force of political circumstances.[5]

The major strategy of denial practiced by the Schmitt apologists has been to try to neatly separate Schmitt the Weimar jurist and political philosopher from Schmitt the legal theorist of the Nazi *Machtergreifung*. According to this revisionist groundswell, Schmitt's writings of the 1920s, rather than pointing the way to March 24, 1933 (the date of the Enabling Act, allowing Hitler essentially to rule by decree), aimed fundamentally at strengthening the presidential system of Weimar and the notorious Article 48 (granting emergency powers to the president), in order to save the fragile republic rather than to hasten its demise. In this reading, Schmitt emerges as a "theorist of democratic legitimacy"—albeit a democratic legitimacy divested of the burdensome fetters of republican institutions. Even if it is a dictator who actually governs, he (or she) must do so only for the sake of upholding the legitimately constituted order. She (or he) may abrogate—but not abolish—the existing constitution. To be sure, there exists a strong basis for such an interpretation in certain of Schmitt's writings of the 1920s; moreover, this is unquestionably the way which the master himself would like posterity to view his historical contribution. At the same time, this approach selectively bypasses significant and troubling facts, both biographical and textual in nature.

One of the most puzzling issues in Schmitt scholarship has been his oscillation between two apparently irreconcilable tendencies: on the one hand, a radical decisionism, emphasizing a decision that is "born out of nothing," and thus enacted ex nihilo, in flagrant disregard of the legal and moral requirements of the existing sociohistorical situation; on the other hand, a concrete *Ordnungsdenken*—a "philosophy of order"—committed to the preservation of the existing system come what may. Schmitt's status as a philosopher of order follows logically from his functional (as well as tautological) definition of legitimacy: a given order is legitimate if it is recognized as such by the majority of its citizens. This definition of legitimacy is a merely logical consequence of Schmitt's abandonment of all moral and philosophical normativism: in the absence of a theoretical concept of justice against which a given political order might be measured, one is ipso facto left with a functional definition of legitimacy.

These seemingly irreconcilable positions—decisionism and a philosophy of order—have been no small source of confusion, with various critics emphasizing one moment to the exclusion of the other. For example, in his excellent essay on Schmitt, Karl Löwith seizes on the contentlessness and irrationalism of Schmitt's decisionism in order to make the point that, insofar as it is deprived of a prior substantive (read: normative) orientation, Schmitt's decisionism ends up as a mere "occasionalism": an ad hoc, opportunistic expression of political will, the self-projection of an arbitrary, authoritarian power—the will of the sovereign—upon political reality.[6] The irony here of course is that "occasionalism" is the term of derision which Schmitt uses to flagellate the German romantics in his 1919 work, *Political Romanticism*. In *Die Entscheidung*, an otherwise standard work on the concept, Christian von Krockow attempts to reconcile these two strands of Schmitt's thought through the convenience of periodization: Schmitt "progressed" from being a decisionist during the 1920s to a philosopher of concrete order during the Nazi years. Yet this solution remains unconvincing insofar as both elements—decisionism as well as *Ordnungsdenken*—are apparent in Schmitt's writing during the Weimar years.

The key to this interpretive quandary is to be found in Schmitt's *political existentialism*. It is this category that serves as the leitmotif of his Weimar writings capable of reconciling irreconcilables—his apparently inexplicable alternation between decisionism and a philosophy of concrete order—and which also goes far to account for the alacrity with which Schmitt converts to National Socialism in 1933. Thus, if the main theoretical question at issue in the interpretation of Schmitt's checkered intellectual career has become: what were the intellectual components of Schmitt's political thought in the 1920s that predisposed him to envisage the Nazi dictatorship as both a deliverance from Weimar and the fulfillment of his innermost political longings?—there are specific existentialist precepts that allow him to unite both a radical decisionism with a concrete philosophy of order. There is little doubt that he perceived the *Führerstaat* of Adolf Hitler as the consummate union of these two doctrines.[7]

The question of the intellectual climate in the Weimar years that prepared the ground for Germany's turn to fascism is a subject that has received much attention.[8] Above all, a crisis mentality prevailed—a fact integrally linked to the dire political and economic uncertainties of the early Weimar years—and a variety of "crisis philosophies" emerged in response. Without doubt, existentialism—or as it was known in the late 1920s, *Existenzphilosophie*—was the most successful. As a philosophy, it managed to formalize thoughts about the "crisis of the West" that had been current in German intellectual life since Nietzsche's day and that had received an apocalyptical formulation for the postwar generation in Spengler's influential *The Decline of the West*. This crisis philosophy seemed to accentuate Nietzsche's insight that all traditional Western values—religious, ethical, as well as political—had lost their validity. Hence, it reinforced the view that all alternatives to the inherited world order, if they were to be real alternatives, had to be radical. In the case of existentialism, the devaluation of all traditional values meant that ***human existence, in its brute facticity***, became a value in and of itself—the only value that remained, as it were. Such insights fed into the "non-normative" nature of decisionism, in both its Heideggerian and Schmittian variants,[9] where the decision must be made ex nihilo—in total disregard of the culturally dominant value paradigms, which merely serve to trap authenticity once more in the nether regions of bourgeois everydayness.

There is yet another aspect of existentialism qua crisis philosophy that merits attention in the context at hand. By emphasizing the brute primacy of human existence, denuded of all supporting value structures, there seems to be only one certainty left in life: the inevitability of death. The extent to which Heidegger here makes a virtue of a necessity is well known: anticipation of death (*Vorlaufen-zum-Tode*) becomes the existential focal point of *Sein und Zeit*, the hallmark of an authentic existence. Heidegger's attempt to correlate death and authenticity, however, was far from an isolated occurrence: in Germany of the interwar period, there arose a veritable "metaphysics of death," with the latter understood as a type of existential culmination of human life itself. The most notable illustration of this tendency occurs in Ernst Jünger's unabashed celebration of the *Fronterlebnis* (front experience) during these years in works such as *Im Stahlgewitter* (*Storm of Steel*), in which enthusiastic battle descriptions often culminate in scenes of glorious death.[10] Similarly, in Spengler one finds the adage that "war is the creator of all great things."[11] And in *The Concept of the Political*, in which Schmitt coins his famous "friend-enemy" distinction as the *ultima ratio* of political life, we find ourselves in close proximity to Jünger's discourse of martial bluster: "War, the readiness for death of fighting men, the physical annihilation of other men who stand on the side of the enemy, *all that has no normative, rather an existential meaning*, indeed, in the reality of a situation of real struggle against a real enemy, and not in whatever ideals, programs, or normative concepts."[12]

Inchoate existentialist impulses colored Schmitt's approach to legal studies very early on. In one of his first published works (*Gesetz und Urteil*—1912), Schmitt vigorously contests the idea that a legal order may be treated as a closed system of norms. He forcefully denies, for example, that in a particular case, one could reach a correct decision by a process of deduction or generalization on the basis of existing legal rules. Instead, he employs the notion of "concrete indifference" to illustrate his contention that in a given case there will always exist a measure of *irreducible particularity* that defies mechanical subsumption under general principles.[13] For Schmitt the moment of "concrete indifference" represents a type of vital substrate, that element of pure life opposed to the formalism of law. The consequences of this emphasis on the irrationalism of the particular case for Schmitt's future as a legal scholar are crucial: they point of necessity in the direction of the paramountcy of the juridical decision itself as a means of surmounting legal formalism. The failings of a consistent normativist stance endow the moment of decision with a certain extralegal arbitrariness: the *decision alone* is capable of bridging the gap between the *abstractness of law and the fullness of life*. The seeds of Schmitt's later decisionistic political philosophy are already fully in place.

The existential cleft between universal and particular is further explored in his 1914 work, *The Value of the State and the Significance of the Individual*, one of Schmitt's first forays into the domain of political philosophy proper. In this phase, Schmitt's early Catholicism is to the fore, as he takes up the question of the relation between the state and civil society. Unsurprisingly, in Schmitt's conception the balance must be totally resolved in the state's favor. Here, the individual is merely "*a means to the essence, the state is what is most important*." Law itself has no validity prior to the state. Instead, it must pass through "the state as a medium" in which it undergoes "a specific modification."[14] The state, in its extralegal capacity as pure "executive authority," is deemed the ultimate arbiter over questions of "concrete indifference": it is the state that must in the last analysis *decide*. By subordinating the autonomy of the legal sphere to "reasons of state," Schmitt strips civil society of any independent, oppositional potential. Such arguments foreshadow the extreme theoretical devaluation of liberal institutions that would characterize so much of his work of the 1920s.

Die Diktatur (1921) represents a transposition of Schmitt's early fascination with the exception in the legal sphere to the domain of political theory. Here, Schmitt establishes one of the themes that would characterize his political thought throughout the 1920s: *politics* must assume primacy over *legality*. The longstanding Western ideal of the *constitutional govern-*

ment (in German parlance, the *Rechtsstaat*)—the idea that it is a certain set of normative principles, as embodied in the constitution qua basis of legality, that account for a state's identity—is thus seriously jeopardized. In *Die Diktatur*, subtitled, "From the Beginnings of the Modern Concept of Sovereignty to Proletarian Class Struggle," Schmitt counterposes "sovereignty" to "class struggle." His point is that it falls due to the state to employ extra-constitutional means to preserve itself against internal disorder (i.e., class struggle) as well as external threats. Hence, it is not so much the constitution but a "logic of the concrete exception" that forms the basis of the state. It is the state alone that retains ultimate power of decision to suspend conditions of political normalcy by declaring a state of exception. In this way, Schmitt transposes Kierkegaard's "teleological suspension of the ethical" from the moral to the political sphere.

However, in Schmitt's view, dictatorship must be distinguished from normal despotism. The former is empowered to suspend the existing constitution, but not to promulgate a new one. To satisfy this condition, Schmitt coins a distinction between "commissarial" and "sovereign" dictatorship—the former is enacted for a specific political purpose, the powers of the latter are in principle unlimited. Regardless of the sincerity of Schmitt's belief in this distinction, it is clear that his interest in the exception over and against the norm results necessarily in a pronounced devaluation of normal conditions of constitutionality/legality and a corresponding overvaluation of "emergency powers." It was these convictions led to his highly influential "latitudinarian" interpretation of Article 48 of the Wemar constitution, in which he concluded that presidential emergency powers should essentially be freed of constitutional restraints.[15]

If one could say that the Weimar Republic's essence or identity was embodied in its consititution, then Schmitt certainly displayed little concern for its identity. He may have been the champion of a dictatorial presidential system, but not of Weimar democracy, as we are told in some accounts.[16] In actual practice the paper-thin distinction between commissarial and sovereign dictatorship would soon fall by the wayside in Schmitt's work of the 1920s. We are left instead with the concept of dictatorship *tout court*, stripped of confusing and extraneous intellectual subtleties.

That in actual practice Schmitt cared very little for the distinction is illustrated by his failure to object to the "sovereign dictatorship" of Adolf Hitler in 1933. As Franz Neumann is quick to remind, "The idea of the totalitarian state grew out of the demand that all power be concentrated in the hands of the president"—precisely Schmitt's strategy. It is important to recall that the National Socialists presented themselves not as the destroyers, but as the saviors of democracy. Neumann goes on to identify none other than Carl Schmitt as "the ideologist of this sham."[17]

Schmitt's next work, *Political Theology* (1922), was one of his most influential. It contains what is perhaps the most consequent formulation of his decisionistic theory of sovereignty: "Sovereign is he who decides on the state of exception," proclaims Schmitt in the book's opening sentence. It is a claim that is in no need of a rational justification. More precisely, it would be incapable of such justification, insofar as in Schmitt's view, "the exception confounds the unity and order of the rationalist scheme" (PT, 14). The power of decision is grounded in an insight superior to the subaltern capacities of human ratiocination, which in any event are only appropriate under the prosaic conditions of normal life. The superior character of the exceptional decision lies in the fact that it proves capable of exploding such mundane parameters of existence. As Schmitt affirms time and again, forcefully and unambiguously, the decision on the state of exception possesses a higher, *existential significance*. It defies the standards of rationalism by virtue of its *sheer existence*. In sum, Schmitt's mature political philosophy is an *existential decisionism*. It persistently withdraws from the tribunal of human reason in order thereby to proclaim with impunity certain higher, existential truths.

One of the most striking features of Schmitt's definition of sovereignty is a consistent employment of existentialist phraseology. For example, he underlines the importance of understanding the state of exception as a *Grenzbegriff* "pertaining to the outermost sphere. . . . Sovereignty must therefore be associated with a border-line case," he observes, "and not with routine" (PT, 14). The border situation is the place in which "Dasein glimpses transcendence, and is thereby transformed from possible to real Existence."[18] By treating the decision on the state of exception in such fashion, Schmitt tries to invest it with a higher, existential meaning as compared with the normalcy of routine life. Its superiority derives from its *sheer existence*: "The *existence* of the state is undoubted proof of its superiority over the valid legal norm. The decision frees itself from all normative ties and becomes in the true sense absolute. . . . The norm is *destroyed* in the exception" he observes (PT, 12; emphasis added).

Schmitt's political philosophy endows the exception with a type of magical omnipotence. This practice allows him to resolve certain intractable ontological problems that plague his framework: above all, the seemingly unbridgeable gulf between the abstract and the concrete, between concept and life, a paramount concern for *Lebensphilosophie* in all its variants. Thus, the state of exception represents the prospect of an existential transformation of life in its routinized everydayness, its elevation to a higher plane. The norm must be "destroyed" insofar as it represents the reign of the merely "conceptual," the "abstract," the "average." Under such conditions, the substance of life in its pulsating fluidity is prevented from coming to the fore. The cardinal virtue of the exception then, from the vantage point of political existentialism, is that it *explodes* the routinization to which life is subjected under conditions of juridical normalcy. For Schmitt, "The exception is that which cannot be subsumed; it defies general codification"; all that remains is the "decision in absolute purity" (PT, 13).

Schmitt's political philosophy represents a plea for what one might call political vitalism. This fact becomes clear when, in the first chapter of *Political Theology*, he explicitly identifies a "philosophy of concrete life" as the conceptual basis of his intellectual enterprise: "Precisely a philosophy of concrete life must not withdraw from the exception and the extreme case, but must be interested in it to the highest degree" (PT, 13). From the standpoint of political existentialism, the rule remains mired in everydayness. It knows no greatness, and merely furthers the rising tide of mediocrity so characteristic of modern democratic societies. Thus, in his decisionistic preference for the exception over the rule, it is clear that Schmitt has drunk deeply from the vitalist philosophical currents of the period: "*The exception is more interesting than the rule*," he declares. "The rule proves nothing, the exception proves everything: It confirms not only the rule but also its existence, which derives only from the exception. In the exception *the power of real life breaks through the crust of a mechanism that has become torpid by repetition*" (PT, 15; emphasis added).

Here, Schmitt purveys many of the standard components of the German conservative-revolutionary critique of modernity as popularized by thinkers such as Spengler and Jünger. The exception, by virtue of its transcendent capacities, possesses the "power of real life" necessary to penetrate the benumbing mechanism of a reified capitalist world. To be sure, such romantic anticapitalist motifs had both their "right" and "left" variants.[19] It is not that the motivational impetus behind such criticisms is itself groundless. In Schmitt's case, however, the emphasis on the exception to the exclusion of all normativism, proceduralism, and institutional checks allows him to degenerate into an advocate of charismatic despotism.

One of the central tenets of *Political Theology* is that all modern political concepts are merely secularized theological concepts. And thus, one of

Schmitt's chief aims as a legal philosopher and political theorist was to reintroduce a strong personal element in modern politics, an element that had fallen by the wayside with the eclipse of political absolutism. Hence, the emphasis on the "personal" aspect of the exceptional decision. But there is something greater at stake. In terms of the theological analogies that Schmitt considers essential, the *exception* should play a role in modern politics comparable to that of the *miracle* in religious life. The practice of political theology aims at nothing less than the "transubstantiation" of the debased body politic—which in the modern age had been shackled by the all-encompassing routine of a legal formalism—into the politically vital ether of the state of exception; a feat, moreover, that can only be accomplished by the charismatic sovereign, the modern-day analog to the divine monarch of absolutist times.[20]

It is of further interest to note that in *Political Theology* the earlier distinction between two types of dictatorship, commissarial and sovereign, vanishes entirely. Instead, one is left with the idea of dictatorship in all its authoritarian starkness. Schmitt contends that in an emergency situation, the powers of the sovereign must be "unlimited." This means that "from the liberal constitutional point of view, there would be no jurisdictional competence at all"; for the sovereign "stands outside the normally valid legal system" (PT, 7). That the sovereign would have to share jurisdictional competence over the question of whether a state of emergency exists or how long it may continue is dismissed by Schmitt as an unwarranted "liberal constitutional interference . . . which attempts to suppress the question of sovereignty by a division and mutual control of competences" (PT, 11). The sovereign's glory must remain indivisible and untainted by power sharing. This conclusion is fully consistent with Schmitt's persistent degradation of liberal institutions, which are capable of "endless conversation" but never an ultimate decision.

Schmitt attempts to provide his theory of dictatorship with historico-philosophical grounding in the discussion of the "counterrevolutionary philosophers of state"—de Maistre, Bonald, Donoso Cortés—that concludes *Political Theology*. According to Schmitt's philosophy of history,[21] political life since the seventeenth century has fallen into a state of permanent decline. Whereas in the absolutist era the two pillars of the state—God and sovereign—occupied their rightful position of supremacy, since then, these concepts have suffered nothing but humiliation and debasement at the hands of the rising bourgeois class and its socialist successors. In the secularizing doctrines of the eighteenth and nineteenth centuries, the concept of God was supplanted by the idea of "man," and the majesty of the sovereign proper was irreparably decimated by the notion of popular sovereignty. As a result of these developments, "the decisionistic and personalistic element in the concept of sovereignty was lost" (PT, 48). More generally, this period of transition witnessed the sacrifice of the sublime virtues of transcendence in favor of the prosaic values of immanence. The concerted assault against traditional religiosity could only end in atheism, disorder, and anarchic freedom. It was the chief merit of the Catholic philosophers of state to have confronted this situation head on and to have never shied away from drawing the logical conclusion: ***dictatorship alone could save the world from the godless era of secular humanism***. Donoso Cortés, "one of the foremost representatives of decisionistic thinking and a Catholic philosopher of the state . . . concluded in reference to the revolution of 1848 that the epoch of royalism was at an end. Royalism is no longer because there are no kings. Therefore legitimacy no longer exists in the traditional sense. For him there was only one solution: dictatorship" (PT, 51–52).

In the reasoning behind Schmitt's praise of Donoso Cortés, one of the standard justifications of fascist dictatorship from a Catholic point of view emerges clearly: the cases of Franco's Spain and Pinochet's Chile immediately leap to mind. Schmitt never tried to hide his view that "all authentic political theories presuppose man as 'evil,' that is, in no way as unproblematical, rather as 'dangerous'" (PT, 61). This undoubtedly accounts in part for his strong personal identification with Donoso Cortés, "whose contempt for man knew no limits," and whom Schmitt lauds as "a spiritual descendant of the Grand inquisitors" (PT, 57–58). In Donoso Cortés' view, evil had triumphed to such an extent in the modern world that only a miracle could deny it ultimate victory. The battle line he saw being drawn in the nineteenth century—that between Catholicism and atheistic socialism—was not just another in a long series of historical struggles; rather, it was Armaggedon. According to Donoso Cortés, therefore, political dictatorship was not only a political, but a ***theological necessity***. At stake was the salvation of men's souls. There is no doubt that Schmitt himself viewed a secularized version of Donoso Cortés' argument as a historical imperative if a decision was to be reached, the prevarications of endless discussion avoided, and the essence of the political saved. Schmitt's own reflections on this theme could hardly be less equivocal:

> The true significance of those counterrevolutionary philosophers of state lies precisely in the consistency with which they decide. They heightened the moment

> of decision to such an extent that the notion of legitimacy, their starting point, was finally dissolved. As soon as Donoso Cortés realized that the period of monarchy had come to an end . . . he brought his decisionism to a logical conclusion. He demanded a political dictatorship. In . . . de Maistre we can also see a reduction of the state to the moment of decision, to a pure decision not based on reason or discussion and not justifying itself, that is, to an absolute decision created out of nothingness. But this decision is essentially dictatorship, not legitimacy (PT 57, 58).[22]

Schmitt's *The Crisis of Parliamentary Democracy* is often cited as evidence of the democratic inclinations of his thought during the Weimar Republic. His basic argument is that liberal institutions essentially invalidate democratic politics, making these two political approaches fundamentally incompatible with one another. Through an extremely selective reading (and mis-reading) of both political traditions, Schmitt builds an effective case. He defines democracy as the "identity of rulers and ruled," thus carefully skirting other historically prominent interpretations of the democratic tradition. Conversely, liberalism—which Schmitt identifies with the institutions of parliament, free discussion, and publicity—in essence subverts the people's right to self-determination, insofar as a variety of cliques and interest groups have seized hold of these institutions merely to exploit them for their own private gain. Hence, "constitutionalism" (here, a code word for liberalism) has forfeited its validity as a political principle in the modern world and stands urgently in need of replacement. The argumentation proceeds seamlessly in the direction of Schmitt's own choice of a successor: plebiscitarian dictatorship.[23]

To understand what Schmitt means by democracy, it is helpful to recall Neumann's claim that the Nazis, too, presented themselves as the champions of democracy, i.e., as the party that represented the authentic embodiment of the popular will. Schmitt's formula for democracy—"the identity between rulers and ruled"—must be understood in a similar vein. Needless to say, the idea of "participatory democracy" could not be further from his mind. Nor the various conceptions of "direct democracy," certainly a logical alternative if one chooses to reject parliamentarianism in toto. Schmitt studiously avoids taking democracy seriously in the etymological sense—"rule of the demos"—nor would he be much interested in the Aristotelian definition of the term, "ruling and being ruled in turn." Hence, like the Nazis' commitment to populism, Schmitt's commitment to democracy is a pseudo-commitment. With the highly tendentious separation of democracy from its supporting liberal institutions—separation of powers, checks and balances, publicity, etc.—he has succeeded in rendering all modern historical incarnations of the term meaningless—precisely his object. To conceive of the democratic revolutions of the eighteenth century minus the substructure of civil liberties (freedom of speech, the press, assembly) that was their necessary concomitant and raison d'être is a monumental non sequitur in historical reasoning (although the tradition of "caeserism" resurrected by Robespierre and the Committee of Public Safety during the course of the French Revolution certainly provides Schmitt with the type of historical precedent he needs).[24]

Via the specious separation of democracy from liberalism, Schmitt has in effect laid out the conceptual and legal groundwork for the turn toward the authoritarian or total state in Germany. Historically, liberal institutions have provided a bulwark for civil society against unwarranted encroachments by the state. In destroying this safeguard, the truly regressive features of Schmitt's political philosophy come to the fore. Thus for Schmitt, the individual ceases to be a point of reference for political theory altogether. Instead, the state is consistently portrayed as the sole embodiment of authority. One cannot even say it is the sole embodiment of "right," since the concept of right loses all its meaning in a situation where the chief virtue of the sovereign is his or her capacity to formulate decisions ex nihilo, in disregard of every normative or juridical precedent.

Lest there be any doubt as to the specific constituents of democracy according to Schmitt, the evidence in *The Crisis of Parliamentary Democracy* is fairly unequivocal. The major criterion, as specified in the Preface to the Second Edition, is the concept of "national homogeneity," a distinct precursor of the National Socialist concept of "racial homogeneity." In Schmitt's framework, "homogeneity" plays the role in democratic theory formerly played by "equality"—a concept Schmitt dismisses outright as part of the conceptual baggage of the liberal mentality. Of course, when the concept of "national homogeneity" is erected as a political ideal, it follows logically that anything that poses a possible threat to its purity must be annihilated. To be sure, Schmitt does not in the least shrink from drawing precisely this conclusion: "Democracy requires, therefore, first homogeneity and second—if the occasion arises—*elimination or eradication of heterogeneity*" (CPD, 9). Schmitt's rhetoric is chilling. He leaves it to the goose-stepping heirs of his political ideas to specify what form such "eradication of heterogeneity" will take. Insofar as his Anglo-American apologists are always arguing for the necessity of understanding his works in historical context, let us take their suggestion to heart in this case by inquiring what ethnic or religious group might have posed a threat to the national integrity of the Germans in the year 1926, and thus might have served as the unspoken target of Schmitt's attack?

"A democracy demonstrates its political power by knowing how to refuse or keep at bay something foreign and dissimilar that threatens its homogeneity," adds Schmitt (CPD, 9), in a formulation that anticipates his insistence a year later in *The Concept of the Political* on the necessity of extirpating the "domestic enemy." It is important to keep in mind that Schmitt's discussion of the need to "eradicate heterogeneity" is in no way an accidental by-product of his political thought. Instead, it follows quite logically from his contempt of political pluralism as part and parcel of the liberal heritage to be jettisoned.

Given these orientations, it is hardly surprising that *The Crisis of Parliamentary Democracy* culminates in a glowing panegyric to the achievements of Italian fascism. As Schmitt observes:

> Until now the democracy of mankind and parliamentarianism has only once been contemptuously pushed aside through the conscious appeal to myth, and that was an example of the irrational power of the national myth. In his famous speech of October 1922 in Naples before the march on Rome, Mussolini said, "We have created a myth, this myth is a belief, a noble enthusiasm; it does not need to be reality, it is a striving and a hope, belief and courage. Our myth is the nation, the great nation which we want to make into a concrete reality for ourselves." (CPD, 75–76)

"The theory of myth is the most powerful symptom of the decline of the relative rationalism of parliamentary thought," he continues, not least of all insofar as it offers the possibility of establishing "an authority based on the new feeling for order, discipline, and hierarchy."

Schmitt's political doctrines consistently attempt to reassert a charismatic dimension that has supposedly been lost in twentieth-century political life. This explains his fascination with the exception as a type of existential boundary-situation, his preoccupation with the sovereignty of decision and its capacity to restore the dwindling "personal element" of politics, and his interest in the irrationalism of political myth. It is curious therefore to note the simultaneous operation of diametrically opposite tendencies in his work, tendencies that push in the direction of a disenchanted functionalism. This functionalism derives in no small measure from Schmitt's agnostic refusal to specify any substantive ends for decisionistic politics. Because his decisionism, as devoid of substantive goals, remains essentially contentless, there is in principle only one end to which the decisionistic sovereign can direct his (or her) energies, and a rather unexalted end at that: the end of political self-preservation. In part this result is a direct consequence of Schmitt's secularization of the political theory of absolutism: when one does away with the "divine right of kings" argument, there is little left for theorists of the authoritarian state to fall back on except Hobbes' "mutual relation of protection and obedience"—a functionalist *Ordungsdenken*, as suggested by Schmitt's praise for the virtues of "order, discipline, and hierarchy" just cited. Of course, the reading of Hobbes here is a highly selective one: retained is the image of the sovereign standing over and above the normally valid legal system; rejected is Hobbes the founder of modern contract theory, since this reading leaves Hobbes vulnerable to liberal interpretations, e.g., as a precursor of the idea of popular sovereignty (precisely the conclusion Rousseau would draw from his reading of Hobbes).

Yet, in the prosaic terminus of Schmitt's political thought—its ultimate emphasis on questions of functional self-preservation–his existentialist point of departure has merely come full circle. When sheer existence is posited as a primary value, whence all other values follow, it is only logical to perceive naked self-preservation as the highest end of political life.

In *The Concept of the Political* (1927) Schmitt thinks through the implications of a political doctrine predicated on the concept of self-preservation with frightening consistency. The result is a glorified social Darwinism in which considerations of foreign policy dominate to the point where domestic politics are stripped of all independence and integrity. But in point of fact, the primacy of foreign policy means "war" as the ultimate, existential limit-condition of politics. The whole analysis leads inevitably toward a justification of the "total state," whose raison d'être is the ever-present possibility of war. Hence, the supremacy of the friend-enemy distinction in politics.

Here, too, Schmitt's ideas must be carefully distinguished from those of Hobbes. For Hobbes, the state of nature or *bellum omnium contra omnes* must be overcome in the contract that establishes civil society. For Schmitt, conversely, the state of war among nations opens up distinctly positive prospects: "war" as the highest instance of the political. This is one of the reasons Schmitt insists time and again that were a single, international federation (foreshadowed by the League of Nations) to supplant the nation-state, the political would disappear from life altogether: for along with the disappearance of the nation-state, the possibility of war too would disappear.[25] In Hobbesian fashion, Schmitt attributes a rather unelevated, functional role to politics in times of political normalcy: the maintenance of internal "peace, security, and order" (BP, 46). It is only in times of war, conversely, that the prospect of existential greatness emerges, prospects unknown to periods of factical normalcy: "Today, the case of war is the 'decisive case' [*'Ernstfall'*]. One can say that here, as elsewhere, the exceptional case has an especially decisive significance in which the inner meaning of things is revealed. For only in actual battle is the most extreme consequence of the political grouping of friend and enemy shown. From this most extreme possibility the life of men gains a specific political tension" (BP, 35).

Thus, for Schmitt, the possibility of war is the ultimate instance, the inherent presupposition of all politics. If, therefore, human life is unavoidably political, *war is the pinnacle of all great politics*. For Schmitt, "politics means *intensive life* [*intensives Leben*]."[26] As the decisive instance of politics, war in Schmitt's eyes takes on the character of an existential boundary-situation, it is the litmus-test as to whether or not a nation possesses political substance.

As the *ultima ratio* of politics, war must be justified in existential terms. Thus, for Schmitt, "The specifically political distinction, to which political acts and motives can be traced back, is the distinction between friend and enemy" (BP, 26). These concepts must be understood "in their *concrete, existential sense*. . . . The concepts of friend, enemy, and struggle receive their real meaning especially insofar as they relate to and preserve the real possibility of physical annihilation. War follows from enmity, for the latter is the *existential negation of another being*" (BP, 27, 28; emphasis added). Dispelling any conceivable ambiguities concerning his program, Schmitt continues by defining the "political enemy" in the folowing terms: "He is the other, the alien, and it suffices that in his essence he is something *existentially other and alien in an especially intensive sense*" (BP, 33; emphasis added). For Schmitt, "War, the readiness for death of fighting men, the physical annihilation of other men who stand on the side of the enemy, all that has no normative, *only an existential meaning*" (BP, 49).

But a closer look reveals that Schmitt's emphasis on the ultimate martial telos of politics merely serves as a cover for the manifest paucity of intrinsic political content in his own thinking. For, despite the colorful existentialist rhetoric, there is no surmounting the fact that the fundamental political value we are left with is naked self-preservation. Indeed, this position follows logically from the original existential point of departure, the unmitigated contingency of all human existence. In pursuing this existentialist tack, Schmitt consciously abandons all higher questions about the meaning of political life, questions he hastily equates with the normativist tradition he is so eager to be done with. The sole important fact is that a state exists, not the specific content or ends of its existence. In this respect, Löwith's critique proves justified: insofar as Schmitt's notion of the political is devoid of independent content, it, too, is a mere "occasionalism." It, too, merely stands in the service of other, "unpolitical powers"—above all, the powers of war. In the last analysis, the specificity of the political sphere, whose preservation Schmitt viewed as his primary intellectual task, is itself eclipsed—sacrificed on the altar of Ares, as it were. Abandoned is a whole series of political questions whose posing accounts for the birth of political philosophy in the West: questions about justice, the virtuous citizen, and, more generally, the "good life." In Schmitt's political theory we trade the "good life" for "mere life": the existential right of self-preservation.

In his writings of the early 1930s, Schmitt discerns a trend at work that presages a return of the political: the reemergence of new *Kampfgebiete* or "areas of struggle" in the modern world. The key variable in this newly emergent equation is technology, which, in the twentieth century, seems to have surpassed economics as the singular determinant of cultural life. Advocates of a religion of technological progress long believed that the rise of technology represented another stage in the neutralization of politics, a verdict Schmitt wishes vigorously to contest. Rather than being "mechanistic" and "soulless," as many of his German contemporaries complained, Schmitt sees "an activistic metaphysic" at work in technology that promises the "unbounded power and domination of man over nature, even over human physics" itself.[27] Rather than representing one more stage in a four-hundred-year process of political neutralization, technology embodies prospects for a momentous return of the political on an unprecedentedly grandiose scale. For the historically unique concentration and accumulation of technology in the twentieth century opens up concrete prospects for the realization of the "total state." Schmitt describes this process as follows:

> The process of the progressive neutralization of the various spheres of cultural life has arrived at its end, because it has arrived at technology. Technology is no longer a neutral basis, in the sense of the process of neutralization, and every strong politics will make use of it. The present century can thus be understood in a cultural sense as a technological century only in a provisional way. Its ultimate meaning will be revealed when it is known what type of politics is strong enough to master the new technology, and what are the real friend/enemy groupings that arise on this new basis.[28]

Schmitt develops his theory of the total state in two key essays from the early 1930s, "The Turn toward the Total State" and "The Continued Development of the Total State in Germany." For Schmitt, the virtue of the total state is that the nineteenth-century neutralization of politics is eclipsed as the state undertakes the self-organization of society. "Politics intervenes in all spheres of life," remarks Schmitt; "there is no neutral sphere." As an example, he cites the modern imperatives of political armament, which concern "not only the military, but also the industrial and economic preparation for war." Even the "intellectual and moral formation of the citizens" is incorporated into this totalizing network. Schmitt sees welcome confirmation of such trends in the theory of "total mobilization" advanced by "a remarkable representative of the German *Frontsoldaten*," Ernst Jünger. "Jünger's formula proves that a self-organization of society into the state is in process, leading from the neutral state of the nineteenth century to the total state of the twentieth century."[29] The only possible obstacle Schmitt envisions to the ultimate triumph of the total state is the residual party pluralism of the Weimar period.[30]

Schmitt's theory of the total state—whose prescience as an analysis of key developments in twentieth-century politics can hardly be denied—was formulated prior to the Nazi seizure of power in 1933. It has been argued that Schmitt's legal opinion on the "equal chance" question in 1932 (suggesting that extremist political parties who did not respect the constitution be denied an "equal chance" of political participation) might have jeopardized his status in the eyes of the Nazi power elite. Whatever the truth concerning these allegations,[31] it certainly did not prevent the Nazi government from summoning their prestigious new convert to draft the infamous *Gleichschaltung* legislation of April 1933. Schmitt cooperated with alacrity.[32]

In his first major work of the Nazi years, *State, Movement, Volk,* Schmitt tried to reconcile his theory of the total state with Party ideology. The tripartite conception of sovereignty expressed in the title of Schmitt's 1933 work represents an attempt to bring his thinking in line with the new National Socialist reality. The opening pages are quick to proclaim the overthrow of the Weimar constitution on the basis of the Enabling Act of March 24, 1933. Ironically, in what at the time possessed the legal status of a temporary, commissarial dictatorship, or limited granting of emergency powers, Schmitt perceived a sovereign or permanent dictatorship. Since the Weimar constitution was incapable of distinguishing friend from enemy, it deserved to perish, argued Schmitt. He chose to view the Reichstag elections of March 5, 1933, in which the National Socialists captured only 43.9 percent of the vote, as a "plebiscite through which the German people recognized Adolf Hitler . . . as the political Führer of the German Volk."[33] Schmitt's arguments here, his alacritous support of the sovereign dictatorship of Adolf Hitler, in no way constitute a break with his earlier positions, but represent their logical completion. As he says at one point with reference to the political pluralism that presented itself as the scourge of Weimar: "In the one-party state of National Socialist Germany, the danger of a pluralistic dismemberment of Germany . . . has been vanquished."[34]

There is no small measure of irony in the fact that despite Schmitt's fawning subservience to Nazi ideology on almost every point in *State, Movement, Volk*—the *Führerprinzip* and racial homogeneity are praised as the substance of National Socialist legality; as is the movement in general for its keen attention to "authentic *Volkssubstanz*"—the book was not entirely successful. Schmitt had lapsed from Nazi ideology on one crucial theme: by considering the movement as the "dynamic" aspect of the tripartite division and the Volk as merely the "passive," "unpolitical" element, he had failed to accord the latter the equal status required for it by official propaganda. Needless to say, the Nazi invocation of the Volk was an immensely fraudulent pseudo-populism, in which popular energies were merely instrumentalized to the advantage of the leadership clique and its expansionist goals. Yet, Schmitt's honesty in owning up to the actual reality of the situation caused his book to be viewed with suspicion.[35]

We have already alluded to the various depths to which Schmitt sunk in his consistent support of the Nazi dictatorship. Certainly the most reprehensible aspect of his collusion with the regime was the avidity with which he supported Nazi racial policies. His article "The Constitution of Freedom" in 1935 was quick to support the Nuremberg racial legislation of the same year, which forbade intermarriage between Jews and non-Jews, and sought to invalidate existing marriages between Jewish and non-Jewish Germans. Schmitt's greatest offenses can probably be found in an article published the following year, entitled "German Legal Science in the Struggle against the Jewish Spirit," in which the standard refrains of Nazi anti-Semitic rhetoric are to be found. Here, Schmitt polemicizes against the "rootlessness" of the Jewish race and the inferiority of the "unproductive and sterile" Jewish intellect.[36] He urged his fellow jurists, when citing from texts written by Jews, to be sure to identify the writer as a "Jewish author."

In 1938, in an otherwise academic work on the political thought of Hobbes, Schmitt gratuitously recites a litany of nineteenth-century Jewish figures who, since the emancipation, have infiltrated and polluted the German nation: "The young Rothschilds, Karl Marx, Börne, Heine, and Meyerbeer" all possess their "spheres of operation" in the various fields of German cultural life.[37] Singled out for special mention is the legal thinker Friedrich Julius Stahl (whom Schmitt insists on calling "Stahl-Jolson" to indicate his Jewish heritage): "The Christian sacrament of Baptism serves him not only as an 'entry-ticket' to 'society,' but also as the identity-card for entrance into the holiness of a still very solid German state," remarks Schmitt. In his advocacy of "constitutionalism," Stahl-Jolson, the treacherous Jew, is charged with seducing the Prussian conservatives "on to the terrain of the enemy"—liberal thinking—"on which the Prussian military state, under the burdensome test of the war, collapses in 1918."[38] In this way, Schmitt attempts to provide a vulgar intellectual-historical grounding for the infamous "stab in the back" myth.

Despite these repugnant efforts to ingratiate himself with the new regime,[39] Schmitt sensed that the alliance was potentially ill-fated and voluntarily resigned from his post in the National Socialist Jurists Association in November 1936. However, he retained his position in the Nazi party, his chair on the law faculty in Berlin, and his position on the prestigious Prussian State Council until the end of the war. His post-1936 writings revolved around the concept of "Grossraum," a perverted version of the Monroe Doctrine which served as a justification of German territorial expansion in the East. In truth, this idea was little more than a pseudo-legalistic variant of the Nazi theory of "Lebensraum."

In Schmitt's political writings of the 1930s, he predictably attempts to back away from the radical implications of his earlier decisionism and instead accords *Ordnungsdenken* conceptual pride of place. For example, in his foreword to the 1933 edition of *Political Theology*, Schmitt warns that decisionism risks succumbing to the exigencies of the moment, and hence overlooks that "restful Being contained in every great political movement." Now, instead of "decision ex nihilo" one finds an emphasis on "völkisch substantiality"—it is no longer the state of exception that concerns Schmitt, but the state of normalcy embodied in the existing fascist order. The latter can now be seen as providing the "concrete basis for decision" in his work, thereby offering a solution to the contentlessness of the decision in its earlier versions. Yet, rather than constituting an absolute break with his earlier work, this move signifies the ultimate union of the two parallel strands of his thought, decisionism and *Ordnungsdenken*. That is, the concrete, racial life of the Volk (*Artgleichheit*) now provides the existential basis for decision—just as in *State, Movement, and Volk*, it was a *Grundentscheidung* of the Volk in the elections of March 1933 that abrogated the Weimar constitution and sanctified Hitler's sovereign dictatorship.

Since the 1920s, Schmitt had been a staunch opponent of formal legality and always advocated the importance of substantive, political criteria in the promulgation of legal decisions. The Nazi revolution thus in many ways merely represented the tangible realization of the basic inclinations of Schmitt's earlier legal and political thinking. For Schmitt it was an essential fact that the "existential-rootedness of all human thought" leads with necessity to a sphere in which human existence is filled with "organic, biological and völkisch differentiations." This remains true insofar as "Man, in the deepest, most unconscious impulses of his soul, but also in his tiniest brain-cell, stands in the reality of völkisch and racial belonging."[40] It was therefore one of Schmitt's deeply held convictions that "all questions and answers intersect with the demand for [racial] homogeneity, without which a total Führer-state could not subsist for a day."[41]

The notion that Schmitt's "no-nonsense approach to concrete power relations can provide a healthy corrective to the predominant leftist moralism," as it has been recently suggested (along with the even more startling claim that "the left can only benefit by learning from Carl Schmitt"),[42] would seem, in light of the foregoing analysis, an extremely tenuous proposition. For wouldn't one of the primary conclusions to be drawn from Schmitt's own intellectual-political itinerary be that all such "transcendent" as opposed to "immanent" critiques of liberal democratic political paradigms—i.e., all attempts to "transcend" without "preserving" this ethico-political legacy—invite historical regressions of the highest magnitude? Schmitt himself was fond of drawing an analogy between his own fate under the National Socialist regime and that of the eponymous hero of Melville's "Benito Cereno"—the ship captain who is forced against his will to carry out the orders of his thuggish captors.[43] But as we have tried to suggest, the elective affinities between Schmitt's own conservative-authoritarian political views and the fascist program of a totalitarian transcendence of liberalism were legion. In truth, it would have been more surprising had Schmitt actually *refused* in 1933 to cast his lot with the victorious National Socialist Party. His post-festum efforts at self-exoneration, therefore, can only strike one as tendentious and self-serving. That the American Schmittians have elected to follow uncritically the version of these events supplied by the master is equally disturbing.

When surveying the intellectual legacy of Carl Schmitt, we are inevitably driven to seek comparisons with the case of Martin Heidegger—who we now know tried in 1933 to solicit Schmitt's involvement in "the gathering spiritual forces" that had recently gained supremacy in Germany.[44] In this connection, perhaps the major risk the impending Anglo-American reception of Schmitt may run parallels those of the Heidegger reception in postwar France: that of a *totally de-historicized reception*. Because the introduction of Heidegger's work in France was completely unhistorical, because the French Heideggerians were under the delusion that the eternal verities of (Heideggerian) philosophy could bear no affinities with the sordid actualities of world history, the world of French letters was wholly unprepared for the shock unleashed by the appearance of Victor Farias' book, *Heidegger et le nazisme*.[45] Similarly, any contemporary rehabilitation of Schmitt's work—be it on the left or the right—must guard against the a-historical illusion that Schmitt's theoretical positions can be innocently lifted out of the socio-historical context in which they originated and applied unproblematically to contemporary world affairs. Schmitt's theories originated at a determinate hour of German history—its most shameful hour—and all future attempts to do justice to the provocative intellectual legacy he has bequeathed must incorporate an awareness of these facts into their analytical perspective. To do otherwise would be both naive as well as intellectually dishonest.

FIVE

Merleau-Ponty and the Birth of Weberian Marxism

> We wanted to begin this study with Weber because, at a time when events were about to bring the Marxist dialectic to the fore, Weber's effort demonstrates under what conditions a historical dialectic is serious. There were Marxists who understood this and they were the best. There developed a rigorous and consistent Marxism which, like Weber's approach, was a theory of historical comprehension, of *Vielseitigkeit*, and of creative choice, and was a philosophy that questioned history. It is only beginning with Weber and with this Weberian Marxism, that the adventures of the dialectic of the past thirty-five can be understood.
>
> —Merleau-Ponty,
> *Adventures of the Dialectic* (1955)

In contemporary French thought, Maurice Merleau-Ponty has inexplicably become something of an "unperson." In *Les Aventures de la liberté*, Bernard-Henri Lévi's panoramic chronicle (and ultimately a television miniseries) of twentieth-century French intellectual life, in which one finds portraits of Malraux, Barrès, Aragon, Breton, Cocteau, Camus, Aron, Mauriac, Blanchot, Bataille, Foucault, Sartre, of course, and many others, Merleau-Ponty doesn't merit a footnote. Those with right-wing political sentiments undoubtedly never forgave him for writing *Humanism and Terror*, which was widely viewed as a Stalinist tract. Those on the left were equally unforgiving when it came to *Adventures of the Dialectic*, which was perceived either as a retreat to liberalism or as an abandonment of the political *tout court*. For structuralists and poststructuralists alike—that is, for virtually anyone writing in France over the course of the last thirty years—he remained identified with the *démodé* paradigm of "expressive subjectivity"; that is, with an outlook that was at the same time excessively Hegelian, Husserlian, and existential-phenomenological; one that remained overly enamored of the delusions of "presence" associated with the forenamed "philosophies of subjectivity." And even though the break with Sartre dates from 1952, since his untimely death in 1961, Merleau-Ponty's intellectual star seems to have been inextricably tied to that of Sartre. Existentialist, fellow-traveler of the Communist Party, founding editor of *Les Temps Modernes*—all characteristics he shares with his illustrious fellow *normalien*—it is by his work of the period 1945–1951 that Merleau-Ponty seems to have been judged by an unforgiving posterity.

All of which is unjust, since many of the preoccupations and concerns of his later work seem to have anticipated poststructuralist thematics. For example, Lyotard's 1971 study, *Discours, Figure*, which argues for the importance of visual form—figures, shapes, images—in exploding the tyrannical hegemony of Western reason and discursive thought, seems very much a lengthy postscript to ideas first developed in Merleau-Ponty's writings on art; to wit, the marvelous phenomenological aesthetic first elaborated in essays such as "Cézanne's Doubt" (*Sense and Non-Sense*). "Before our undivided existence, the world is true; it exists," remarks Merleau-Ponty in a text from the early 1950s. "We experience in it a truth which shows through and envelopes us rather than being held and circumscribed by our mind," he continues; a characterization of the priority of "world" and "truth" to "mind" and "thought" that is of classically (late) Heideggerian vintage. To its discredit, "critical thought"—disembodied, unfeeling, objective—commits the intellectual sin of breaking with "the naive evidence of things."[1] With such insights, Merleau-Ponty begins the project of a systematic reexamination of the relationship between "thought" and "world"—one he will refer to as "The Origin of Truth" and whose posthumous fruits are texts such as *The Prose of the World* and *The Visible and the Invisible*—in which "the body" plays the all-important role of mediating agency or *tertium quid*; an undertaking which, in many essential respects, prefigures the deconstruction of truth, subjectivity, and "presence" that would attain such prominence in French intellectual life in the decades to follow.

Such conjectures concerning the course and import of Merleau-Ponty's philosophical development have been borne out by Claude Lefort:

> From 1952 to 1959 a new task imposes itself, and his language is transformed. He discovers the delusions in which "philosophies of consciousness" are trapped. . . . The truth is that, in Merleau-Ponty's last years, metaphysics no longer

appeared to him to be the ground of all his thoughts. He allowed himself to be carried beyond its frontiers and entertained an interrogation of Being which shattered the former status of the subject and of truth.[2]

■ ■ ■ ■ ■ ■

I

In the history of dialectical thought every now and then one encounters a conceptual oxymoron that, upon closer scrutiny, reveals itself as an intellectual breakthrough of the highest order: Kant's "disinterested pleasure" in the third *Critique*; Hegel's characterization of freedom as "insight into necessity" in the *Philosophy of History*. Such is also the case with the epithet "Weberian Marxism" coined by Merleau-Ponty in *Adventures of the Dialectic*. Seldom, it would seem, were two intellectual stances more thoroughly opposed than those of Marx and Weber. One need only survey their respective etiologies of capitalist development: for Marx, primitive accumulation; for Weber, the Protestant ethic. Yet, for Merleau-Ponty, not only were the theoretical enterprises of Marx and Weber compatible; each represented the necessary historical corrective of the other. For Merleau-Ponty, dialectical thought that remained uninformed by the self-critical categories of the "understanding" congealed into the worst form of conceptual dogmatism—Sartre's "ultra-bolshevism" in *The Communists and Peace* (1952) being only the most recent in a long line of historical offenders. Hence, viewed epistemologically, *Adventures of the Dialectic* attempts both a metaphysical salvation of nominalism and a nominalist salvation of metaphysics: Merleau-Ponty attempts both to relativize Marxian conceptual absolutism and radicalize Weberian value-relativism. For only when infused with Weberian doubt will the adventures of the dialectic be prevented from terminating in misadventures of a catastrophic and gruesome nature—"ultra-bolshevism." And only when Weberian relativism yields to the Marxian insight that a society predicated on reification, one that functions blindly and unconsciously, behind the backs of its members, is unconscionable, will the possibility exist of rescuing history from an abyss of contingency and non-sense. In this respect, for Merleau-Ponty historical materialism remains very much the categorical imperative of the present age.

The ensuing inquiry proceeds from the following conviction: *Adventures of the Dialectic* represents one of the most important discussions of Marxism in our century; it achieves this status, however, only insofar as it remains, strictly speaking, non-Marxist. The theoretical significance of *Adventures of the Dialectic* can only be fully appreciated when viewed in the context of Merleau-Ponty's lifework in its entirety; specifically, as a lengthy self-criticism of his earlier position on revolutionary violence in *Humanism and Terror* (1947). Finally, the curious relationship between the two texts cannot be understood apart from Merleau-Ponty's early philosophy as a whole, which receives its fullest articulation in *The Phenomenology of Perception* (1945).

Interpreters of Merleau-Ponty have been at odds over the relationship between politics and philosophy in *Humanism and Terror*. Martin Jay, for example, contends that "Merleau-Ponty's philosophy, indeed his entire outlook on the world, was deeply holistic from the beginning."[3] Proceeding from this insight, he suggests that it was only a short step from the phenomenological holism of his early philosophy to the political holism of *Humanism and Terror*—where the proletariat becomes the seemingly infallible Archimedean point of history. Conversely, James Miller comes to the diametrically opposite conclusion, observing that "such an essentialist vision of the proletariat and its historical mission contradicted the chief import of Merleau-Ponty's phenomenology of perception, with its emphasis on the contingency and open-ended nature of meaning."[4]

It is Miller, it seems, who has pinpointed the extreme tension underlying Merleau-Ponty's early political thought: its incompatibility with the epistemological standpoint of the *Phenomenology of Perception*, which seemed inimical to the affirmation of philosophical first principles and absolutes. Yet the disquieting justification of proletarian violence in *Humanism and Terror* was based on precisely such an affirmation: a wager on the proletariat as the potential incarnation of "reason in history." Let us briefly reconstruct the nature of the politico-philosophical dilemma at issue.

The Phenomenology of Perception boldly attempts to weave a path between the Scylla and Charybdis of traditional epistemological standpoints, rationalism and empiricism. For Merleau-Ponty, both approaches are inauthentic insofar as both are equally one-sided. Whereas rationalism prefers to view human experience as disembodied and eviscerated for the sake of the purity of the "I think," empiricism, with excessive humility, ultimately devalues the specificity of human existence to the level of merely a "thing among things." For Merleau-Ponty, like his predecessor Edmund Husserl, both perspectives are insufficiently "prescientific," both obfuscate the pristine quality of the "natural attitude" through which things themselves in their precategorial givenness make themselves known to us. Hence, following

Husserl, Merleau-Ponty seeks out a third path, a via media between philosophical extremes. Yet it becomes increasingly clear to him that the path adopted by Husserl—the doctrine of *Wesenschau*, the phenomenological "intuition of essences"—ultimately retains too many affinities with the metaphysical illusions of first philosophy. Consequently, Merleau-Ponty makes common cause with the existential phenomenology of the early Heidegger. And it was the late Husserl—the Husserl who has discovered history in the *Crisis*—who became for him the "authentic" Husserl.[5]

The increasing distance from Husserl and proximity to Heidegger can be seen most clearly in Merleau-Ponty's renunciation of the time-honored telos of philosophical rationalism: the idea that the entirety of human knowledge can be grasped within the confines of the philosophical system. From this vantage point the Husserlian desideratum of "philosophy as rigorous science" can only appear as merely another effort to "out-Hegel Hegel."[6] Merleau-Ponty himself renounced philosophical systematics in favor of the ideal of an open-ended system. However, of equal importance in understanding his relation to the philosophical tradition is his rejection not only of the metaphysical ideal of emphatic truth, but also his relinquishment of the idea of epistemological transparency: the idea that somehow our knowledge of things could ever be exhaustive, consummate, and pure. It is the perennially situated nature of the knowing subject that mocks omniscience and suggests finitude as the true transcendental ground of cognition. In this respect Merleau-Ponty's epistemological perspectivism, which derives from the *Gestalt* notion of the phenomenological field, has more in common with Nietzsche than Husserl. And thus he has frequently been referred to as a "philosopher of ambiguity."[7] The rejection of epistemological transparency and the partisanship for existential finitude are perceived as significant philosophical gains. For what has been sacrificed in epistemic exactitude and precision is recovered with dividends in phenomenological richness and diversity—Weberian *Vielseitigkeit*. Hence, via a curious twist, the emphasis on "finitude" proves capable of recapturing a virtually "infinite" array of existential meanings and resonances that remain barred to us as a result of the closures of traditional idealist or empiricist epistemologies.

Although Merleau-Ponty's references to Husserl are unfailingly dutiful, it is clear that for him the pre-*Crisis* Husserl remains too beholden to the rationalist camp. Above all, this can be seen in Husserl's insistence on the "constitutive" function and "intentionality" of consciousness as in the last instance meritorious of epistemological primacy.[8] Although the battle cry of the phenomenological movement had been "back to the things themselves,"[9]

Merleau-Ponty recognized that, despite its professed intentions, Husserlian phenomenology remained most comfortable when operating on the plane of mind or thinking substance.

By virtue of his thoroughgoing rejection of the transcendental ego as an unproblematical point of departure for sound philosophical inquiry, Merleau-Ponty parts company with Husserl and makes common cause with Heidegger, for whom subjectivity becomes Dasein or Being-in-the-world. "Probably the chief gain from phenomenology," observes Merleau-Ponty, "is to have united extreme subjectivism and extreme objectivism in the notion of the world or rationality. . . . To say that there exists rationality is to say that perspectives blend, perceptions confirm each other, a meaning emerges." "Because we are in the world, we are *condemned* to meaning," he adds.[10]

For Merleau-Ponty, in lieu of the epistemological primacy of thinking substance, it is *the body* that provides the key to our Being-in-the-world, our perspectival situatedness, our very capacity for experience and meaning. The body represents nothing less than the inner-worldly locus wherein *res extensa* and *res cogitans* intersect. As such, it facilitates the determinate overcoming of philosophical dualism in all its forms. As Merleau-Ponty explains, from it we learn that all subjectivity is a situated or *embodied subjectivity*; and thus it is the body, and not the scientific construct of a pure ego, that discloses our modes of relatedness vis-à-vis objects and other (embodied) subjectivities or selves.

"Our constant aim," remarks Merleau-Ponty at one telling juncture in *The Phenomenology of Perception*, "is to elucidate the primary function whereby we bring into existence, for ourselves, or take hold upon a space, the object or the instrument, and *to describe the body as the place where this appropriation occurs*."[11] It is his claim that all perception, all experience and cognition, are mediated through the body that represents his unique contribution to both the phenomenological movement and the field of epistemology in general.[12]

And yet Merleau-Ponty's rethematization of the body in no way bespeaks a return to an epistemological standpoint that is in the least physicalist. Instead, as the earlier description of our being "condemned to meaning" as the essential existential feature of human Being-in-the-world suggests, Merleau-Ponty's conception of human action remains staunchly interpretive and anti-positivist.

Thus, for example, at one point in *The Phenomenology of Perception*, Merleau-Ponty goes so far as to suggest that the body be "compared not to a physical object, but to a work of art."[13] This is true insofar as, phenomenologically speaking, the body is neither the "other" of a pure "I think," nor the mere physiological locus of a network of neurological functions, but rather a grouping or nexus of lived-through meanings: it is the medium through which we both impart and receive meaning from a pregiven environing world.[14] The body is the irreducible existential prism through which alone we make sense (*Sinn*, *Sens*) of the world. It suggests comparison with a work of art insofar as, phenomenologically, it exhibits a structural indeterminacy, a concatenation of meaning-structures, that proves inimical to apodeictic certitude of the mathematico-geometrical type. Instead, like a work of art, the structure of human experience yields symbolic, conceptual meaning only after one has first proceeded through the detour of sensuous-somatic being: the gesture and perception in all their existential concretion and variety. Both human and aesthetic meanings only reveal themselves through the ontological medium of sensuous embodiment; and it is for this reason that both present themselves as an inexhaustible "play" of meanings rather than as a sequence of logical postulates to be stated once and for all. Herein, too, we discern the "uniquely ambiguous" character of all human Being-in-the-world that is revealed from the standpoint of a phenomenology of the body; as well as the intellectual grounds behind Merleau-Ponty's emphatic renunciation of a Platonic-Cartesian "metaphysics of certitude."

The interpretive enigma that implores decipherment, then, is: how does one proceed from the philosophy of ambiguity in *The Phenomenology of Perception* to the self-righteous justification of proletarian violence in *Humanism and Terror*, Merleau-Ponty's response to Koestler's eschatologico-political agnosticism. For it would seem that the standpoint of proletarian violence, based as it is on a series of historico-philosophical certitudes, on an "ethic of ultimate ends," is a standpoint that would tolerate few ambiguities. Ambiguities only threaten to impede the revolutionary course; and it is revolutions, after all, that serve as the "locomotive of history" (Marx).

Yet another question regarding proletarian violence as seen through Merleau-Ponty's eyes must be posed: does *Humanism and Terror* proffer a normative or empirical justification of proletarian violence? Does it purport to justify proletarian violence as an ideal or in merely historical terms?

It is clear that Merleau-Ponty's initial intent in *Humanism and Terror*—and it is perhaps here that his argument remains on its firmest ground—is to censure the duplicity of "bourgeois" critiques of proletarian violence, which hypocritically object to violence unconditionally on ethical grounds.

Here, bourgeois Tartufferie manifests itself in the denial of the struggles and bloodletting of its own historical origins: 1640, 1776, 1789, colonialism, imperialism, and so forth. Nor are the affinities between liberalism and violence by any means confined to the past, argues Merleau-Ponty. Liberalism, too, proceeds via the systematic exclusion of certain social classes and groups from public life (e.g., Marx's description of the proletariat as a class that is "*in* civil society but not *of* civil society"). Its hands too are unclean. And thus, self-serving claims to moral superiority disintegrate upon careful scrutiny. As Merleau-Ponty argues:

> A regime which is nominally liberal can be oppressive in reality. A regime which acknowledges its violence *might* have in it more genuine humanity. To counter Marxism with "ethical arguments" is to ignore what Marxism has said with most truth and what has made its fortune in the world; it is to continue a mystification and to bypass the problem. Any serious discussion of communism must therefore pose the problem in communist terms, that is to say, not on the grounds of principles but on the grounds of human relations.[15]

"The purity of [liberal] principles not only tolerates but even requires violence," he concludes.[16] As an ethical and political thinker, Merleau-Ponty seems rigorously un-Kantian. In a world of unbridled circumstantial contingency, his version of the categorical imperative can, like that of Ernst Bloch, only function effectively when it is backed up with revolver in hand.[17] It is not through one's intentions that one acts ethically—as the critique of ideology shows, intentions come cheap. Instead, it is only by way of the ultimate consequences and effects of action that the latter can be actually judged. As a political thinker, Merleau-Ponty shows himself to be a thoroughgoing realist. Since politics is primarily a sphere of indeterminacy, contingency, and chance, it remains at an unbridgeable remove from the purity of the moral realm. As Weber once suggested, those desirous of a clear conscience should go elsewhere. Politicians who tell us that their hands are clean are only the worst sort of apologists and connivers.

Thus, in an essay from the same period, Merleau-Ponty praises Machiavelli as the political theorist of the modern age par excellence. Instead of sugar-coating the issue of politics and violence, "Machiavelli introduces us to the milieu proper to politics and allows us to estimate the task we are faced with if we want to bring some truth to it."[18] The fallacy of a politics of principle is that, in its steadfast allegiance to a higher order of truth, it fails to concern itself with the consequences of action, which must come to fruition in the mundane empirical world. This type of politics—the Crusades of the Middle Ages, for example—in the end always proves guilty of the greatest excesses. As Merleau-Ponty concludes:

> If by humanism we mean a philosophy of the inner man which finds no difficulty in principle in his relationships with others, no opacity whatsoever in the functioning of society, and which replaces political cultivation by moral exhortation, Machiavelli is not a humanist. But if by humanism we mean a philosophy which confronts the relationship of man to man and the constitution of a common situation and a common history between men as a problem, then we have to say that Machiavelli formulated some of the conditions of any serious humanism.[19]

The question then remains and must be posed in the starkest terms possible: which variety of humanism is represented by Bolshevism? In Bolshevism does one find a new crusade or Cesare Borgia?

The difference between *Humanism and Terror* and *Adventures of the Dialectic* will hinge on the answer to this question. In *Humanism and Terror* Merleau-Ponty still perceives Bolshevism as a form of "Machiavellian humanism." Proceeding from this assumption, he has no problem with the doctrine that the ends justify the means. Since politics is a sphere of struggle, *all* politics of necessity employ violent means. One is never faced with a simple moral choice between a violent politics and one that shuns violence. Hence, all questions concerning violence in politics can only be questions of degree. And it may well prove the case that a politics that renounces violence out of "principle" (that of Chamberlain at Munich, for example) is responsible for unleashing a greater evil than one that openly recognizes its central place in the world of human affairs (thus, despite its sanguinary dénouement in 1793–94, Jacobinism also "saves the Revolution"). For Merleau-Ponty, Bolshevism is justified and immune to all liberal criticism insofar as the ends it embodies are humanistic. Violence is a fact of life, and hence justified "in an epoch . . . where the traditional ground of a nation or a society crumbles and where . . . the liberty of each man is a mortal threat to others."[20] If "the violence it exercises is revolutionary and capable of creating human relations between men,"[21] then Bolshevik violence is fully licit.

Yet *Humanism and Terror* is by no means a crude vindication of Stalinism. Merleau-Ponty himself is only too aware of the fact that "the Revolution has come to a halt: it maintains and aggravates the dictatorial apparatus while renouncing the liberty of the proletariat in the Soviets and its Party and abandoning the humane control of the state."[22] The mistake made by Koestler and others was to have conflated this particular historical embodiment of communism with communism as a normative principle. In this context, ironically, it is Merleau-Ponty who emerges as the consummate anti-Machiavellian in berating a recalcitrant communist reality with the sublimity of communism as an ideal, a *verité à faire*. In effect, he risks succumbing to a Fichtean voluntarism which holds that if the facts fail to measure up to the idea, so much the worse for the facts ("um so schlimmer für die Tatsachen")—which is itself a recipe for ultra-Bolshevism:

> Marxist politics is formally dictatorial and totalitarian. But it is a dictatorship of men who are men first and foremost and a totalitarianism of workers of all kinds who repossess the state and the means of production. The dictatorship of the proletariat is not the will of a few officials who are the only ones initiated in the secret of history, as in Hegel; it follows the spontaneous movement of the proletariat in every country and relies upon the "instinct" of the masses.[23]

Merleau-Ponty is trapped (he has trapped himself) at a historical juncture with no exit. How does one react to an era in which it is simultaneously "impossible to be an anti-communist and not possible to be a communist"?[24] The reason it is impossible to be a communist has already been stated: the Revolution has come to a halt. However, the reason it is impossible to be an anti-communist is that, in Merleau-Ponty's view, historical materialism still represents the only concrete possibility of overcoming the injustices of the present age, the only prospect of surmounting history as the sphere of pure contingency, of Weberian *Sinnlosigkeit*, and of establishing the reign of reason in history, by virtue of which humanism becomes a reality instead of a liberal shibboleth. However, when Merleau-Ponty invokes the "spontaneous movement of the proletariat" and the "instinct of the masses," one detects a desire not merely to transcend the contingencies of history, but a desire to escape from history *tout court*. One detects a search for absolutes and guarantees that can never be found in history as lived, but which would only exist in some extraterrestrial intelligible realm—a realm that could never be realized *by us*. One senses a—Hegelian—desire to bring the dialectic to a premature halt: to proclaim once and for all the convergence of the "real" and the "rational," to celebrate the "end of history" as an accomplished fact.

What Merleau-Ponty failed to recognize in his attempt to rescue Bolshevism qua norm from its actual historical debasement was the constitutive role of the norm in the fact itself. The distinction between the "dictatorship of the officials" and that of the "proletariat" ("spontaneous," "instinctive") will not wash. For part of the reason the officials can claim a monopoly of historical power and knowledge is because of a philosophy of history that lends itself to precisely such an appropriation. That is, if the proletariat as a class can be said to possess insight into the "secret of history," it stands to reason that a historical vanguard might seize the reins of power in the name of that secret to hasten its realization—especially in historical situations in which the "empirical" proletariat seems reluctant to assume the world-historical role that had been ascribed to it by revolutionary theoreticians. In the proletariat Merleau-Ponty desires more than an infusion of rationality in history; he desires a transcendental force that will purge history of its accidental character, of its *ambiguity*. A greater contradiction with his phenomenological writings of this same period would be difficult to imagine.

Nevertheless, one can agree with *Humanism and Terror*'s critique of the false alternative posed by Koestler: the choice between the "yogi" or the "commissar."[25] First, Koestler offers us a caricatural version of Marxism—a Marxism equivalent to the crudest form of "diamat," in which the Moloch of historical necessity parasitically feeds off the corpses of innocent individuals. He deceives a second time by claiming that an ascetic withdrawal from history—the attitude of the yogi—would be a praiseworthy alternative to Marxist terror. And although he attempts to deny that the attitude of the yogi suffices as an alternative to that of commissar—inasmuch as the yogi's otherworldliness promotes an unconscionable tolerance vis-à-vis the violence and evils of this world—for want of any existing alternatives as to how one could successfully intervene in the world as it is presently constituted, he tilts decisively toward the position of the yogi. Koestler's yogi longs for the balm of an all-enveloping religiosity; a sentiment that echoes in his conviction that "the age of Enlightenment has destroyed faith in personal survival, the scars of this operation have never healed. There is a void in every living soul a deep thirst in all of us."[26] For Koestler history becomes the proverbial night in which all cows are black, a "tale told by an idiot," in which the hiatus between intention and action is elevated to the level of a tragic ontological constant.

II

The transformation in theoretical perspective from *Humanism and Terror* to *Adventures of the Dialectic* is a consequence from Merleau-Ponty's having brought the standpoint of his "philosophy of ambiguity" in *Phenomenology of Perception* to bear on his political thinking. However, the concerted reevaluation of the legacy of historical materialism he undertook between 1947 and 1955 was by no means a strictly conceptual affair. Unconscionable instances of communist aggression in the Korean War precipitated his change of heart regarding the Soviet Union.[27] In his eyes, from this point onward, the higher claim to justice once embodied in Marxist doctrine had become all but chimerical. Power blocks on both sides resorted equally to conceptions of *Realpolitik* in the domain of international relations. For this reason no individual side could claim superiority over the other.

Merleau-Ponty was faced with several political alternatives. He could abandon politics in toto; but, of course, this would have meant a capitulation to the standpoint of Koestler's yogi. He could relinquish any and all partisanship for existing socialist societies and yet retain allegiance to Marxism as a type of normative touchstone or regulative ideal—an alternative he entertains seriously but ultimately rejects. Or, he could finally renounce the (bad) contemporary political alternatives (USSR vs. USA) and, along with them, the historical materialist legacy, in favor of a new nondogmatic theory of political transformation—"Weberian-Marxism."

The essential question raised by Merleau-Ponty's later political philosophy thus becomes: does Weberian-Marxism possess a content that in the last analysis points beyond "mere" liberalism—the standpoint he subjected to such unrelenting criticism in *Humanism and Terror*?

At the outset of *Adventures of the Dialectic* he inquires, what does it mean to speak of politics in an era in which both liberalism and historical materialism have been discredited? Or: does there somehow exist a via media between a "politics of understanding" and a "politics of reason"; that is, between a politics that knows only discrete particulars and rigorously shuns all totalization, on the one hand, and a politics that knows only totalization and for which particularity is reducible to a negativity to be surmounted, on the other? For Merleau-Ponty, liberalism has been discredited insofar as it rejects out of hand historical synthesis and instead rests content with a discrete series of random assaults against contingencies of historical life. In this way it makes its peace with what is by its own admission a world that is both unjust and unreconciled. "It is fine to do all that is possible step by step and leave the rest to the gods," says Merleau-Ponty of liberalism, "but how is one to know where the possible stops?"[28] He continues: "By its inflexible manner of leaving a pure value and a factual situation face to face, this politics must give in, sometimes to one side, sometimes to the other; and this patient action, which was little by little to construct the world, can only keep the world as it is or destroy it" (5).

Yet, for its part, a politics of reason succumbs to an equally debilitating fallacy: it proceeds according to the fatal conviction that there exists the possibility of attaining an end of history; an end of history that, for Merleau-Ponty, would return humanity to the "immobility of nature" or death. With Sartre in mind, he suggests that "this idea of an absolute purification of history, of an inertialess regime without chance or risk, is the inverse reflection of our own anxiety and solitude" (5).[29] He is nonetheless surprisingly quick to defend Marx against his ultrabolshevist interpreters: Marx spoke of an end of *prehistory* rather than an end of *history*, he reminds. (However, one cannot help but wonder about this qualification, for was it not clearly the original Marxian claim concerning the end of prehistory that in effect facilitated all future illusions concerning the end of history itself?) Moreover, insofar as all politics are "undemonstrable"—that is, possess no ultimate grounds or foundations—Marxist politics deserves praise because it "understands this and . . . has, more than any other politics, explored the labyrinth" (6).

Yet, in almost the same breath, Merleau-Ponty speaks of the "liquidation of the revolutionary dialectic" as a self-evident truth and sees it as his task to bring this liquidation to its conclusion (7). In 1955, his relationship to Marxism has become ambiguous. In *Adventures of the Dialectic* he seems to be of two minds. One of the most telling inconsistencies is his contrasting evaluations of the Marxisms of Lukács and Sartre. Bluntly put, whereas the former can seemingly do no wrong, the latter can do no right. Of course, what strikes one as contradictory is that the line of development between Lukács and Sartre forms a continuum, not a breach—the continuum established by Western Marxism.[30]

Merleau-Ponty's dilemma is the following: how does one proceed to infuse history with intelligibility once the worldview that seemed to promise most in this respect—historical materialism—has discredited itself? His answer seems to be that dialectical reason needs a critique in the Kantian sense of establishing boundaries or limits to the faculty of knowledge. For in its philosophy of history, Marxism—like the dogmatisms of old—has posited assurances and guarantees in an essentially fluid historical world. It has regressed to myth. It is in order that the relationship between "interpreting" and "changing" the world might be reconstituted on a basis free from myth that he undertakes this scrutiny of the dialectic's adventures.

It is far from accidental that Merleau-Ponty seizes upon the work of the neo-Kantian Max Weber in his efforts to set limits to dialectical thought's voracious capacity for synthesis. It is above all Weber's insistence on the subjective constitution of historical meaning that Merleau-Ponty values and in turn counterposes to the orthodox Marxist claim that meaning in history is objectively given once and for all. Weber thus emphasizes the hypothetical, fallible, and contingent character of all historical knowledge and in this way undermines the penchant of dialectical thought to cast its truth claims in a categorical mode. He characterizes Weber's attitude toward historical knowledge as follows: "We know history in the same way that Kant says we know nature, which is to say that the historian's understanding, like that of the physicist's, forms an 'objective' truth to the degree that it constructs, and to the degree that the object is only an element in a coherent representation which can be indefinitely corrected and made more precise but which never merges with the thing in itself" (9–10).

This description, which is derived from the Weberian theory of ideal types, suggests that amid the infinitely variegated flux of historical life, we find in history only what we as investigators have ourselves put into it; that our ideational constructs—such as Weber's *Grundbegriffe*—inevitably abstract from the full wealth of historical concretion in order to serve our own willful scientific ends; that our choice of a vantage point from which to view the course of historical becoming is never *unconditioned*, but instead always determined (in a noncausal sense) by the here and now of my own historical situatedness; and that, therefore, the values and meaning I seek in historical research are never suprahistorical or objective, but instead inescapably suggested to me by the values, problems, and dictates of my contemporary historical standpoint.

Merleau-Ponty's advocacy of the Weberian ideal-type model signifies his first critical departure from materialist methods of historiography in the direction of Weberian Marxism. To appreciate the radical nature of this shift of emphasis, one might inquire: what does it mean to conceive of the proletariat as an "ideal type" rather than the "solution to the riddle of history" proclaimed by Marx?[31] To begin with, it suggests that the proletariat, though by no means reduced to the status of a mere subjective construct, can no longer be said to possess the emphatic character attributed to it by Marx; that is, it can no longer claim to be the simultaneous normative and empirical embodiment of reason in history. This conclusion follows directly as a result of the shift from an Hegelian to a Kantian view of history; that is, the rejection of an a prioristic, teleological *philosophy* of history in favor of an open-ended or hypothetical or *theory* of history.[32]

Yet Merleau-Ponty stops short of endorsing Weber's theory of ideal types wholesale. Above all, he seeks to surmount the theory's relativistic implications. For there may well still be cogent and compelling reasons for our electing to view history through the eyes of the proletariat; and hence, the standpoint of the proletariat might not ultimately be reducible to merely "one value standpoint among many" in the land of Weberian "warring idols." Such a conviction will nevertheless be one that falls far short of the a priori guarantee of correctness usually posited in materialist philosophies of history.

The reasons Merleau-Ponty is attracted to Weberian historiography are clear: only a standpoint such as Weber's that avoids predetermined historical schemas, that remains open to the chance conjunctures of historical meaning—such as the peculiar elective affinity between the Protestant ethic and capitalism—will be open to the fullness and plurality of historical variability or *Vielseitigkeit*. One's historiographical choices inevitably influence one's political choices; and only an approach such as Weber's remains capable of conceptualizing history according to the potentialities of freedom: in view of which men and women struggling for meaning in history are free to fail and are not condemned—at an unconscionable cost—to succeed:

> The ambiguity of historical facts, their *Vielseitigkeit*, the plurality of their aspects, far from condemning historical knowledge to the realm of the provisional (as Weber said at first), is the very thing that agglomerates the dust of facts, which allows us to read in a religious fact the first draft of an economic system or read, in an economic system, positions taken with regard to the absolute. (18–19)

The praise of Weberian methodology in terms of its receptiveness to ambiguity strongly suggests that Merleau-Ponty perceives a significant theoretical convergence between his own earlier "philosophy of ambiguity" and Weber's approach.

Yet there are questions a philosophy of ambiguity or a politics of the understanding will remain incapable of answering; and at times these appear as the most vital questions. Weber himself appears to oscillate between two extremes. On the one hand, there are his significant ties to German historicism and the *Geisteswissenschaften* school (Ranke, Dilthey, etc.). Here, an appreciation of historical specificity is recaptured at the expense of our capacity to evaluate and judge: the expanse of historical meaning is resuscitated in the form of unique and incomparable historical "individuals," all of which are "equally close to God." Historical determinism is sacrificed on the altar of historical contingency as a type of Hegelian "bad infinite."[33] Ultimately, by refusing to judge history, we end up by merely affirming its course.

On the other hand, there is the Weber who inquires into the purported value universalism of the West, who is preoccupied with questions of developmental logic and social evolution. Here, Weber readily admits that our orientation toward the past is inevitably derived from the value orientations of the present. Hence, in his *Collected Essays on the Sociology of World-Religions* he poses the problem of why capitalism developed in the West and not elsewhere. Yet this is a question that could only appear meaningful to a citizen of the West; a capitalist West, one might add, that has fallen upon times of crisis, as the thesis of the "iron cage" would suggest. In historical research the process of value selection derives from the historical vantage point of the researcher—his or her situatedness—rather than from the historicist "wie es eigentlich gewesen ist" ("the way it really was"). Weber's historiographical method can thus be said to weave a skillful—meaningful—course between two bad extremes: "The path which he seeks lies precisely between history considered as a series of isolated facts, and the arrogance of a philosophy which lays claim to have grasped the past in its categories and which reduces it to our thoughts about it. What he opposes to both of them is our *interest* in the past: it is ours and we are its" (19–20).

The virtue of Merleau-Ponty's phenomenological reading of Weber is that, unlike Hegelian phenomenology, it does not terminate in absolute knowledge. It is not a closed system. Instead, it recognizes that all philosophical attempts to define a final solution to the problems of human contingency are secretly desirous of an end of history. As such, they have more in common with the annihilation of the specifically human than its emancipation. Were there to be an inner *telos* to history it would consist not in the extirpation of human plurality and multifariousness, but rather in its unimpeded proliferation. In opposition to Vico and Marx, the quest for an unambiguous finality to knowledge would characterize the study of the natural not the social world. For nature is the domain in which we seek causes and invariable regularities, whereas society is the locus of contestable shades of value and meaning. It is the Weberian thesis of "unintended consequences"—an "iron cage" of bourgeois rationalization paradoxically resulting from a religious ethic—that reminds us of the inherent futility and inappropriateness of expecting results from history that are properly sought in the natural world. As Merleau-Ponty observes: "A historical solution of the human problem, an end of history, could be conceived only if humanity were a thing to be known—if, in it, knowledge were able to exhaust being and could come to a state that really contained all that humanity had been and all that it ever could be" (22–23). Here, the recourse to an epistemology of ambiguity dovetails with the existential implications of Weber's own work—most notably, with the doctrine of unintended consequences. It is, consequently, the Weberian "critique of historical reason" that becomes a sine que non not only for all future historical study but for all political action as well. The ethical and political implications of the Weberian approach to history are felicitously encapsulated in the following claim:

> It is the destiny of a cultural epoch which has tasted of the tree of knowledge to know that we cannot decipher the meaning of world events, regardless of how completely we may study them. We must, rather, be prepared to create them ourselves and to know that worldviews can never be the product of factual knowledge. Thus the highest ideals, those which move us most powerfully, can become valid only by being in combat with the ideals of other men, which are as sacred to them as ours are to us.[34]

At this point in the analysis an alarm sounds; one that proclaims the problematical implications of Weberian historiography and ethics. For Weber's vision of history founders in an attitude of stoical pessimism; an attitude that is a invitation to inaction and passivity. For once the hypothesis that we cannot decipher the meaning of world events is raised to the level of an ontological constant, history seems condemned a priori to objective meaninglessness, to chaos; and the inherent futility of intervening in history for the sake of "rational ends" is treated as self-evident. Equally devastating is the fact that from the standpoint of Weberian ethics—which are in essence decisionistic—there remains no objective basis upon which one could ground a partisanship for rational ends. Instead, one is faced with an irreconcilable plurality of value choices; and though Weber suggests that one make one's value choices responsibly—with the consequences of one's actions fully in mind—in the last analysis these value choices themselves boil down to matters of personal conviction or preference.

Herein lie the intrinsic limitations of a politics of the understanding as elaborated by Weber and endorsed by Merleau-Ponty. Merleau-Ponty would like to contrast Weber's "heroic liberalism"—which allows room, under responsible circumstances, for an "ethic of ultimate ends"—with traditional liberalism. The latter remains complacently convinced that to act moderately and to remedy social ills piecemeal is to do all that one can do; its conscience is clean, or so it believes.

Weberian liberalism, conversely, by becoming self-critical has ceased to be insular. It recognizes that the attitude of liberalism remains acceptable only under certain historical conditions—conditions of sociopolitical normalcy. However, in critical historical periods, such as eras of momentous historical transition, a greater degree of practical resolve or commitment is morally obligatory.

Where, then, does Merleau-Ponty stand with respect to the potentially quietistic implications of a "politics of the understanding"? Undoubtedly, in its steadfast refusal to posit an end of history as a desirable—or even attainable—goal, the standpoint of the understanding serves as an important corrective to the synthetic impulses of dialectical reason. At the same time, because of its extreme rejection of historical totalization, the understanding seems willing to rest content with the bad facticity of the here and now. The question that returns to haunt Merleau-Ponty's treatise on dialectics remains: is Weberian Marxism in the last analysis a position that is capable of transcending mere liberalism?

But perhaps this question is itself a pseudo-question or even prejudicially phrased. Perhaps it bespeaks—and, worse still, promotes—a false opposition, one which itself only makes sense from the standpoint of a "politics of reason." The basic question Merleau-Ponty raises in *Adventures of the Dialectic* points to the indispensability of forcing Marxism to take a Weberian turn if it is to prevent itself from congealing into a dogma. That question runs: "If history does not have a direction like a river, but has a meaning, if it teaches us, not a truth, but errors to avoid, if its practice is not deduced from a dogmatic philosophy of history"—then what can it mean realistically speaking to transcend the standpoint of the understanding? In truth, such an act of transcendence proves merely a regression to myth under another name. In light of these findings, Weber's admonition that as individuals we ground our choice of ultimate ends in an ethic of responsibility cannot help but appear sobering.

At the same time, Merleau-Ponty refuses to rest content with Weberian liberalism and the attitude of stoical pessimism that is its signature. He realizes that to hypostatize the standpoint of the understanding is to create a pretext for shunning effective historical action. The understanding can never wholly escape the suspicion of secretly underwriting accommodationist tendencies. Its fear of historical totalization forever runs the risk of acquiescing to the existing state of things. It is not true, as ethical decisionists would claim, that moral choices can be judged formally or aesthetically. Nor is it true, as Weber at times suggests, that our choice of ultimate ends cannot be rationally adjudicated. To be sure, our choices are always difficult;

they never possess the self-evidence a politics of reason would have us believe they have. Yet perhaps this much must be conceded to a politics of reason: at times it is in fact possible to distinguish forces of greater historical freedom from those of historical oppression. On such occasions, the former merit of unqualified political commitment. Whether the ethical relativism and historicist agnosticism of the understanding would prove capable of such unhesitating engagement remains to be seen.

Merleau-Ponty's critique of the Weberian understanding proceeds precisely along these lines. Relativism itself needs to be relativized. Weber elevates relativism to the status ontological condition. As Merleau-Ponty observes:

> He always considers the circle of the present and the past, of our representation and real history, a vicious circle. He remains dominated by the idea of a truth without condition and without point of view. By comparison with this absolute knowledge, with this pure theory, our progressive knowledge is degraded to the rank of opinion, of simple appearance. Would not a more radical criticism, the unrestricted recognition of history as a unique milieu of our errors, and our verifications, lead us to recover an absolute in the relative? (31)

To "recover an absolute in the relative"—with this phrase the Marxist component of Merleau-Ponty's Weberian Marxism emerges in full force. It is by no means fortuitous that this component reemerges in the context of his discussion of Lukács' Hegelian Marxist classic, *History and Class Consciousness*. For Merleau-Ponty this is a work that embodies all the advantages of a politics of reason, while remaining free of its dogmatisms. It accomplishes this feat by ceasing to conceive of the problem of human freedom in objectivistic terms—a logic proper only to inanimate objects—but rather in terms of the capacities of human consciousness and volition as bounded by the parameters of determinate—yet fluid and malleable—social conditions. In this sense, Lukács, in his emphasis on the moment of the "subjective constitution" of history, has retrieved the dialectic from its sedimentation in nature, in things, and rendered it serviceable for emancipatory ends once more. In this sense, despite the pronounced residual idealism in his conception of the proletariat as the "identical subject-object of history," he has reproached his former mentor from Heidelberg with a prospect of human emancipation that remained imperceptible from the value-standpoint of inner-worldly asceticism gone haywire—the iron cage of capitalist rationalization. It is on the basis of this truth that Merleau-Ponty seeks to point to the potential deficiencies of the understanding—lest it risk turning into a "pillow for the intellectual sloth, which soothes itself with the idea that everything has been proved and done with."[35]

Merleau-Ponty would be the last to deny that the dialectic has suffered serious, well-nigh lethal reversals in the twentieth century, as his criticisms of Lenin, Trotsky, and Sartre make clear. However, the understanding of dialectics with which he leaves us is in no way resigned. His conclusion, rather, is that "what then is obsolete is not the dialectic but the pretension of terminating it in an end of history, in a permanent revolution, or in a regime which, being the contestation of itself, would no longer need to be contested from the outside and, in fact, would no longer have anything outside it" (206). In many respects, his words have proved prophetic.

Sartre, Heidegger, and the Intelligibility of History

> If, as he fears, he has become an "institution," then it would be an institution in which conscience and truth have found refuge.
>
> —Herbert Marcuse, Postscript to "Sartre's Existentialism" (1965)

Now that we have some measure of distance from the turbulent controversy surrounding Heidegger's National Socialist involvements, it would seem fair by way of summary to draw four conclusions:[1]

1) To suggest that Heidegger's 1927 magnum opus *Sein und Zeit* would in some way be "disqualified" by his political misdeeds of six years hence would be to profane that "love of wisdom" that informs the spirit of all authentic philosophical inquiry.

2) Nevertheless, one must at the same time make sense of the fact—and this is a "fact" that cannot help but give pause—that Heidegger understood his political commitment of the early 1930s as an "authentic" transposition of the fundamental ontology adumbrated in *Sein und Zeit* to the plane of "ontic life." That is, it signified for him a *realization of authenticity*. And whereas this particular ontological-ontic transposition certainly does not exhaust the philosophical essence of Heideggerian *Existenzphilosophie*, it suggests emphatically that we examine in detail the intrinsic conceptual shortcomings of Heidegger's early work that may have facilitated (or at the very least: did not prevent) such a perverse historical realization of philosophical substance.

3) Beginning with the 1929 lecture series *Die Grundbegriffe der Me-*

taphysik, fundamental ontology ceases to be a pristine *prima philosophia*; it becomes simultaneously a "worldview." That is, Heidegger's subsequent reflections on the "history of Being" (*Seinsgeschichte*) are inexorably tied to an ongoing series of meditations on the present age as an epoch that is defined primarily by the category of *Seinsverlassenheit*—"abandonment by Being." From this point hence, the eminently worldly, ontico-historical concerns that remained for the most part merely implicit in his great work of 1927 attain a position of centrality in his thought.

4) Heidegger at first viewed National Socialism in Nietzschean terms as an authentic overcoming of European nihilism; that is, as a radical historical response to "the decline of the West." And although his disillusionment with the actual practice of the movement dates roughly from 1936, until the end of his life he continued to believe (as he avows in the concluding pages of *Einführung in die Metaphysik*) in the "inner truth and greatness of National Socialism"—that is, when the movement is understood from the superior vantage point of "the history of Being."

The perspective advanced above—which I would propose as a necessary framework for any future Heidegger interpretation—has been confirmed by Germany's leading Heidegger scholar, Otto Pöggeler, who suggests: "Was it not through a definite orientation of his thought that Heidegger fell—and not merely accidentally—into the proximity of National Socialism, *without ever truly emerging from this proximity*?"[2]

It is Pöggeler's concluding observation that is most suggestive, disconcerting—and most deserving of consideration. For what would it mean to say that Heidegger "never truly emerged" from his earlier "proximity to National Socialism?" It can only mean that in the last analysis, Heidegger never completely abandoned certain habits of thought that were responsible for his delusory conviction that National Socialism represented the "saving power" (Hölderlin's *das Rettende*) for which the West longed in an age of total *Gottesverlassenheit*—"abandonment by the gods." As an external confirmation of this fact, one might cite his persistent refusal in the postwar era to publicly renounce his earlier Nazi allegiances; or, as has often been pointed out, his refusal to utter a word of contrition for the crimes against humanity committed by a regime which Heidegger himself once vigorously supported. Thus Heidegger, as late as 1942, could still speak in good conscience of the "historical uniqueness of National Socialism."[3]

But, in truth, these "external confirmations"—the sensational veneer of "l'affaire Heidegger"—fall wide of the mark. Instead, at issue is a longstanding *philosophical habitus* that prevented Heidegger from emerging completely from the fateful "proximity" of which Pöggeler speaks. An important clue to the way in which one might go about identifying the dubious habits of thought in question has been provided by Karl Jaspers, who once observed that Heidegger's "way of thinking [is] essentially unfree, dictatorial, and incapable of communication [*communikationslos*]." Thus, concludes Jaspers, "[Heidegger's] manner of speaking and his actions have a certain affinity with National Socialism; these alone begin to make his 'error' comprehensible."[4] However, if Jaspers' characterization is correct, then there was no "error."

At a later point in our inquiry, we will need to return in no small detail to the suggestive insights of Pöggeler and Jaspers concerning the unregenerate character of Heidegger's later philosophy. For now, however, these observations—admittedly hypothetical and tentative—suggest some important consequences concerning the reception of Heidegger's work in postwar France. For this reception has been fundamentally dominated by a rejection of the "existentialist" Heidegger of *Sein und Zeit*—that is, of that phase of Heidegger's development associated with the name of Jean-Paul Sartre—and an exaltation of Heidegger *the critic of metaphysics*: the Heidegger of the 1947 "Letter on Humanism" and related writings. Indeed, the entire critique of "logocentrism," of the intrinsic and inalienable link between "reason" and "power," which has become such a predominant feature of French philosophical culture since the late 1960s, would be nearly unthinkable in the absence of Heidegger's influence as a critic of metaphysics.

A reexamination of the different philosophical paths pursued by Heidegger and Sartre in the postwar period must call into question the tenability and one-sidedness of this reception of Heidegger's work. And thus, a reevaluation of the Sartre-Heidegger nexus must challenge the intellectual commonplace that it is the author of the "Letter on Humanism," rather than that of *Sein und Zeit*, who somehow represents "the authentic Heidegger." The value of this reexamination is not qua exercise in theoretical clarification or "the history of ideas." Instead, by reevaluating the basic philosophical premises of what has become a dominant intellectual paradigm, we seek to clarify (in a quasi-Kantian spirit) the unspoken conceptual limits of that paradigm; and thereby to identify the point at which this frame of reference becomes unserviceable for the purposes of critical intellectual discourse.

Thus, if our initial suspicions as supported by the observations of Pöggeler and Jaspers prove correct, this would suggest the need for a sweeping reappraisal of the dominant "metaphysico-critical" (in German: *metaphysikkritisch*) paradigm via which Heidegger's work has been received in France.

Conversely, this approach would also imply that Sartre's (qualified) fidelity to the thought of the "existential Heidegger" represents a distinctly more promising theoretical avenue for understanding the historical and practical dilemmas of twentieth-century social life.

■ ■ ■ ■ ■ ■

We know that in the cases of both Heidegger and Sartre, the experience of the war mandated a reconsideration of basic philosophical premises. In this regard their respective courses of development are superficially parallel. In addition, the parallels extend to one crucial area of substance. As a result of the war experience (though in Heidegger's case, the reevaluation is more narrowly tied to the encounter with National Socialism), both thinkers were forced to reexamine the adequacy of their initial, quasi-solipsistic epistemological starting points: for Heidegger, *Dasein*, and for Sartre, consciousness or the *Pour-soi*. In sum, as a result of the war, both thinkers felt firsthand *the weight of history as destiny*; and it was in consequence of this experience that the standpoint of an a-historical, "first philosophy"—in its post-Husserlian guise of "phenomenological ontology"—became manifestly untenable. The conclusions Heidegger drew as a result of these experiences cannot help but seem in retrospect inordinately extreme: he reduces the multifariousness of historical becoming to so many epiphenomenal expressions of a superordinate *Seins-geschick*—the "destiny of Being." However, in opting for this approach, Heidegger runs a grave risk: that of mystifying or "explaining away" the immanent trajectory of historical experience by attributing responsibility for its course to an a priori, otherworldly determination. For Sartre, too, the question of the "intelligibility of history" becomes the central motif around which his future theoretical labors revolve. The limitations of a quasi-Kierkegaardian "choice"—which, when all is said and done, changes nothing—and of a quasi-Kantian "intelligible freedom"—where the problem of "dirty hands" need never arise—have become self-evident.

For with the conclusion of *L'Etre et le Néant* we are left with a disconcerting paradox: that of an "unhappy consciousness." The latter, according to Sartre, is the essential lot of *la réalité humaine*: "The being of human reality is suffering because it rises in being as perpetually haunted by a totality which it is without being able to be it, precisely because it could not attain the in-itself without losing itself as for-itself. Human reality therefore is by nature an unhappy consciousness with no possibility of surpassing its unhappy state."[5] Thus, it is the unenviable fate of the *Pour-soi*—that "hole of being at the heart of Being"—to see its most essential strivings ontologically condemned to failure. For as a "being-what-it-is-not and not-being-what-it-is," its essential reality is that of *self-alienation*. In medieval ontology all created being is separated into existence and essence, and God alone exists perfectly or essentially. The secularized ontology of existentialism does away with the perfection of the creator, thus separating Being-in-the-world from the (albeit delusory) security of its former ground. The absence of "ground"—of a prior ontological determination—is the source of the intoxicating freedom that pervades the being of consciousness or the *Pour-soi*. And thus, the priority of "existence" over "essence" allows it, via the self-assertion of existential choice, potentially *to become its own ground*. Yet this absence of ground is simultaneously the source of the acute and pervasive *anxiety*—or in Sartrian parlance, *la nausée*—that is such a prominent feature of *Existenzphilosophie* in both its French and German variants.

The paradox of the human condition then lies in the fact that the *Pour-soi* finds its own freedom—its "groundlessness"—unbearable and thus seeks at every turn to do away with it. And thus, the temptation of bad faith—of "inauthenticity"—lies ever-present at the heart of *la réalité humaine*. For consciousness, the only apparent way beyond the irresolvable uncertainties of existential ambiguity and choice seems to lie in attaining the stability of "thinghood"—that is, the stability of what is other than consciousness, the *en-soi*. The inherent nature of consciousness is thus to seek its own undoing. Or as Sartre himself expresses this thought, the *Pour-soi* yearns to become an *En-soi-Pour-soi*. Which is only another way of saying that the *Pour-soi longs to become God*, to remedy its own groundlessness by becoming a ground:

> Each human reality is at the same time a direct project to metamorphose its own For-itself into an In-itself-For-itself and a project of the appropriation of the world as a totality of being-in-itself, in the form of a fundamental quality. Every human reality is a passion in that it projects losing itself so as to found being and by the same stroke to constitute the In-itself which escapes contingency by being its own foundation, the *Ens causa sui*, which religions call God. Thus the passion of man is the reverse of that of Christ, for man loses himself as man in order that God may be born. But the idea of God is contradictory and we lose ourselves in vain. Man is a useless passion.[6]

But if man is a "useless passion," if all his attempts to bestow meaning upon the world—that is, to overcome alienation by making the world a habitable and familiar place—are predestined to failure, then there can certainly be no intelligibility to history; nor would there be any point in trying to give meaning and direction to history by attempting to influence its course. The profound risk of an ontologically induced resignation and passivity arises. Sartre, moreover, proceeds to bestow a peculiarly *ennobling* character upon humanity's condition of self-alienation and the "anguish" that accompanies it. Thus, to live with a heightened awareness of the impossibilities of *la réalité humaine*—that is, an awareness of the essential ambiguity of the human condition—becomes a hallmark of the existential elect.

To be sure, with his magisterial analysis of "bad faith," Sartre has provided us with a perceptive and enduring critique of humanity's boundless capacities for self-deception. Yet his thoroughgoing debunking of *l'esprit de sérieux* risks condemning all human projects to an a priori ineffectuality and meaninglessness. But this condemnation—its ontological devaluation of the possibility of human solidarity ("ma chute originelle c'est l'existence de l'autre")[7]—could itself be an act of faithlessness. As Sartre's wartime treatise builds to its climax, we read in an oft-cited passage: "Thus it amounts to the same thing whether one gets drunk alone or is a leader of nations. If one of these activities takes precedence over the other, this will not be because of its real goal *but because of the degree of consciousness which it possesses of its ideal goal*; and in this case it will be the quietism of the solitary drunkard which will take precedence over the vain agitation of the leader of nations."[8] Here, in the self-canceling attempt to understand reality from the worldless standpoint of "degrees of consciousness," the transcendental solipsism of Sartre's early philosophical program reaches its predictably absurdist dénouement.

And yet there is another dimension of *L'Etre et le Néant* that transcends the apparently facile emphasis on the axiomatic "sovereignty of consciousness," a dimension that goes to the heart of its status as a *résistance* work. For the summons to human freedom that is the governing impulse behind Sartre's inquiry is more than an abstract and timeless appeal to the "indomitability of the human spirit." It is simultaneously a bold philosophical summons to *resistance in the here and now*, both despite and because of the oppressive conditions of the German occupation. For the latter only served to highlight the necessity of freedom as a moral-ontological imperative.[9]

By now Sartre's retrospective self-criticism of his early philosophy of freedom, as exemplified with undeniable brilliance in *La Nausée* and *L'Etre et le Néant*, has become part of the common lore of twentieth-century intellectual history. In "The Itinerary of a Thought" he observes: "The other day, I re-read a prefatory note of mine to a collection of these plays—*Les Mouches*, *Huis Clos* and others—and was truly scandalized. I had written: 'Whatever the circumstances, and wherever the site, a man is always free to choose to be a traitor or not. . . .' When I read this, I said to myself: it's incredible, I actually believed that!"[10] And six years earlier in *Les Mots* he offers a parallel series of reflections on the simplistic credulity of his early convictions:

> At the age of thirty, I executed the masterstroke of writing in *La Nausée*—quite sincerely, believe me—about the bitter unjustified existence of my fellowmen and of exonerating my own. I *was* Roquentin; I used him to show, without complacency, the texture of my life. At the same time, I was *I*, the elect, the chronicler of Hell, a glass and steel photomicroscope peering at my own protoplasmic juices. Later I gaily demonstrated that man was impossible. . . . Fake to the marrow of my bones and hoodwinked, I joyfully wrote about our unhappy state. Dogmatic though I was, I doubted everything except that I was the elect of doubt. I built with one hand what I destroyed with the other, and I regarded anxiety as the guarantee of my security; I was happy.[11]

But the experience of the war compelled Sartre by degrees to revise his youthful belief in the a priori capacity of subjective freedom to triumph over external circumstance. Or as he would later observe: "As for the fine little well-scrubbed atom I believed myself to be, powerful forces seized him, and sent him to the front with others without asking his opinion. The duration of the war, and above all of internment in Germany . . . was for me the occasion for a lasting immersion in the crowd, which I believed I had escaped and which I had in fact never left."[12]

However, it took the philosophical writings a good bit of time to catch up with implications of the literary analyses. Thus, although *L'Etre et le Néant* and *Le Sursis* are written contemporaneously, the content of the novel—which, in the manner of Dos Passos or Döblin, employs a panaramic, "wide-screen" technique to illustrate the preponderance of historical circumstance vis-à-vis the diminutive individual will—belies the celebration of transcendental subjectivity that governs the philosophical work.

The contradictory imperative confronting Sartre's existentialism after the war has been accurately summarized by Jeanson: "Here, existentialism finds itself at a dangerous crossing. It is tempted to capitulate either in the direction of a transcendental philosophy ignorant of individual historical situations or in the direction of exclusive preoccupation with historicity, where the risk is great that one will give up all concern for authenticity. The ambiguity can be maintained to the end only on condition that it establish some synthesis between radical conversion and historical development or, if you will, between the realism of authenticity in Husserl, or even in Heidegger, and the realism of history in Marx."[13] Indeed, from these years date Sartre's first attempts to reconcile Marxism and existentialism; a long and intense encounter that was meant to provide both the dimension of historical concretion so lacking in the transcendental ontology of *L'Etre et le Néant*, as well as the sensitivity to the requisites of human autonomy absent from Marxism-Leninism qua "diamat." As a materialistic thaumaturgy that erroneously believes that the conditions of human freedom can be deduced from the laws of necessity—that the "ground" of the *Pour-soi* could somehow be deduced from the *en-soi*—Marxism has historically lapsed into a monumental instance of bad faith. Nevertheless, because of its insights into the historical conditions of social injustice that govern the contemporary world, Sartre would dub Marxism the "unsurpassable" "philosophy of our time."[14] Or as he would opine later in a somewhat different context: "It is not my fault if reality is Marxist."

But in the context at hand it is worthy of note that at one point Sartre believed—mistakenly as it turned out—that he could derive the dimension of historicity that was missing in his early work from the philosophy of Heidegger. Sartre's first intensive study of Heidegger dates from 1939.[15] What drew Sartre to Heidegger (and, one might add: away from Husserl) were the same conditions of "existential urgency" that had made Heidegger an object of fascination in Germany for the generation of 1914: *Heidegger as a theorist of crisis*, whose *Existenzphilosophie* seemed capable of addressing the paramount, "epochal" questions of *lived experience*—Being and nothingness, historicity and everydayness, authenticity and death—that seemed a matter of utter indifference to the reigning variants of academic philosophy—Husserl's included. Thus, in *Les Carnets de la drôle de guerre* (1940), Sartre writes: "[Heidegger's] infuence has in recent times sometimes struck me as providential, since it supervened to teach me authenticity and historicity just at the very moment when war was about to make these notions indispensable to me." And by way of explaining his "conversion" from Husserl to Heidegger, he continues: "I was in exactly the same situation as the Athenians after the death of Alexander, when they turned away from Aristotelian science to incorporate the more brutal but more 'total' doctrines of the Stoics and Epicureans, who taught them to *live*. Furthermore, *History* was all around me."[16]

The move toward Heidegger in the years predating *L'Etre et le Néant* signified an attempt to overcome Husserl's transcendental idealism: an attempt to go beyond the naiveté of his theory of "intentionality" and "constitution," and, more generally, the impoverishment of "world-relations" that has always afflicted eidetic phenomenology. Heidegger, in contrast, argued for the ontological primacy of a *situated Dasein*—a Being-in-the-world standing in a relation of equiprimordial thrownness vis-à-vis tools, things, situations, and other human beings. It was this standpoint that, in principle, allowed greater access to an entire series of concerns related to questions of existence, authenticity, and history; questions that seemed unapproachable from the vantage point of transcendental phenomenology per se.

Nevertheless, the philosophical framework of *L'Etre et le Néant* remains governed by an uneasy synthesis between Husserl and Heidegger. For in point of fact, Sartre could not fully abandon the sovereign intentionality of the Husserlian *cogito* without forsaking the essential principle on which the success of his entire enterprise depended: ***the ontological irreducibility of human freedom***. Thus, despite the omnipresent and fearful encroachments of "existential contingency" (the *En-soi*, the "other," even our own bodies), in the last analysis it is *we*—qua *Etre-pour-soi*—who endow our thrownness with existential significance and meaning. A perspective that reaches its *credo ad absurdum* with the conviction that "even the executioner's tools cannot dispense us from being free."[17] Or, to cite another example from *L'Etre et le Néant*: "The slave in chains is free *to break them*; this means that the very meaning of his chains will appear to him in the light of the end he will have chosen: to remain a slave or to risk the worst in order to get rid of his slavery."[18] The synthesis between Husserl and Heidegger is "uneasy" insofar as Sartre strives after two goals which are incompatible given the essentially static, a-historical methodology of phenomenological ontology: the vindication of a subject that is both radically situated (i.e., world-related) and radically free (i.e., world-constituting).

At the same time, Sartre's expectation, dating from 1939, that the apparently contradictory demands of history and freedom could be reconciled by recourse to categories drawn from Heideggerian *Existenzphilosophie* (e.g., the category of historicity) rapidly came to naught. This failure had less to do with material interpretive differences between Sartre and Heidegger (e.g., Sartre's spirited rejection in *L'Etre et le Néant* of central Heideggerian categories such as "Mitsein," "Sein-zum-Tode," etc.) than with the conceptual limitations of Heidegger's version of fundamental ontology itself. In essence, the ontological gulf between "historicity" and real history proves metaphysically unbridgeable. The understanding of history falls victim to an ontologically mandated devaluation: the onto-ontological difference (the difference between "Being" and "beings") debases the ontic—which is the domain of history proper—as epiphenomenal, "vulgar," and "existentiell." Moreover, as the existential analytic of *Sein und Zeit* shows convincingly, the sphere of ontic life—history included—has been colonized by the "They" (*das Man*) and, as such, has become a ***bastion of inauthenticity***. Thus, Sartre reaches essentially the same negative verdict as Herbert Marcuse concerning the prospects of rendering fundamental ontology serviceable for the ends of historical study. Or as Marcuse, in a 1974 interview, reflects on his philosophical apprenticeship in Freiburg:

> I soon realized that Heidegger's concreteness was to a great extent a phony, a false concreteness, and that in fact his philosophy was just as abstract and just as removed from reality, even avoiding reality, as the philosophies which at that time had dominated German universities, namely a rather dry brand of neo-Kantianism, neo-Hegelianism, neo-Idealism, but also positivism. If you look at Heidegger's principal concepts . . . *Dasein, das Man, Sein, Seindes, Existenz*, they are "bad" abstracts in the sense that they are not conceptual vehicles to comprehend the real concreteness in the apparent one. They lead away.[19]

Thus, for Sartre, the encounter with Marxism took on the character of a categorical imperative if the problem of human freedom was to be posed authentically, that is, historically. Which is only another way of saying that for freedom to become actual, it must be realized historically—that is, *in the world*. By means of this theoretical approach, Sartre sought to avoid what he once called the "Immoralité de la morale": that is, "les valeurs conçues comme objectivité"—disembodied, formalistic abstractions that function in disregard of the concrete reality of a given historical situation. To the abstract humanism of universalistic morality, Sartre counterposes "a concrete morality," which he defines as a "synthesis of the universal and the historical." And thus, "morality must be historical, that is, it must find the universal within History and reappropriate it within History."[20]

It is from this period, in which his confrontation with the demands of history begin in earnest, that one may date Sartre's quest for the "singular universal." And it would not be too much of an exaggeration to claim that it was this quest that permeated virtually everything he thought and wrote from 1945 on—his biographies, his plays, his essays and philosophical works. Thus, already in the "Morale" of 1947–48, in opposition to an ethical formalism of the Kantian stamp, Sartre announces, "In truth, we choose the concrete universal."[21] The quest for the singular universal becomes the guiding inspiration behind the "progressive-regressive method" (cf. *Questions de Méthode*) and as such the philosophical modus operandi that informs virtually all of Sartre's later work.

At the root of this search stands the question of the *intelligibility of history*; that is, the question of how one can reconcile the prior historical determination of lived experience with humanity's quest for freedom. Sartre thereby attempts to account for the everyday miracle of how an individual human life—isolated, idiosyncratic, and subject to the immense causality of historical conditioning—can nevertheless emerge in its irreducible singularity. It is, then, in the works of this period that the philosophy of freedom first adumbrated in *L'Etre et le Néant* finds its authentic realization; for it is here that Sartre recognizes that for freedom to be meaningfully conceived and understood, its historical situatedness must be given its full due. Nowhere are these precepts better illustrated than in the great biographies of Genet and Flaubert. Or as Sartre avows:

> The idea which I have never ceased to develop is that in the end one is always responsible for what is made of one. Even if one can do nothing else besides assume this responsibility. For I believe that a man can always make something out of what is made of him. This is the limit I would today accord to freedom: the small movement which makes of a totally conditioned social being someone who does not render back completely what his conditioning has given him. Which makes Genet a poet when he had been rigorously conditioned to be a thief.[22]

"Man is nothing but what he makes himself," observes Sartre in "L'Existentialisme est un humanisme."[23] Ultimately, though, Sartre will have to temper this observation with an insight derived from Marx: "Men make their own history, but they do not make it just as they please; they do not make it under circumstances chosen by themselves, but under circumstances directly encountered, given and transmitted from the past."[24] But already in 1945, the conception of "existentialist humanism" set forth by Sartre represents a significant advance over the version of 1943. For there has been a determinate gain in both worldliness and humanity. In this version, existentialism no longer finds its terminus in the isolated subjectivity of the "unhappy consciousness"; instead, it *opens out onto the world*. This proves, moreover, to be an *intersubjective world*, a world inhabited by a plurality of human consciousnesses, whose categorical imperative is one of *collective solidarity*. In this respect, Sartre has clearly taken the lessons of the *résistance* to heart. For he realizes that when one reflects seriously on human Being-in-the-world, it makes no sense to speak of my projects in isolation from the projects of other men and women. And thus the precondition for our freedom—the freedom to which we have been "condemned," but which remains as yet *unrealized*—is our *Being-with-others*. The bourgeois image of "negative freedom," which, based on the ethos of free competition, suggests that my being free can only come at the expense of the freedom of others, must be transcended in the direction of human solidarity. And it is this credo that stands as the inspiration behind the ethos of "engagement" Sartre advocates in the postwar years. "When we say that a man is responsible for himself," observes Sartre, "we do not only mean that he is responsible for his own individuality, but that he is responsible for all men. . . . Therefore, I am responsible for myself and for everyone else. . . . In choosing myself, *I choose man*."[25] The desire for freedom "springs from a recognition of other freedoms and it demands recognition on their part. Thus, from the beginning, it places itself on the level of *solidarity*."[26] And further: "It goes without saying that a conversion is possible in theory, but it implies not only a transformation within the self but a real transformation of the other. Without this historical transformation, there can be no absolute moral conversion. . . . One cannot make the conversion alone. In other words, morality is not possible unless the whole world is moral."[27]

Similarly, the critique of bourgeois aestheticism in *Qu'est-ce que la littérature?*—and the defense of a literature of engagement that accompanies it—aims not at harnessing literature to a set of predetermined political goals. Rather it tries to ensure that artistic creation, instead of succumbing to the living mortification of "eternal verities" and "timeless values," remains faithful to the ends of freedom and worldliness that are its origin and raison d'être. To this end, Sartre cautions against the pitfalls of the bourgeois institution of art and the hypostatization that results when aesthetic values, that are the result of an immanent, this-worldly exchange between an author and his or her public, are elevated to the status of a new, tyrannical secular absolute. The existentialist credo that insists on the priority of existence over essence thereby assists in demystifying an inverted social world in which values that are the result of inner-worldly dealings among men and women are exalted to a position of superiority vis-à-vis their human recipients and creators. This is Sartre as *critic of reification*. The critique of *l'art pour l'art*, of an idle belle-lettrism, thus seeks to restore the *worldliness of the word*, its power to shape and give meaning to everyday human conduct. For Sartre is aware in advance of analytic philosophy (Wittgenstein and Austin) that to give voice to practical utterances, to put pen to paper, is simultaneously to be engaged in speech-*acts*: it is to assume a practical posture vis-à-vis the totality of inherited world-relations: namely, that of an ethically conditioned refusal to accept the world in its indigent immediacy, as something "given" and "present-at-hand." As such it is an act of human freedom that aims at ***remaking the world***: "the creative act aims at a total renewal of the world. Each painting, each book, is a recovery of the totality of being. Each of them presents this totality to the freedom of the spectator. For this is quite the final goal of art: to recover this world by giving it to be seen as it is, but as if it had its source in human freedom."[28] Hence, like all other acts and forms of action, to write is an undeniably ***moral*** act. Or as Sartre expresses it, "at the heart of the aesthetic imperative we discern the moral imperative."[29] For here, too, by choosing our positions, we choose universally, we implicitly establish a relation with all other living beings. Thus, "there is no art except for and by others." And if it would be a fatal error (precisely the error of bourgeois aestheticism) to mistake art for a type of sublimated "kingdom of ends," as a concrete anticipation of human freedom, "it must at least be a stage along the way . . . toward that city of ends." In sum, "the work can be defined as an imaginary presentation of the world insofar as it demands human freedom."[30]

■ ■ ■ ■ ■ ■

An evaluation of the philosophical legacies of Heidegger and Sartre will turn on a key point: their respective efforts to reevaluate the heritage of Western humanism. Neither Sartre nor Heidegger wishes to appropriate that heritage in its traditional form whereby the "cult of man" supplants the "cult of God." Sartre explicitly warns against this logic of substitution as another form of value hypostatization or reification. As a totem before which humanity must prostrate itself, the abstract "cult of mankind" proves to be merely another form of human self-abnegation: "The existentialist will never consider man as an end because he is always in the making. Nor should we believe that there is a mankind to which we might set up a cult in the manner of Auguste Comte. The cult of mankind ends in the self-enclosed humanism of Comte, and, let it be said, of fascism. This kind of humanism we can do without."[31] Sartre criticizes traditional humanism, therefore, insofar as by erecting humanity-in-the-abstract as a static, timeless ideal, it detracts from human freedom as a yet-to-be-realized, immanent historical value.

For Heidegger, on the other hand, the tradition of humanism is essentially a dead letter: it culminates in a metaphysical theory of the "will to will" whose ultimate manifestations are the "events of world history in this century": the "collapse of the world," the "desolation of the earth," the "unconditional objectification of everything present"; all of which are the result of what Heidegger calls "the consummation of metaphysics" (*die Vollendung der Metaphysik*). As a result of the metaphysical "world-picture" that holds sway over Western modernity, Heidegger continues, "Collapse and devastation find their adequate occurrence in the fact that metaphysical man, the *animal rationale*, gets fixed as the laboring animal"; this animal is then "left to the giddy whirl of his products so that he may tear himself to pieces and annihilate himself in empty nothingness."[32] Heidegger's apocalyptical image of modernity is one of *total nihilism*. For according to his way of thinking, "nihilism" is merely the consequent and necessary outcome of an age of total *Seinsverlassenheit*: the total forsakenness of man by Being.

But there is no small irony in the fact that the doctrine of *Seinsgeschick*, which subtends Heidegger's theory of modernity and which explicitly aims at the "overcoming of metaphysics" (*die Überwindung der Metaphysik*), proves in the last analysis to be at least as metaphysical as any of the theories Heidegger criticizes. In his later work, the "destining of Being" appears as an unshakable, primordial force that willy-nilly determines the shape and character of all human life. Thus, in stark contrast to Sartre's postwar efforts to reconcile his concern for human freedom with the constraints of history, with Heidegger, a meaningful analysis of the *immanent* course and trajectory of human history is rendered superfluous, since all has been predestined by "Being" qua "implacable fate"—that is, qua *Seins-geschick*. Here, Heidegger's fascination with the pre-Socratics has served him poorly. For he willfully sacrifices the capacities of human freedom and autonomy on the altar of a primal, Eleatic totem: the totem of Being qua *physis*. Once again, the onto-ontological difference that was first stressed in *Sein und Zeit* tends to diminish the intrinsic value of ontic life, which is the sphere of human history and practice. Everything in this sphere seems disqualified in advance insofar as it receives a prior, meta-ontological determination by the mysterious powers of *Seinsgeschichte*. Thus, whereas for Heidegger, a quasi-religious exaltation of Being qua *physis* appears as an unequivocal philosophical desideratum, for Sartre, conversely, the preponderance of Being qua *physis* symbolizes the realm of "natural necessity" which must be overturned for human freedom to be realized: "Nature would be the historical fact that men have a nature, that humanity, in choosing oppression at the beginning of its history, has chosen to begin with nature. In this sense the perennial dream of anti-physis would justifiably be the historical and perpetually utopian possibility of making a different choice"—that is, the choice of freedom.[33]

Consequently, it is difficult to disagree with the verdict expressed by the philosopher Hans Blumenberg concerning Heidegger's later work: "*The absolutism of 'Being' is in truth only the continuation of medieval results by other means.*" By "medieval results" Blumenberg is referring to the shackles of scholastic ontology, whose static categorical hierarchies closely mirror those of the social milieu whence it emanates. And in this respect, Heidegger's later recourse to the doctrine of *Seinsgeschick* constitutes a deliberate regression behind the potentials for human autonomy and freedom that are provided by the modern age. As Blumenberg explains, in Heidegger's work: "The [modern] epoch appears as an absolute 'fact'—or better: as a 'datum'; it stands, sharply circumscribed, outside any logic, adapted to a state of error [*Irrnis*], and in spite of its immanent pathos of domination (or precisely on account of it) finally permits only the one attitude that is the sole option that the 'history of Being' leaves open to man: *submission*."[34]

The points raised by Blumenberg—above all, his concluding remark concerning "submission" as the "only option that the 'history of Being' leaves open to man"—cannot help but recall to mind the suspicion already voiced by Pöggeler that Heidegger "never truly emerged" from his earlier proximity to National Socialism. And in this connection, it is necessary to inquire whether it is not in fact those same antidemocratic habits of thought that precipitated his turn to Nazism in the early 1930s—viz. a characteristically German conservative-revolutionary disparagement of reason, enlightenment, and the tradition of political liberalism—that continue to dominate his later philosophy via the nebulous theory of *Seinsgeschick*. Thus, when in a 1943 lecture we come across the claim, "Thinking begins only when we have come to know that reason, glorified for centuries, *is the most stiff-necked adversary of thought*"—we see how integral such habits of thought have remained for Heideggerian "essential thinking."[35]

Thus, in face of the inflexible and omnipotent "destinings" (*Schickungen*) of the history of Being, the possibilities of human freedom become purely epiphenomenal and uncognizable. And in a manner that parallels the remarks by Blumenberg just cited, another commentator suggests that the latent authoritarianism of Heidegger's doctrine of the history of Being lies in the fact that it inculcates in its recipients a "diffuse readiness to obey" a series of unnamed, "pseudo-sacral powers":

> Because Being withdraws itself from the assertive grasp of descriptive statements, because it can only be encircled in indirect discourse and "rendered silent," the destinings of Being remain undiscoverable. The propositionally contentless speech about Being has, nevertheless, the illocutionary sense of demanding resignation to fate. Its practical-political side consists in the perlocutionary effect of a diffuse readiness to obey in relation to an auratic but indeterminate authority. The rhetoric of the later Heidegger compensates for the propositional content that the text itself refuses: it attunes and trains its addressees in their dealings with pseudo-sacral powers.[36]

But is not this infatuation with "pseudo-sacral powers"—so well exemplified in Heidegger's infamous proclamation in the 1966 *Der Spiegel* interview that "only a god can save us"—in point of fact *metaphysics at its purest*: namely, the attempt to account for the "totality of beings" or "what is" on the basis of another theoretical *fundamentum inconcussum*—the "destining of Being"? And in this respect, the charge Heidegger levels against Nietzsche's philosophy—that instead of being the first genuinely *antimetaphysical philosopher*, Nietzsche is in truth *the last metaphysician*—can easily be turned against his own putatively postmetaphysical thinking as well.

According to the conventional wisdom of the French Heidegger reception, the philosopher's political "error" of the early 1930s may be attributed to a surfeit of metaphysico-humanist thinking. As Derrida observes with reference to Heidegger's 1933 Rectoral Address: "He engages in a voluntarist and metaphysical discourse, which he will subsequently [i.e., in his later antimetahysical writings—R. W.] view with suspicion."[37] Similarly, for Philippe Lacoue-Labarthe, one is justified in attributing Heidegger's "engagement" during the early 1930s to "the pressures of a thought insufficiently disengaged from metaphysics" (although Lacoue-Labarthe immediately qualifies this point by confessing that metaphysics "is at the most secret heart of thought itself").[38] To be sure, the Heidegger interpretation suggested here is one that closely follows the self-interpretation of the master himself: viz., that his early philosophy of existence in *Sein und Zeit* remained excessively beholden to the standpoint of the western "metaphysics of subjectivity." That is, it remained inordinately reliant (e.g., in its privileging of "authentic Dasein") on the metaphysical paradigm of the "will to will" that has dominated Western philosophy from Descartes to Nietzsche; a paradigm which relates to "objectivity" ("beings") imperiously, that is, only insofar as it can be appropriated and manipulated according to the whims of the "subiectum." And thus, it was because of this mistaken indebtedness to *subjectivist metaphysics*—a paradigm with which Heidegger will break definitively during the *seinsgeschichtliche* "Turn" of the 1930s—that Heidegger could erroneously project his hopes for inner-worldly salvation on an actual, empirically existing historical subject: the National Socialist movement and its Führer.

But this interpretation of Heidegger's "error" goes awry on an essential point: it is undoubtedly the case that Heidegger's residual reliance on the tradition of Western metaphysics, instead of abetting his allegiances to the National Awakening of 1933, *prevented him* from identifying *tout court* with the genocidal imperialism of National Socialism—for example, with aspects of Nazi doctrine such as "racial thinking." Thus, even at those precarious moments of the Rectoral Address where Heidegger is tempted to fully merge his thought with National Socialist ideology, it is his fidelity to the legacy of Western humanism—here, the category of "the Greek beginning"—that prevents him from losing touch with the authentic impulses of his early philosophy. "Metaphysics" is less to blame for the philosopher's political misdeeds than the "conservative revolutionary" aspects of Heidegger's early thought; aspects he inherits from the likes of Nietzsche, Spengler, and Ernst Jünger and which figure so prominently in the critique of "everydayness" of *Sein und Zeit*, Division I.

Moreover, the attempt to redeem the later Heidegger at the expense of the early Heidegger runs the risk of playing into the philosopher's own complex strategy of intellectual subterfuge in the postwar period.[39] And in this regard it is important to realize the paramount role played by the theory of *Seinsgeschichte* in Heidegger's own psychology of denial. For doesn't this doctrine—which instructs that all occurrences in the world of human affairs have their ultimate source in the activities of an unnameable, higher power—conveniently serve to deny all individual and collective historical responsibility? If it is true, as Heidegger claims in "Überwindung der Metaphysik," that it is *Western metaphysics* and the technological nihilism it promotes (*das Gestell*) that is responsible for the events of contemporary history, then what sense would it make to hold the German people accountable for the untold destruction of the Second World War—for millions of civilian deaths, the enslavement of entire peoples, and, to be sure, the Holocaust? If "error," which Heidegger ontologically ennobles as "*Irrnis*," is in truth produced by the unpredictable "sendings" of Being, then one would be foolish to await a word of contrition from the philosopher himself. For the flipside of Heidegger's later abandonment of a "philosophy of the subject" is a renunciation of the category of personal responsibility *in toto*. Thus, Heidegger's own "error" has also been "sent" by Being.

Dismay over the fact that Heidegger, in the course of his voluminous reflections on the course of modern nihilism, never condescended to address the Holocaust can only seem naive.[40] For his refusal to pursue this subject was itself *philosophically overdetermined*: the Holocaust, too, was merely another manifestation of *Seinsgeschick*, for which no individual nor any nation bears special responsibility. Moreover, qua manifestation of *Seinsgeschick* it is thoroughly unexceptional. Thus, in the sole published instance where he indeed deigns to comment on the Nazi politics of genocide, one finds the predictable tergiversations: when viewed from the lofty standpoint of the history of Being, the annihilation of the Jews cannot be qualitatively distinguished from "mechanized agriculture," the manufacture of atomic weapons, or economic blockades.[41]

I would like to suggest that the bankruptcy of Heidegger's later philosophical program—ironically, that phase which his French defenders peculiarly deem most worthy of redemption[42]—lies precisely in its philosophically overdetermined capacity for historical mystification: thus, from the standpoint of "the history of Being" *questions of historical intelligibility cannot be raised*. And from this perspective, it seems that the later philosophy of Being, instead of representing a triumphant "overcoming" ("Überwindung") of his early philosophy of existence, in truth constitutes a distinct regression. Even the critique of technology for which Heidegger's later work has become known remains essentially unserviceable for the ends of human emancipation. Instead, it proves a prescription for human inaction and passivity: in light of our fate of total *Seinsverlassenheit*, all we can do is await the "god" who will "save us" and initiate the "other beginning." In the end, the philosophy of the later Heidegger consistently displays an incapacity for making essential historical distinctions. Thus, according to the theory of *Seinsgeschick*—which combines "metaphysics," "the will to will," "technology," "das Gestell," and "nihilism" into an undifferentiated and seamless ensemble—when they are viewed "essentially" there is no real difference between "communism," "fascism," and "democracy": "Today everything stands under this reality ["the universal domination of the will to power"] whether it is called communism or fascism or world democracy."[43] As such, they are all "equiprimordial" manifestations of *Seinsvergessenheit*. Similarly, the triumph of world democracy over the forces of fascism has from the standpoint of the "history of Being" decided nothing "essential." Or in Heidegger's own words: "What has the Second World War actually decided—not to speak of its terrible consequences for our fatherland, especially the laceration down its middle? This World War has decided nothing, if here we take decision in the strong sense, as it pertains uniquely to the essential destiny of man on this earth."[44]

Here, too, the phenomenal, the historical, and the ontic withdraw from the grasp of Heideggerian essential thinking. In the present age, all historical change is condemned a priori as meaningless, insofar as it cannot help but appear under the sign of *Seinsverlassenheit*—which constitutes a sign of *perdition*. The category of *Seinsgeschick* presents itself as a universal construct by means of which everything is *explained*—but nothing is *understood*. Thus, in the later work, the misguided Nietzschean critique of modernity—of "Western values," "progress," the democratic tradition, and social egalitarianism—that motivated his engagement of 1933 has never been reevaluated. Instead, restyled as the abandonment of modern man by Being, it has in effect been radicalized (despite the intensive confrontation with Nietzsche in the late 1930s and early 1940s).

The foregoing analysis leads us to conclude that with the later Heidegger we are presented with a *philosophy of heteronomy*. This position receives its consummate articulation in his debate with Sartre in the 1947 "Letter on Humanism." The early Heidegger, as a theorist of *Mitsein*, at least had not ruled out in principle the prospect of genuine human intersubjectivity—and thus the prospect of a meaningful this-worldly existence. The uniqueness of the human condition was preserved insofar as Dasein—which is distinguished by "care," that is, "by the fact that, in its very Being, that Being is at issue for it"—proved an indispensable locus of meaning and truth.[45] But with the ontological-historical "Turn" of the 1930s, these achievements are placed at risk. Dasein is degraded to the purely passive status of the "shepherd of Being." On the stage of world history qua *Seinsgeschichte*, it has become a supernumerary, a pliable conduit for the Being's autonomous and unpredictable "presencings." Or as Heidegger declares: "Man does not decide whether and how beings appear, whether and how God and the gods or history and nature come forward into the lighting of Being, come to presence and depart. *The advent of beings lies in the destiny of Being*."[46] In face of this all-consuming, heteronomous destiny, the meager powers of human volition—and thus the possibilities of a meaningful, intersubjective human *praxis*—pale as accidents before substance.

For the later Heidegger, man is not the neighbor of man. Rather, "man is the neighbor of Being."[47] Or as Heidegger defines it, "Being is *transcendens* pure and simple." But qua *transcendens*, Being itself proves unapproachable, unnameable, and undefinable. Thus, to the question "what is Being?" the only answer Heidegger can provide is the quasi-biblical, "It is It itself"—a self-identical, first unmoved mover.[48] Heidegger's infatuation with "pseudo-sacral powers" has never been more evident.

The foregoing analysis suggests a number of critical conclusions concerning the philosophy of the later Heidegger, especially with regard to the much vaunted "overcoming" of Western humanism on which so much of his later work depends. Beginning with the Nietzsche lectures of 1936, Heidegger attempted to work through his "error" of 1933–34; that is, to account for the fact that National Socialism, instead of embodying that self-overcoming of Western nihilism prophesied by Nietzsche, constituted merely a further instance of nihilism. Yet, until the end of his life, Heidegger never abandoned the seminal distinction elaborated in *Einführung in die Metaphysik* (1935) between "the inner truth and greatness of National Socialism" (which consists in "the encounter between global technology and modern man") as opposed to its debased historical actuality.[49] For when understood "ontologically"—that is, according to the sublime perspective of Heideggerian *Seinsgeschichte*—National Socialism indeed harbored the seeds of such an "overcoming"; a potentiality, however, to which its "ontic" reality never measured up. Thus, he could state as late as the 1966 *Spiegel* interview: "I see the task of thought to consist in helping man in general, within the limits allotted to thought, to achieve an adequate relationship to the essence of technology. *National Socialism, to be sure, moved in this direction*. But those people were far too limited in their thinking to acquire an explicit relationship to what is really happening today and has been underway for three centuries."[50]

But this claim confirms the suspicion that Heidegger's efforts to think through the essence of National Socialism on the basis of the theory of the "history of Being" never went far enough. Instead, this doctrine itself represents in truth only a further mystification of the historical reality of National Socialism; a movement that in truth has its roots in the peculiarities of German history rather than in the suprahistorical "presencing" of "Being" as "destiny."[51] The attempt to explain the essence of National Socialism as an outcome of *Seinsgeschichte*, therefore, must be traced back to the aforementioned strategy of denial. For by virtue of this strategy, Heidegger perversely succeeds in rendering the failings of other nations "equiprimordial" with the misdeeds of Nazism. For be they communist, democratic, or fascist, they, too, have equally succumbed to the afflictions of "technological nihilism" and the "forgetting of Being." As such, nonfascist regimes constitute no "essential" improvement over National Socialism—which, by virtue of its "confrontation between global technology and modern man," at least had the merit of staging a heroic struggle against nihilism. According to this contorted, Heideggerian vision of *Heilsgeschichte* (the history of salvation), Nazism's failure symbolizes the tragedy of modern humanity in general in its struggle with the realities of technological nihilism. In the end, the philosopher of Being leaves us with a perverse nostalgia for an essentialized version of Nazism—our century's last chance in the long struggle against nihilism.

Both Gorz and Sartre correctly recognized the dangers of the "history of Being" as a philosophy of heteronomy. Both realized that such a doctrine threatens to suppress the conceptual parameters through which alone freedom can be thought. Nor can such a theory be of much value for addressing the problem of the intelligibility of history. Ironically, both thinkers learned about the perils of a philosophical hypostatization of Being via their respective encounters with "Marxist scholasticism": that is, with Soviet Marxism qua "diamat." As such, they were acutely aware of the ethico-political repercussions of a philosophical doctrine in which human existence is viewed as a function of a primordial ontological destiny—be it the destiny of "matter" or the destiny of "Being." Both realized that the basic impulse guiding such a doctrine could only be a hidden *scorn for things human*. Here, both the inverted idealism of the "dialectics of nature" and Heidegger's exaltation of Being qua absolute *transcendens*—to be sure, unlikely bedfellows—betrayed a similar longing: a premodern desire to have quit with the project of human autonomy, the "democratic invention," the "self-institution of society." This was a philosophical dogmatism that remained fully imprisoned in metaphysics. As such, it was a philosophy that merely reproduced on a conceptual plane the conditions of unfreedom that governed contemporary social life. Thus, according to Gorz: "The fact is that any discourse on Being that tries to abstract from the speaker and to grasp Being beyond the cognitive situation (i.e., the practical relations) of the speaker, is implicitly *a metaphysical discourse*: it claims to pronounce on Being in the absence of men. Any certainty that lacks the criterion of being certain for me (of being evidence) on the basis of lived experience, is an act of faith that sooner or later leads to dogmatism. Conversely, the only way to eliminate metaphysics is always to refer the affirmation or the investigation to the praxis—historically situated, methodologically defined, oriented towards determinate goals—of the investigator."[52]

And in a similar spirit, Sartre will inquire: "How can we ground *praxis*, if we treat it as nothing more than the inessential moment of a radically non-human process? How can it be presented as a real material totalisation if the whole of Being is totalised through it?. . . . But any philosophy which subordinates the human to what is Other than man, whether it be an existentialist or Marxist idealism, has hatred of man as both its basis and its consequence."[53]

In honor of the tenth anniversary of his death—but, more importantly, in honor of his exemplary life—we conclude by allowing Sartre to have the last word.

PART III

Neopragmatism and Poststructuralism

SEVEN

Recontextualizing Neopragmatism: The Political Implications of Richard Rorty's Antifoundationalism

> It is natural to feel victimized by philosophy, but this particular defensive reaction ["a rebellion against the philosophical impulse itself, which is felt as humiliating and unrealistic"] goes too far. It is like the hatred of childhood and results in a vain effort to grow up too early, before one has gone through the essential formative confusions and exaggerated hopes that have to be experienced on the way to understanding anything. Philosophy is the childhood of the intellect, and a culture that tries to skip it will never grow up.
>
> —Thomas Nagel,
> *The View From Nowhere*

I

Ten years ago, Richard Rorty's *Philosophy and the Mirror of Nature* sent ripples of controversy throughout the usually staid American philosophical community by boldly proclaiming the obsolescence of the epistemological model that has dominated Western thought for the last 2,400 years. That model, based on the primacy of the faculty of vision, (the ancient Greek verb "to know," *noein*, is also integrally related to the word for "sight" or "vision"), conceived of knowledge as a correspondence between intellect and object—*adaequatio intellectus et rei*, as the scholastics re-phrased it—such that "truth" would emerge once a harmonization between mental image and objective reality occurred. To be sure, over the course of the last two and one-half millennia, philosophers have disagreed violently over which half of the equation was to be privileged: idealists from Plato to Hegel have staked their wagers on the side of mind or the ideal factor; empiricists, from Locke to twentieth-century positivism, have emphasized the primacy of the objective world, to which mind in turn must conform. The disruptive nature of Rorty's contribution to this long-standing controversy lay in his strident declaration that the very terms of this debate were themselves fallacious; that every attempt to posit a definitive answer to this age-old quest for metaphysical certainty—from Plato onward—was a priori condemned to futility. The very idea of a timeless, suprahistorical, objective claim to truth was said to be a delusion peculiar to a specific human type—*homo philosophicus*; and according to Rorty, this metaphysical urge—in essence, a secularized version of the religious longing for divinity—is a "hang-up" we must exorcise and bury. Only in this way can we be ultimately freed from an entire series of false steps that, in the opinion of Rorty, constitute the history of philosophy.

The essential character of these false steps is felicitously conveyed by Rorty's title metaphor. Throughout the ages, philosophy has sought to produce a body of unimpugnably accurate representations of the external world, a perfect "mirror-image" of reality, as it were. And it is from this grandiose compunction that Rorty wishes to emancipate us.

The tone of Rorty's enterprise is nothing if not Promethean: we are meant to feel as if a discovery of epochal significance has been made. That Rorty offers a penetrating and lucid rereading of the history of philosophy since Descartes is uncontestable. That the claims to originality of his undertaking are inflated is similarly undeniable. In part, this is the case insofar as the villain of Rorty's narrative—the old-fashioned correspondence theory of truth—turns out to be rather a straw-person. The foundationalist mode of philosophizing, against which Rorty rails, lost its hegemony in Europe with Hegel's demise in 1831. It was, to be sure, revived in our century with Edmund Husserl's doctrine of the "intuition of essences"; but orthodox Husserlians are few and far between these days. The "mirror of nature" metaphor has, since Hegel, prospered in the empirically oriented natural and social sciences. But even this situation has changed with the rediscovery of interpretive sociology in the 1960s. And as far as the discipline of philosophy itself is concerned (which is, after all, the original target of Rorty's polemics), the analytical tradition that dominates the contemporary Anglo-American scene, and whence Rorty himself hails, can only be categorized as "foundationalist" in a qualified sense. Whereas the analytical school still believes in something like "truth," this truth bears little resemblance to the Cartesian, metaphysical variety. Instead, it is mediated by a theory of ordinary language in a way that potentially renders conventional mirror imagery invalid: once language is viewed as an insuperable mediating variable between our capacity for representation and the truth "out there," the purity of our representations is never quite the same. Hence, while Rorty's polemics against the atavisms of first philosophy are not quite object-less, and thus pointless, one must concede (and perhaps Rorty himself would not deny this fact) that the tide had essentially turned before the appearance of his book in 1979. His own undertaking consequently must be viewed more as a type of mopping-up operation, an attempt to synthesize various criticisms of metaphysics that have been circulating for quite some time (at least since Nietzsche). Many of his points had already been forcefully made by his three "heroes of modern philosophy"—Dewey, Heidegger, and Wittgenstein.

That Rorty's book was so phenomenally successful may have been at least partially conditioned by a number of extra-philosophical, contextual factors. Indeed, the book's main thesis concerning the definitive obsolescence of all strong claims to truth is strikingly reminiscent of a book with a parallel thesis that had an analogously controversial impact in the early sixties: Daniel Bell's *The End of Ideology*.[1] Bell's thesis, which is by now well known, alleged that advanced industrial societies were witnessing an ultimate disillusionment with "utopian political claims" (read: "Marxism"), and that in their stead, a mentality prizing technocratic/managerial efficiency (which was purportedly *non-ideological*) had come to prominence. Indeed, in a recent paper on the "Priority of Democracy to Philosophy," Rorty includes a flattering reference to Bell's theory, as well as a ringing endorsement of the profoundly conformist, neoconservative implications of the argument in general: Rorty's ideal polity, like Bell's, "will be a society that encourages the 'end of ideology,' which takes reflective equilibrium as the only method needed in discussing social policy."[2]

Might one not, without too much strain, view Rorty's work as performing an intellectual function analogous to that of Bell's book some twenty years earlier? Is it not a saga of disillusionment concerning the utopian mission of thought—to know things as they ultimately and truly are—and a sober admonition for us to rest content with the inevitably partial, relative, and parochial character of even our deepest intellectual insights? In a word, isn't there something profoundly neoconservative about Rorty's philosophical program? In the last analysis, isn't his historicist-inspired credo—viz., the relativist conviction that all truth is ultimately a phenomenal manifestation of the historical-intellectual matrix in which it originates—extremely resigned and quietistic? Is it not a philosophy of "adjustment," decidedly appropriate for an age of "retrenchment" and "lowered expectations"? One arrives at these conclusions, ironically, merely via a consequent application of Rorty's historicist methodology to his own thought—by historicizing his historicism, as it were.[3]

The central antifoundationalist maneuver of Rorty's treatise is a rejection of all claims to universal and objective value. The logical consequence of this move is the adoption of a thoroughgoing relativism—which Rorty (and here, one can only admire his consistency) freely embraces.[4] Relativism is not as bad as it seems, Rorty informs us; for it is, after all, conducive to tolerance. But Rorty cannot have it both ways. Once all claims to universal value have been discredited, how can we justifiably praise tolerance as the one value that has survived the skepticist onslaught? Here, too, Rorty is consistent. Tolerance, he is forced to admit, has no higher moral status than intolerance. His own preference for tolerance is just that, a "preference" or a "decision." All attempts to inscribe this principle objectively in the "natural order of things," as seventeeth- and eighteenth-century philosophers of natural right sought to do, are bound to fail. Rorty has nothing to fall back on but his own parochialism, something he does with increasing frequency: as someone raised in a bourgeois, Western environment, tolerance is a value *he* happens to *like*. But the fact that he and other members of these societies incline in such a direction says nothing about the objective worth of this value. Indeed, were one to attempt to convince, e.g., a member of the Hindu caste system or an Islamic mullah of the "objective superiority" of this and other Western ethical precepts, one would abruptly realize the inherent limits of one's own way of thinking. Rorty thus reiterates for our benefit the arguments of another accomplished metaphysical dragon-slayer, David Hume. According to Hume, our morals are merely a product of custom and habit; but for the sake of our own convenience, out of a narcissistic impulse that seems endemic to every culture, we choose to stylize them as "universal" as a way of enhancing our own self-importance.

But in truth, Rorty is largely doing battle with a series of metaphysical ghosts who put up little resistance. As we have suggested earlier, orthodox believers in old-style metaphysics are today few and far between. Moreover, this calculated strategy of pursuing the line of least resistance allows him to avoid coming to grips with more sophisticated contemporary attempts to justify universalist convictions, attempts which, moreover, avoid the foundationalist traps of traditional metaphysics.[5] That is, one can be a nonrelativist, a believer in rationality and truth, without being a metaphysician or a foundationalist in the traditionalist sense, a possibility that Rorty refuses to consider. One can certainly talk justifiably about the "universality" of certain Western values (as Max Weber did)—of the rational concept, methods of scientific discovery, human rights, and even Rorty's "tolerance"—without falling back on specious metaphysical claims that such ideas are somehow God-given or rooted in a transhistorical human essence. Instead, it is possible to argue that in the various spheres of human endeavor—scientific, ethical, political—certain institutions and principles that happened to originate in the West represent the most "efficient" or "just" means of solving problems, and that they have been recognized as such increasingly even by cultures with opposed fundamental value structures. Hence, if one wants to master nature efficiently, one has recourse to the methods of Western science. If one wants to criticize tyrannical forms of government, one has recourse to theories of justice and human rights. Similarly, if one wants to convince readers about a given theoretical or practical stance—as does Rorty—one employs the customary procedures of rational argumentation. In an important sense, the superior "rationality potentials" of these various methods of solving problems have received a type of universal approbation.

Rorty's penchant for paradox and provocation cannot help but remind one of the sophists of fifth-century B.C. Athens against whose adeptness at making the weaker argument appear to be the stronger Socrates dedicated his exemplary life. At the same time, this tactic moves him to the defense of not a few rather unwholesome points of view—for example, that of the Italian Cardinal Bellarmine in his criticisms of Copernican heliocentrism. Of course, Rorty, as a self-satisfied, ethnocentric Westerner, is quite pleased that Copernican standards of rationality eventually triumphed. The rhetoric of science "has formed the culture of Europe. It has made us what we are today." Nevertheless, Rorty inquires, "Can we really find a way of saying that the considerations advanced by Cardinal Bellarmine—the scriptural descriptions of the fabric of the heavens—*were* 'illogical or unscientific?'" In essence, "no," he responds: "To proclaim our loyalty to these distinctions [between what is scientific versus what is unscientific] is not to say that there are 'objective' and 'rational' standards for adopting them."[6] But here, Rorty gives up the fight too quickly. And in doing so, he makes things too easy for himself—and for us. For whatever relative merits Rorty's argument might have (certainly, our criteria governing what counts as scientific, as Thomas Kuhn has pointed out, have changed over the course of time and are still changing) seem ill-served by the example he has chosen: despite all the Kuhnian talk about "paradigms," there can be no denying the "objective fact" that the earth indeed revolves around the sun; that water is composed of hydrogen and oxygen; or even that a great European conflagration took place between 1939 and 1945. Nor would such "facts" be in any way altered if the scriptural cosmology of Cardinal Bellarmine had won the day.

And in this respect, Rorty's profound aversion to strong, context-transcendent claims to truth is misguided. This is true, ironically, even if one accepts the same pragmatic definition of truth to which he incessantly appeals. For one need only demonstrate the untenability of the idea of the absolute insularity/impermeability of context, on which Rorty bases his strong case for cultural relativism, and the entire argument for cultural incommensurability (which is most likely based on a faulty understanding of Wittgenstein's notion of "language-games" or "forms of life") disintegrates. Thus, given the only standards on the basis of which we might judge—those of the rules of public argumentation and reason—Cardinal Bellarmine was, in a far from trivial sense, indeed "illogical and unscientific"; a claim that could be upheld regardless of whichever side of the dispute happened to factually triumph. Ironically, it is precisely this case that seriously undermines Rorty's efforts to banish all representational claims to truth. For Copernicus is "right" precisely insofar as his account is superior in virtue of the way things really are.

Hence, Rorty's attempts to banish once and for all the correspondence theory of truth, to have quit with all species of metaphysical realism, seem (at least in this and similar instances) ill-conceived and precipitate. His thinking displays a confusion between epistemology and ontology: between *how* we know that something is and *that it is*. In this sense, even if we cannot convincingly give an account of the former, we can, it seems, point to a wealth of everyday, nonscientific practices that would literally *collapse* were they to be suddenly deprived of the basic assumption of metaphysical realism—the existence of an independently existing, external world. Thus, there exists a mass of everyday circumstances and disputes that can only be resolved (or, as the case may be, begin to be resolved) by recourse to a conventional logic of empirical verification that presupposes some notion of correspondence: whether or not a student has turned in a paper on time; whether or not the bridge I am crossing is structurally sound, and so forth. Of course, the hermeneuticists may be perfectly correct in saying that, taken by themselves, these "facts" are meaningless; that it is only once we begin integrating them in some larger interpretive framework that they become significant for us; an explanation that even lends plausibility to Derrida's oft-cited, only apparently inflammatory claim that "there is nothing outside the text."[7] But this is not to deny that an essential segment of human experience (both scientific and nonscientific) depends on the assumption that there is, at some fundamental level, a meaningful correspondence between our understanding of reality and reality itself. It is not, as Rorty intimates in his relativizing polemic against mirror imagery, as if anything goes.

The example of the Cardinal Bellarmine/Copernicus dispute is significant insofar as it is emblematic of one of the major deficiencies of Rorty's narrowly contextualist version of neopragmatism: by entirely ceding the power of "right" or "normativity" to context, he studiously ignores the context-transcendent powers of reason and critique, and thereby ends up with a *de facto* endorsement of an essentially neoconservative position: "what is real is rational, what is rational is real." For, according to this way of thinking, there is nothing *de jure* that could transcend what is given to us *de facto*. But not even Rorty can get around the fact that this is an essentially *foundationalist claim about the nature of contexts*. His argument about contexts is based on a context-transcendent—hence, quasi-metaphysical—presupposition about the nature of contexts, all contexts: that they are insular, self-enclosed, and impermeable. But it is very doubtful that such a claim could withstand sustained empirical scrutiny. Can we really say in advance and with certainty that disputes between worldviews or cultures do not admit of adjudication by rational argumentation that aims at agreement? In the last analysis, Rorty remains a prisoner of precisely that epistemological tradition he seeks to expose.[8] For he, too, must posit an absolute claim about the nature of knowledge as such (that it is contextual, self-referential, etc.) in order to uphold his critique of epistemological realism. He believes, erroneously, that he can step out of the language-game of philosophical truth-positing, whereas his only hope for success lies in besting others who have played it according to their own rules. And these rules presuppose standards of "universal agreement and validity" to which Rorty, as a philosopher making arguments, must himself implicitly appeal. Moreover, one could easily point to a wealth of everyday linguistic practices that depend on precisely those context-transcendent idealizations that Rorty is at such pains to deny. And thus, is it not the case that

> our ordinary common-sense truth talk and reality talk is shot through with just the sorts of idealizations that Rorty wants to purge. In everyday talk we do not normally mean by "true" anything like "what our society lets us say," but some-

> thing closer to "telling it like it is—like it *really* is." And by "real" we don't normally mean anything like "referred to in conformity with the norms of our culture," but something closer to "there anyway, whether we think so or not."[9]

In the course of his plea for a disenchanted, contextualist, "post-Philosophical" culture, Rorty insists: "when the secret police come, when the torturers violate the innocent, there is nothing to be said to them of the form, 'There is something within you which you are betraying. Though you embody the practices of a totalitarian society which will endure forever, there is something beyond those practices which condemns you.'"[10] But here one gets the impression that Rorty has too readily become a prisoner of his own epistemological cynicism. One need be no less skeptical than he about the prospects of deterring torturers by recourse to rational argument to grant that there is indeed something "beyond those practices" that condemns them: the nonempiricial idealizations of an ethos of "justice" that have become part of a (counterfactual) universally shared, posttotalitarian moral ethos. The self-justifications of torturers and inquisitors become self-negating *as soon as they are put into language*: for they fail to measure up to the context-transcendent, moral idealizations inherent in the linguistic expectations of a posttraditional culture based on universalizable—hence, non-particularistic—norms. According to this logic, as soon as such particularistic worldviews partake of the language-game of "justice and validity"—a necessity for all modern, as opposed to traditional despotisms—they have lost—which does not of course mean that they automatically cease to exist. The stunning collapse of bureaucratic communism in 1989, moreover, is attributable to the effectiveness of precisely such "ideal" factors. Their demise, in the first instance, reflected a crisis of legitimacy. The claim to justice staked by these regimes succumbed to a classical dialectic of appearance and essence: the former stood in such blatant contradiction to the latter that ultimately the regimes disintegrated from within. To be sure, that the "ruse of reason" triumphed is less attributable to a preordained "dialectics of spirit" than to the idealizing, context-transcendent force of something like the democratic idea. It is an idea which certainly has a determinate context and a history. But as the dramatic events of 1989 revealed so well, it also possesses a capacity to transcend the empirical circumstances of its own historical emergence.

Rorty's efforts to extirpate the last remnants of correspondence theory from intellectual discourse repeatedly force him to defend self-contradictory and untenable positions. He reiterates an important insight that twentieth-century philosophers of language (e.g., Saussure and Wittgenstein) have reached concerning the limitations of linguistic representation: that language is a semantic system in which words refer primarily to other words rather than entities in the world. But from this fact he draws the erroneous, poetic/Derridean conclusion that the referential function of language is nonexistent: "We have to drop the notion of correspondence for sentences as well as for thoughts, and see sentences as connected with other sentences rather than with the world," observes Rorty. "To think of Wittgenstein and Heidegger as having views about how things are," he continues, "is not to be wrong about how things are exactly; *it is just poor taste*. It puts them in a position which they do not want to be in and in which they look ridiculous."[11]

The aestheticist aspect of Rorty's position—the idea of philosophy as an elite parlor game in which questions of "taste" matter more than considerations of "truth"—gradually assumes pride of place in his argument. Thus, as the foregoing citation indicates, we are forced to admit that Wittgenstein and Heidegger, in their criticisms of traditional theories of representation, have arrived at a more "accurate" (more "objective"?) conception about the way things are. But to call attention to this fact makes them look "ridiculous" (worse still: it is "bad manners") insofar as their intention was to get beyond such notions of representational accuracy in their entirety. We have caught them in the act—to transcend old theories of representation, they are forced essentially to posit new ones with a higher claim to "veracity"; hence, there is no way of honestly escaping the self-referential game of epistemology—but to point this fact out in good company is to be guilty of bad table manners and *impolitesse*.

Rorty's book revolves around a central binary opposition: that between "objective" philosophy (which is bad, serious, and exclusionary) and Rorty's own conception of "edifying" philosophy (which is good, playful, and open). But, as is the case with all such oppositions, by virtue of their rigidity, they commit a serious injustice at the expense of their lesser term. We still stand to learn much from the doctrines of those systematic philosophers on whom Rorty heaps so much opprobrium—Plato, Descartes, and Hegel. Rorty concedes that after the revolution of the "edifiers" has been completed, we would still read the others. But I suspect we would not read them much differently than we do at present and as they have been read for quite some time. Few persons today reach for these texts with the expectation of assimilating something like ultimate truth. Instead, their contributions are viewed as profound meditations on the central problems of human life and thought; such thinkers are revered as gifted spirits who have in the course of cultural history established the terms of debate over precisely what matters to us as beings with spiritual and practical needs. Perhaps Rorty would not fundamentally disagree with these formulations; but if this is the case, then the manifold, apocalyptical warnings about the imminent prospects of "metaphysical closure" would seem guilty of rhetorical overkill.

Rorty constantly tells us he is trying to free us from a number of stifling metaphysical prejudices. But to what end are we to be freed? And do we really want Richard Rorty as our liberator? At the risk of ingratitude, I'd like to suggest that were Rorty's notion of edifying philosophy to become hegemonic, we would in fact be worse off. For in his cheery American debunking of the spirit of philosophical seriousness, he essentially leaves philosophy without substance, without any higher aims. As a result, his thought comes close to becoming a "have a nice day" philosophy tailored to suit the needs of a postmodern era, in which we react with relief at no longer having to confront the intellectual responsibilities of earlier epochs—responsibilities that revolve around our capacity to make "strong evaluations."[12] It is an era which, according to Fredric Jameson, is dominated by a hyperanesthetized sensibility in which the distinction between "appearance" and "essence" has been effaced, resulting in an overidentification with mass media-engendered *simulacra*—that is, with the illusion-proffering powers of the "culture industry." In consequence of this situation, we have, as it were, even lost the capacity to feel our own alienation.[13]

Rorty's thought thus risks becoming a philosophy appropriate to the shallow narcissism of an era that refuses to be convinced that its precursors had something important to say. Its credo is a pathetic and timorous hedonism, in which matters of philosophical conviction are reduced to considerations of taste.[14] It is after all Rorty's own text, and not just the imagination of this writer, that is teeming with dinner-party metaphors. As he observes, "the point of edifying philosophy is to keep the conversation going. . . ."[15] He defines "philosophical progress" as the capacity "for human beings to do more interesting things and to be more interesting people."[16] Whereas formerly philosophers naively occupied themselves with the search for truth, they must now become "generators of new descriptions," seekers of "new, better, more interesting, more fruitful ways of speaking."[17] The post-Rortian philosopher is a passionate advocate of "free and easy conversation," a self-professed "post-modern bourgeois . . . ready to offer a view on pretty well anything."[18] He (or she) is a self-satisfied "name-dropper" who uses these names "to refer to sets of descriptions, symbol-systems, ways of seeing."[19]

It is hard not to sympathize with the powerful and telling criticisms Rorty makes of the Western philosophical tradition. The problem, however, is that he too readily conflates "metaphysics" with "thought" or "reason" *simpliciter*. As a result, he gives up too quickly on the stuggle to determine how in a postmetaphysical era we will decide on the true, the meaningful, and the good; that is, how we will make decisions about those things that really matter to us. For these are not themes and concerns that will simply cease to exist once the delusions of foundationalism have been overcome. It is precisely these decisions that remain the important ones. And now that we have, with the help of Rorty and others, abandoned the idiom of philosophical essentialism and the accompanying ontotheological urge for an irrefragable "ground" of all thought and being, the struggle to establish via argument and discourse the *immanent* parameters of meaning and truth has become, as it were, a type of existential imperative.

As many commentators have pointed out, Rorty's philosophical aims are in the main therapeutic.[20] He wants to free us from the illusion that there might be a suprahistorical ground or basis for knowledge. But to say that there is no such ground does not mean there are no *grounds*. Rorty wants to skirt this dilemma—the "Cartesian anxiety" according to which either we possess an epistemologically unimpeachable basis for certainty or else we succumb to the nihilistic abyss of intellectual and moral meaninglessness—through the ruse of what he calls "epistemological behaviorism": the idea that "context" is sovereign, that, in the last analysis, it is the historically given norms of the day that will out. It is these quasi-sociological norms, then, that function as the virtual ground for our actions and beliefs. Yet this solution is merely a sophisticated form of question-begging. It risks becoming a celebration of historical contingency—of what is sociologically merely "given," of facticity as such; one which in effect accepts the bad opposition between "objectivism and relativism" and complacently rests content with the latter term.[21] For just when things begin to get interesting, when therapeutic philosophy has accomplished its defetishizing mission and the project of philosophical reconstruction promises to get underway, Rorty leaves us in the lurch. When it comes to addressing the question of how we are to go about reconstituting the relationship between philosophy and public life, between our "considered convictions" (Rawls) and our inherited "forms of life" (Wittgenstein), Rorty has very little to say to us—apart from a timorous reaffirmation of the basic tenets of bourgeois liberalism.[22] The problem is that

> Rorty writes as if any philosophic attempt to sort out the better from the worse, the rational from the irrational (even assuming that this is historically relative) must lead us back to foundationalism and the search for an ahistorical perspective. . . . He keeps telling us that the history of philosophy, like the history of all culture, is a series of contingencies, accidents, a history of the rise and demise of various language games and forms of life. But suppose we place ourselves *back* into our historical situation. Then a primary task is one of trying to deal with present conflicts and confusions, of trying to sort out the better from the worse, of focusing on which social practices ought to endure and which demand reconstruction, of which types of justification are acceptable and which are not.[23]

When confronted with such questions and themes, all Rorty has to offer us is the resignation of the traditional philosophical skeptic who wears his epistemological perplexity like a scout merit badge. As Hegel realized, we are left with a situation in which "the fear of falling into error sets up a mistrust of knowledge itself." But as Hegel rejoins appropriately: "Should we not be concerned as to whether this fear of error is not just the error itself?"[24]

II

Philosophy and the Mirror of Nature has been the object of a number of pointed critiques, many of which have accused Rorty of implicitly promoting a neoconservative worldview.[25] He has responded, in turn, in a number of essays and books that have attempted to provide a more favorable account of the political implications of his metaphysical agnosticism, but the results have been less than persuasive.[26] The problem is that in his consequential efforts to do away with context-independent, nonrelativist truth claims, Rorty leaves himself, so to speak, without a critical leg to stand on. His position is a self-professed contextualism, whose absolute point of departure is society as it is presently ordered. And because of his neonominalist distrust of any standpoint that might transcend the nature of contemporary bourgeois America—Rorty's absolute, ethnocentric point of reference—his position turns into a de facto glorification of the world as it is. Rorty is constantly telling us that his rejection of first philosophy means that now political principles and convictions must be gleaned from the actual practices of contemporary (American) society, rather than from ethereal philosophical treatises. But ironically, this is not how he himself proceeds. In traditional fashion, he has written his own book on "first philosophy" (albeit a type of anti-epistemology) and then has attempted to come up with a political theory to fit his philosophical conclusions.

A good example of the intrinsic ideological conformism of Rorty's avowed contextualism is his essay "The Priority of Democracy to Philosophy." The article consists of a contrast between two basic positions in contemporary political philosophy, the universalist (represented by the early Rawls and Ronald Dworkin) and the neopragmatist (represented by Rorty himself and the later Rawls). Whereas the former group insists on an a-historical notion of human rights that is independent of context, the latter group believes that what counts as right and rational "is relative to the group to which we think it is necessary to justify ourselves" and thus entails "a quasi-Hegelian identification with our own community." For this latter group, "truth is simply irrelevant."[27] Or, to echo the immortal pragmatist clarion call of William James, "Truth is what is good for us to believe."

Much of the essay consists of a familiar replay of themes and issues already covered in *Philosophy and the Mirror of Nature*. However, an interesting development occurs with the appearance of a third group comprised of thinkers who are neither universalists nor neopragmatists (though they do have more in common with the latter position than the former). This group, which includes thinkers such as Alasdair MacIntyre, Michael Sandel, and Charles Taylor, is often referred to as the communitarians. They pose an interesting dilemma from the standpoint of Rorty's framework. Whereas they, like Rorty, reject ahistorical theories of truth, nevertheless, unlike Rorty, they are anything but apologists for the status quo. Instead, their work has been the source of some of the most trenchant social criticism of recent years.[28] While their respective positions are in truth diverse, they all attempt to measure contemporary liberal, possessive individualist societies against various historically derived notions of community; and, according to this standard, they find these societies highly wanting.

But Rorty hardly knows what to do with these theorists. The fact that they are able to offer intelligent, immanent social criticism while abandoning a universalist perspective makes them an immediate threat to his own complacent contextualism. It is not so much the specific content of their various criticisms that poses an immanent threat to Rorty's framework. It is the fact that, while rejecting ahistorical standards of criticism, they possess something that Rorty does not: a point of view. To be sure, when Rorty discusses problems of contemporary society, one often has the feeling that he is out of his depth; that despite all his obeisances toward "pragmatism" and making philosophy "worldly," he is somewhat ill at ease once he steps out of the insular confines of the faculty lounge. Yet his main problem is an eminently theoretical one. He really believes the anti-epistemology elaborated in *Philosophy and the Mirror of Nature* to the point where he is incapable of questioning his own ideology. And thus what began as an allegedly critical philosophical enterprise, an effort at "unmasking," turns into an unthinking affirmation of current social relations and all their failings. Rorty himself is all the while merely remaining faithful to his own avowed ethnocentrism.[29]

Hence, Rorty is merely being consistent (that is, consistently *ethnocentric*) when, disregarding his cherished maxim of tolerance, he expresses the conviction that in our model liberal-democratic polity, "there is no place for the questions which Nietzsche or Loyola would raise."[30] For they are not sufficiently *like us* in terms of their political preferences (one cannot help but wonder what other intellectual nonconformists will be next added to the list). "We heirs of the Enlightenment," Rorty continues, "think of enemies of liberal democracy like Nietzsche or Loyola as . . . *mad*." Since Rorty has already eliminated considerations of truth or justice as atavistic "pseudo-concepts," he must resort to the clinical notions of madness and sanity to characterize his political opponents. But like all parochialisms, Rorty's too backfires: in the hypothetical territories governed by Loyola and Nietzsche, the situation would be merely reversed, and he would stand equally condemned. And according to the strictures of his own self-canceling ethical ethnocentrism, theirs would be a "just" verdict. Only the hope offered by a nonfoundationalist and fallibilistic view of the "tribunal of reason"—that is, some minimal effort to preserve recourse to principles of argumentation, force of the better argument, and so forth, as a fair and nonprejudicial basis of adjudicating disputes—could come to his rescue. But Rorty has already abjured this tribunal as a false idol. Yet to claim that the ideal of rational justification can never provide us with an unproblematical ground of justice and truth is to miss the point. For we are still faced with the task of providing "good reasons" to support our convictions and beliefs. Indeed, even Rorty, in his guise of anti-philosopher, constantly appeals to such principles of argumentation in order to make his self-professed epistemological behaviorism seem more convincing, more plausible—and, ultimately, more "true."

A self-avowed parochialism such as Rorty's risks both arrogance and moral complacency. Rather than taking the "other" seriously and attempting to hammer out some middle ground for the sake of mutual understanding, other points of view may be simply dismissed on the basis of their dissimilarity. For example, the so-called communitarians pose a major challenge to Rorty's self-satisfied liberalism with their claim that the type of individual produced under Rorty's model—for the most part, smug, egoistic, self-seekers—falls short of a nobler, more positive ideal of the human self—for example, MacIntyre's criticism that the major character types produced under late capitalism are "the Rich Aesthete, the Manager, and the Therapist." There is no way that Rorty can rebut these charges, so he chooses simply not to answer them. Thus, instead of acknowledging the possible deficiencies of the liberal model, Rorty practices a strategy of avoidance: his philosophical framework, which has already ruled out the possibility of addressing questions of truth, deems all questions concerning an "ideal self" likewise illegitimate: "Accommodation and tolerance must stop short of a willingness to work in any vocabulary which one's interlocutor wishes to use, to take seriously any topic which he puts forward for discussion," Rorty confesses—in what surely must be one of the strangest characterizations of "tolerance" on record. In certain cases, he continues, we must "simply *drop* questions and the vocabulary in which these questions are posed."[31]

Rorty himself tirelessly sets forth his own conception of the self as "a centerless web"—a remarkably ingenuous confession as to the shallowness of the contemporary bourgeois character type. It is as if Musil's "man without qualities" has, in an era of liberal apologetics, gone from a satirical figure to a respectable social role model.

In a recently published response to Rorty's essay, Richard Bernstein has remarked that for Rorty, the idea of tolerance "is close to indifference"; that Rorty's emphasis on "play" and "light-minded aestheticism" is ultimately "facile"; that his conception of liberalism is woefully simplistic in view of the complexity of historical and contemporary debates over the heritage of this concept; and that, in the end, his defense of liberalism offers little more than "an *apologia* for the status quo."[32] Finally, upon considering Rorty's glorification of the "liberal ironist" as the quintessential modern character type, Bernstein suggests that "when we turn to Rorty's attempt to privatize irony, to encourage the playing out of private fantasies, it is difficult to understand why anyone who becomes as narcissistic as Rorty advocates would be at all motivated to assume public reponsibilities."[33]

It is hard to disagree with Bernstein's conclusions, especially when, while reading Rorty, one comes across sentences such as these: "There seems no particular reason why, after dumping Marx, we have to keep repeating all the nasty things about liberalism he taught us to say. . . ."[34] Or again: "We should be more willing than we are to celebrate bourgeois capitalist society as the best polity actualized thus far," as "the best example of solidarity . . . we have yet achieved."[35] Philosophy, and the spirit of criticism that is its raison d'être, which in the eighteenth century laid the foundations for a global assault against despotic forms of government, have been reduced by Rorty to the insular role of buttressing "the hopes of the North Atlantic bourgeoisie."[36] If the late Hegel was the philosopher of the Treaty of Vienna, Rorty has become the philosopher of the North Atlantic Treaty Organization.

At the risk of uncharitableness, one is tempted to say that Rorty's reflections on the tasks of political thought today constitute an elaborate exercise in bad faith. For even if one accepts his philosophical starting point—the rejection of all suprahistorical conceptions of reason—one is by no means driven to the timorous, neoliberal apologetics that Rorty freely embraces. Instead, there is ample space *within* the liberal-democratic tradition for criticism of those empirical bourgeois institutions whose honor Rorty wishes to safeguard at all costs. For the constitutions of these societies all enunciate ideal claims to freedom, egalitarianism, and happiness that are to be realized—however imperfectly and counterfactually—in the institutional life of those societies. And it is precisely the fruitful tension between the "ideal" and the "real" that is the driving force behind all progressive social change.

But this distinction remains imperceptible from the standpoint of Rorty's framework. Constitutional ideals are too redolent of first principles or essences, and thus must be viewed with inherent mistrust. It is common knowledge that Western constitutional principles are inordinately indebted to the vocabulary of modern natural law (or, as it is commonly characterized today, of "rights talk") that is mere grist for Rorty's antifoundationalist mill. His critique of metaphysics is thus purchased at the price of a positivistic ban on all utopian thinking; that is, on all thought capable of articulating the difference between "ought" and "is." We are instead left with the "is" in its indigent immediacy, which Rorty celebrates as the best of all possible worlds.

Rorty's thought suffers gravely from a lack of precisely that transcendentalism he believes he can so readily do without. He prematurely renounces the prospect of having to convince a wider, more cosmopolitan public of his conclusions by falling back on the conceit of parochialism. In this way, he maintains his fidelity to the definition of pragmatism coined by William James one hundred years ago which we have already cited: "Truth is what is good for us to believe."

But it does not require much philosophical sophistication to see that this precept is essentially a vindication of moral complacency: it is a functionalist definition of truth that confers philosophical legitimacy on whatever beliefs happen to be dominant. Admittedly, if one lives in a cultural environment in which toleration and respect for the rights of others are the rule, one can't stir up too much mischief by following this maxim. Conversely, if one hails from a milieu in which the persecution of minorities and the suppression of free speech are deemed "good" (from the standpoint of majority interests or for the sake of the preservation of political order), one is deprived, from the standpoint of Rorty's neopragmatist contextualism, of the conceptual means necessary for a moral indictment of such practices—Western-type moral criticisms simply do not happen to coincide with what is "good to believe" in these particular contexts. "Pragmatist morality" is thus a contradiction in terms. In its scorn of universal moral principles—in the sense of maxims that could be freely or consensually adhered to by all those who would be subject to their influence—it ends up as a de facto justification of the empirical moral practices that are currently prevalent.

The unfortunate irony throughout all this is that there are aspects of the pragmatist tradition Rorty might have drawn upon in order to provide his position with more critical substance; reflections culled from the experiences of nineteenth-century American participatory democracy and elaborated by John Dewey in the 1920s and 1930s, a time when the integrity of these political values was threatened with eclipse.

In a series of pathbreaking works of immanent social criticism—*The Public and its Problems, Democracy and Education, Individualism: Old and New*—Dewey demonstrated how a new constellation of social forces had emerged to endanger the essence of American political life. He argued that the very basis and life-blood of democracy—an informed, educated public, given to a passionate and free exchange of opinion—was being eroded as the "machine age" came into its own. Dewey observed and criticized an era in which "mechanical forces" began to dominate life in all its aspects, resulting in unprecedented "intellectual and social uniformity," a "standardization favorable to mediocrity."[37] He showed how "our intricate and interdependent economic relations" have led to the disintegration of "face-to-face communities." The latter, in turn, were the indispensable foundation of those vital and autonomous "publics" that have historically served as the basis of all healthy democratic polities. In an age of large-scale organizations, politics are increasingly taken over by party bosses and machines, and thus further withdrawn from the control of the citizenry—which thus ceases to be sovereign.

As one of the first critics of a consumer society, Dewey polemicized against the proliferation of "cheap amusements"—a natural outgrowth of the machine age—which in his opinion served as a powerful diversion from political concerns. As members of a "society of consumption," we increasingly exchange our identities as "citizens" for one as "consumers." Ours is an era, according to Dewey, conducive to passing "amusements" rather than profound "attachments," a way of life that is becoming increasingly shallow and superficial. He would undoubtedly have seconded Max Weber's ominous description of twentieth-century social life as dominated by "specialists without spirit, sensualists without heart, this nullity imagines it has reached a level of civilization never before achieved."[38]

Rorty's theoretical framework proves inattentive to such concerns. Society, along with objective reality as such, disappears from the purview of his theoretical framework as a casualty of his assault against metaphysical realism and mirror metaphors in general. In his attempt to reduce philosophy to a drawing-room pastime, to the civilized pursuit of aesthetic frivolity, Rorty assimilates philosophical inquiry to that same passion for "cheap amusement" that was the object of Dewey's criticisms. His philosophy is a rehabilitation of that weak, toothless version of pragmatism that was in the last analysis merely a mirror image of the nineteenth-century American spirit—a type of codified "know-how."

Rorty would do well to heed the warning of the philosopher Max Horkheimer, who once observed: "[The pragmatist] has made it his business to justify the factual criteria as supreme. As a person, as a political or social reformer, as a man of taste, he may oppose the practical consequences of scientific, artistic, or religious undertakings in the world as it is; his philosophy, however, destroys any other principle to which he could appeal."[39]

■ ■ ■ ■ ■ ■

POSTSCRIPT: ON THE SUMMARY BANISHMENT OF POLITICAL THOUGHT FROM PUBLIC LIFE

Rorty is a self-professed liberal. His definition of liberalism is borrowed from Judith Shklar: liberals are people who think that cruelty is the worst thing we can do. In his view, Western social and political thought has had "the last *conceptual* revolution it needs" with J. S. Mill's *On Liberty*. Hence, for Rorty, Mill's recommendation that "governments devote themselves to optimizing the balance between leaving people's private lives alone and preventing suffering seems . . . pretty much the last word."[40] The social structure of contemporary Western industrial democracies—despite recurring cycles of high unemployment and inflation, structurally endemic patterns of racial and sexual discrimination, urban decay, meaningless work, widespread political venality, a growing discrepancy between "haves" and "have-nots," ostentatious displays of private wealth coupled with increasing public squalor—represents the best of all possible worlds. Trenchant theoretical criticism has in our day become socially superfluous, since no large-scale, fundamental reorientation is needed. "Discoveries about who is being made to suffer can be left to the workings of a free press, free universities, and enlightened public opinion"[41]—institutions that, in Rorty's view, must also remain "free" and unencumbered by the influence of any theoretical legacy that might disturb the reigning distribution of social power. However, one cannot but suspect that only someone whose privileged existence has remained relatively untouched by the aforementioned social ills would so readily embrace such a program.

By imperiously consigning the social philosophies of, for example, Rousseau, Hegel, Marx, Weber, Gramsci, Arendt, Habermas, and so forth to the proverbial dustbin of history—at least insofar as their "public" importance is concerned—Rorty's neoliberal panacea, "negative freedom," betrays a profound underlying social conformism. It is as if once formal equality has been assured, nothing further is left to be publicly said or debated. It is as though Rorty really believed Anatole France's maxim, "Capitalism is democratic: it forbids to rich and poor alike the right of sleeping under bridges." Rorty gives a new lease on life to the notion of passive citizenship. Professional politicians and social engineers are to manage the ship of state. All that remains for members of the demos is that we privately cultivate our gardens. We are left with the isolated and monadic joys of "aesthetic self-creation" *simpliciter*. The "solidarity" that appears in the title of Rorty's book (*Contingency, Irony, and Solidarity*) is a grotesque misnomer. Not only can the values of publicness, fraternity, and participatory democracy *not* be deduced from his negative definition of freedom ("cruelty is the worse thing we can do"); the rigid separation he wishes to maintain between philosophical reflection and politics, as well as the kindred claim that the values of self-realization and authenticity have no place in the sphere of public life, in fact militate against the attainment of meaningful collectivities.

Essentially, then, there are two points at issue, one theoretical, the other material. Theoretically, Rorty's argument for the obsolescence of political philosophy follows from his anti-epistemology, which calls into question the cogency of all claims to truth or normative rightness. There is nothing essential or authentically true about such claims. "In truth," they express nothing but a post hoc confirmation of our contextually derived inclinations or preferences. The theoretical argument for the superfluousness of theory is then buttressed by Rorty's material estimate of the degree to which social justice has been adequately realized in contemporary Western liberal societies. And as I've indicated already, the portrait of these societies that emerges—a portrait that is remarkably unencumbered by empirical description, analysis, or detail—is one that is decidedly complacent and uncritical.

Rorty's desire to eliminate social theory from public discourse cannot help but strike one as one of the more peculiar—if not ouright "illiberal"—features of his neopragmatism. One may grant that it expresses an appropriate disillusionment with the brand of nonfallibilistic philosophical posturing that usually subtends political messianism, a legacy that must be rejected. "I agree with anti-Marxist writers such as Popper and Kolakowski," Rorty once remarked, "that the attempt to ground political theory in overarching theories of the nature of man or the goal of history has done more harm than good. We should not assume that it is our task, as professors of philosophy, to be the avant-garde of political movements."[42] But it is hardly the case that all, or even most, modern social philosophy—that of Arendt, or Habermas, or Michael Sandel, for example—is or has been messianic in tenor. Hence, wherein lies the imperative for excluding their strong, yet fallibilistic claims—which have often been quite critical of inherited "liberal" political pradigms—from the domain of public discussion? What act of hubris has impelled Rorty, a self-professed liberal ironist, to proclaim that some 2,500 of Western political thought has been suddenly rendered obsolete?

Rorty is compelled to make this far-fetched and improbable exclusion of political philosophy from the polis for reasons of internal consistency; that is, in order to remain consistent with the anti-epistemology he has elaborated in earlier works. For the more closely we regard his tortured efforts to reconcile politics and epistemology, the more impossible it seemingly becomes for him to effect the desired reconciliation between that anti-epistemology and his liberal political leanings. For what cannot help but strike even the most casual observer is that, with the notable exception of Dewey, Rorty's philosophical heroes—Nietzsche, Heidegger, Foucault, and Derrida—are anything but convinced democrats. On the contrary, to a man they have advocated an iconoclastic, radical ethos of transgression, rupture, overturning, and so forth; an ethos that is hardly compatible with the prosaic, reformist, managerial democratic political sensibility that Rorty himself has sought to promote. Conversely, many of the philosophers to whom he feels the closest politically—staunch republicans such as Kant, Habermas, and the early Rawls—fail to pass Rorty's anti-foundationalist epistemological litmus test. This situation leaves him in a true bind, one which emerges in full when Rorty tries to stake out a political position that is compatible with his theory of knowledge. Instead of trying to reconcile the unreconcilable—epistemology and politics—he seeks, like the positivists of yore, to dismiss the entire dilemma as a pseudo-problem; hence, his extremely idiosyncratic conclusion that philosophy is and should remain an entirely private matter which one must prevent from contaminating the public sphere. For Rorty is all too keenly aware that were one to transpose the aforementioned ethos of radical transgression directly to the realm of political life, the liberal values he cherishes would be the first to suffer.

EIGHT

Michel Foucault and the Search for the Other of Reason

> The world of *intimacy* is as antithetical to the *real* world as immoderation is to moderation, madness to reason, drunkenness to lucidity. There is moderation only in the object, reason only in the identity of the object with itself, lucidity only in the distinct knowledge of objects. The world of the subject is the night: that changeable, infinitely suspect night which, in the sleep of reason, *produces monsters. I submit that madness itself gives a rarefied idea of the free "subject," unsubordinated to the "real" order and occupied only with the present.*
>
> —Georges Bataille, *La Part maudite*

Among the group of thinkers commonly associated with French poststructuralism, the cultural criticism of Michel Foucault undoubtedly comes closest to the concerns of the Frankfurt School. Whereas other poststructuralists have had repeatedly to defend themselves against the charge of hypertextualism, Foucault, like the Critical Theorists, is committed to an anti–idealist research program which holds that "truth is a thing of this world."[1] Both Foucault and the Frankfurt School believe that the "dialectics of spirit" must be subjected to the techniques of material analysis. In this way alone might spirit's pretension to Being-in-itself be unmasked. Thus, for Foucault, "'Truth'"—note how the very word must be placed in inverted commas—"is to be understood as a system of ordered procedures for the production, regulation, distribution, circulation, and operation of statements." As such, "it is linked in a circular relation with systems of power which produce and sustain it, and to effects of power which it induces and which extends it."[2]

From the remarks just cited it becomes clear that Foucault and the Frankfurt School share not only a set of methodological concerns, but a number of substantive interests as well: above all, an interest in the mechanisms whereby domination and power implacably consolidate their hold on us. Foucault's special genius lay in his capacity to ferret out the manifestations of power where few prior to him had thought to look, in the capillaries and interstices of modern society: in hospitals, asylums, prisons, schools, army barracks, the confessional, training manuals, as well as in ancient and modern discourses on sexuality. Whereas liberals and Marxists alike concentrated on the state, qua locus of sovereignty, as the primary repository of power, Foucault contends that in political theory "the king's head still hasn't been cut off."[3] The juridical model of power—the "repressive hypothesis," according to which power is primarily the capacity to refuse, to deprive, to forbid—must be supplanted by a notion of power as *productive*. Thus, as Foucault puts it, in truth state power is "superstructural in relation to a whole series of power networks that invest the body, sexuality, the family, kinship, knowledge, technology, and so forth." State power is only effective insofar as it is "able to gain access to the bodies of inidividuals, to their acts, attitudes, and modes of everyday behavior. Hence the significance of methods like school discipline. . . . [Hence] the problems of demography, public health, hygiene, housing conditions." These new techniques of power undertake the "administration, control, and direction of the accumulation of men." Similarly, the extensive thematization of human sexuality by troops of professionals and experts is attributable to the fact that "sex is located at the point of intersection of the discipline of the body and the control of the population."[4] Foucault's masterful uncovering of the normalizing "micro-physics of power" by means of which we moderns are constituted as "docile bodies"—pseudo-autonomous, pliable selves—undoubtedly remains the most provocative dimension of an intellectual oeuvre that was tragically cut short in mid-course. The parallels between this aspect of Foucault's work and the Frankfurt School program of a critique of instrumental reason are many and profound.[5]

Moreover, toward the end of Foucault's life, it seemed that prospects of a more genuine intellectual rapprochement between him and the Frankfurt School was in the offing. In part, this development was motivated by his renewed interest in the philosophy of Kant: not in the transcendental philosopher who inquires into the "conditions of possibility" of experience, but in Kant qua exponent of the philosophical discourse of modernity. For in texts such as "Answer to the Question: What is Enlightenment?" Kant sets in motion an unprecedented reflection on the nature, meaning, and import of the historical present. For the first time, observes Foucault, "a philosopher has connected . . . the significance of his work with respect to knowledge, a reflection on history and a particular analysis of the specific moment at which he is writing and because of which he is writing."[6] It is perhaps less the content of Kant's reflections—the definition of enlightenment as "the emergence from self-incurred tutelage" and the concomitant emphasis on "the public use of reason"—that Foucault esteems than the process of reflection as such. Nevertheless, denuded of its legalistic implications, the Kantian formula for autonomy ("Act only on that maxim through which you can at the same time will that it should become a universal law") becomes a crucial harbinger of Foucault's own later ethic of aesthetic self-fashioning: the attitude of the "dandy" who turns his or her life into a work of art (although, as we shall see, Foucault's attempt to base ethics on aesthetics ultimately proves unsuccessful). Moreover, Kant's relentless critique of "heteronomy," of the "inability to use one's reason without the guidance of another," is a position that bears certain affinities with Foucault's own critique of the power of professional expertise in modern society. Or, as Kant observes in a remarkable anticipation of several Foucauldian themes: "The guardians who have kindly taken upon themselves the work of supervision will soon see to it that by far the largest part of mankind (including the entire fair sex) should consider the step forward to maturity not only as difficult but as highly dangerous." Hence, "if I have a book to have understanding in place of me, a spiritual adviser to have a conscience for me, a doctor to judge my diet for me, and so on, I need not make any efforts at all."[7]

It is, then, this characteristically modern interrogation of the content and nature of the historical present—"philosophy as the problematization of a present, and as the questioning by the philosopher of this present to which he belongs and in relation to which he has to situate himself"[8]—that accounts, according to Foucault, for the profound affinities between his own project of "genealogy" and the "critique of instrumental reason" advanced by the critical theorists. Hence, in one of the last texts published while he was still alive, Foucault situates his own intellectual project squarely in line with the Critical Theory tradition. One must opt, Foucault asserts, "for a critical thought that will take the form of an ontology of ourselves, an ontology of the present; it is this form of philosophy that, from Hegel, through Nietzsche and Max Weber, to the Frankfurt School, has founded a form of reflection in which I have tried to work."[9] This remark, coupled with Foucault's remarkably enthusiastic revaluation of both the enlightenment as well as Kant's place in the history of philosophy (after all, in *The*

Order of Things, Kant is rather unflatteringly portrayed as the intellectual progenitor of the nefarious, anthropocentric "human sciences") indicates, I think, a striking directional shift in Foucault's later thinking. According to Habermas, it drew Foucault back "into the circle of the philosophical discourse of modernity which he thought he could explode."[10] Unfortunately, we'll never know precisely how influential this directional shift might have proved for his subsequent work.

"THE SOVEREIGN ENTERPRISE OF UNREASON"

Toward the conclusion of *Madness and Civilization*, Foucault presents us with a fervid appeal to the "sovereign enterprise of unreason"—"forever irreducible to those alienations that can be cured, resisting by [its] own strength that gigantic moral imprisonment which we are in the habit of calling, doubtless by antiphrasis, the *liberation of the insane* by [the nineteenth-century reformers] Pinel and Tuke."[11]

If ever it could be said that a single passage in an oeuvre as fertile and voluminous as Foucault's possessed foundational status, it would undoubtedly be this one. For it might be said that Foucault's guiding pursuit as a writer and critic was none other than a quest for the *other of reason*. And even though circa 1970 Foucault announces a type of *coupure epistémologique*—the "break" between archaeology and genealogy—in this respect his work, from *Madness and Civilization* to the *History of Sexuality*, displays a remarkable degree of thematic consistency. For the impassioned appeal to the "sovereign enterprise of unreason" with which his provocative study of 1961 concludes is a trope that will reappear in virtually all his subsequent writings.

Foucault was always a harsh critic of the *episteme*, of the inflexible limits to thought that are inevitably imposed upon us by our inherited conceptual schemes. But it is not at all clear that he was ever able truly to account for the conceptual status of his own discourse, of genealogy as a type of "meta-episteme" charged with laying bare the unacknowledged conceptual foundations of various epochs in the history of thought, Renaissance, classical, and modern (the age of "Man"); of that "discursive practice" —his own—that is somehow able to unmask the hidden theoretical presuppositions of all others without succumbing to their illusions, limitations, and prejudices.

Attention to the trope of the "other of reason"—Foucault's "alteriotropism," as it were—might help us gain access to the unspoken schemata that govern his own conceptual framework; schemata, moreover, that may enable us to account for the value orientation underlying his methodological self-understanding qua "felicitous positivist."[12] For upon closer examination, it is not hard to see that in his search for the "other of reason," Foucault inserts himself within an intellectual and cultural lineage dominated by an *anti-civilizational ethos*, whose origins date back to Rousseau's first *Discourse*. In the twentieth century, the major inspiration behind this ethos has been a strain of anthropological romanticism, whose seminal exponents have been Marcel Mauss, Georges Bataille, and Claude Lévi-Strauss. In his early writings, moreover, Foucault explicitly relates this influential anti-civilizational current to another tradition: that of *literary modernism*, whose aesthetic critique of modernity proves an indispensable complement to the anthropological perspective of Mauss and company.

In *Madness and Civilization* we witness the first employment of a classificatory scheme that would become determinative for Foucault's entire subsequent project of a "history of the present."[13] For it is in this book that the "power-knowledge" dyad that would henceforth become a type of epistemological signature makes its first tentative appearance. Or, as Foucault himself observes in retrospect: "When I think back now, I ask myself what else it was that I was talking about, in *Madness and Civilization* or *The Birth of the Clinic* but power?"[14] And thus, in the perennial hostilities between reason and its other (or *unreason*), "knowledge" consistently sides with the powers of reason, its fraternal term. Relatively benign in the classical age of Descartes and the "great confinement" owing to its indeterminacy, reason reaches maturity with the age of positivism in the nineteenth century, an era that coincides with the dual emergence of the asylum and the human sciences. In language that unambiguously foreshadows the power-knowledge thematics of *Discipline and Punish* (1976), Foucault observes, "The asylum of the age of positivism [read: the human sciences] . . . is a juridical space where one is accused, judged, and condemned. . . ."[15] Thus, should the object of study consist of madness, punishment, or the order of classification itself, the periodization remains the same: a relatively benign preclassical period (Middle Ages and Renaissance) is followed by an incipient triumph of reason (the classical era), which is succeeded in turn by a third epoch in which the potentials for social control implicit in the knowledge-power nexus are diabolically consummated, resulting in the "disciplinary society" of the modern era—in whose grasp we remain today.

But once reason, which for Kant and the Enlightenment was to act as the universal solvent vis-à-vis all unwarranted claims to authority, has itself been unmasked as fully complicitous with the social organization of power—as its basis and *ne plus ultra*—to what countervailing forces might one appeal in order to remedy reason's hegemony?

Enter Foucault's embrace of "the sovereign enterprise of unreason" (the allusion to Bataille is intentional and profound). *Madness and Civilization*, to be sure, is a *Verfallsgeschichte*, a story of decline, that recounts the undoing of madness at the hands of the "party of reason"—the troop of experts, clinicians, and psychiatrists who sally forth to subdue and "normalize" the insane. Hence, Foucault tells us, since the triumph of psychiatry in the nineteenth century and the pseudo-liberation of the insane, the no-longer sovereign enterprise of unreason has of necessity undergone an immense sublimation. Transmogrified, it has migrated into "the lightning-flash of works such as those of Hölderlin, of Nerval, of Nietzsche, or of Artaud."[16] And in this form, it has become *écriture*: *poésie pure*, a chain of self-referential signifiers whose "sovereignty" consists in their capacity to burst asunder the trammels of referentiality, the semiotic prison-house of the *episteme*. Here, the conclusion of *Madness and Civilization* foreshadows concerns with language and power that will only become explicit in Foucault's subsequent work. The madness that appears in Goya's paintings, such as the felicitously titled *The Sleep of Reason Produces Monsters*, is no longer the structurally produced madness of Bosch and the Renaissance, but a new sovereign madness, born out of nothingness, where "man communicates with what is deepest in himself, and with what is most solitary." The obverse of reason's prosaic sobriety, it is at once intoxicating and terrifying: "man's possibility of abolishing both man and the world," "the end and the beginning of everything," "the ambiguity of chaos and the apocalypse"—these are some of the terms Foucault uses to describe it.[17] It is this same madness that will reappear in the work of Nietzsche and Artaud. It generates the ethos of "total contestation" that becomes the signature of their work, thereby restoring to it a dimension of "primitive savagery";[18] a dimension that has been occluded owing to the triumph of our "instrumentally rationalist" culture (Weber).

The Marquis de Sade represents, unsurprisingly, a key figure in the intellectual lineage valorized by Foucault. It is Sade, moreover, not Locke or Rousseau (with his facile celebration of natural innocence), who proves to be the ultimate philosopher of natural law. For it is Sade who poses the crucial question: what human act can be declared contrary to nature, since *all have their basis in nature itself?*—thereby besting the *philosophes* at their own game. Foucault, who appropriately identifies the Sadean enterprise as "a gigantic *pastiche* of Rousseau," understands that at issue in Sade is a daring retrieval of sovereignty, a desire that has been muted amid the Enlightenment training manuals—such as the *Emile*—that serve only to denature their instructees. With his Society of the Friends of Crime, Sade restores "the sovereign rigor of subjectivity" to its rightful position of primacy by rejecting "all natural liberty and all natural equality." We are left instead with the "uncontrolled disposal of one member by the other, the unconditional exercise of violence, the limitless application of the right of death"; that is, Sade as harbinger of Nietzsche's "transvaluation of all values" in the *Genealogy of Morals*.[19]

In this way, Sade effects his own transvaluation of eighteenth-century natural law. Instead of a social contract that artificially redresses the inequities (and iniquities) of the state of nature, Sade heroically restores to the latter their "right" vis-à-vis the "unnatural" mores of a civil society that has become effete and decrepit. Here is Sade the precursor of Bataille. Through repeated acts of ritual profanation, he succeeds in reestablishing the affinities between nature and a type of primordial madness, thereby—at least temporarily—restoring nature's omnipotence, its *sovereignty*. As Foucault concludes: "Through Sade and Goya, the Western world received the possibility of transcending its reason in violence, and of recovering tragic experience beyond the promises of dialectic."[20]

But Foucault must also know that there is a direct line of development between Sadean "natural law" and the Republic of Salo as depicted by Pier Paolo Pasolini; that is, between a restoration of the state of nature qua "right of the strongest" and the ethos of twentieth-century fascism, a form of transgression that was also a consequent rejection of "all natural liberty and all natural equality." And thus, in *Histoire de Juliette*, one of Sade's heroes, Francavilla, presciently outlines the methods of a new political science as follows: "The government must control the population, and must possess all the means necessary to exterminate them when afraid of them, or to increase their numbers when that seems desirable. There should never be any counterweight to the justice of government other than that of the interests or passions of those who govern."[21] But is this the price we must pay for a return of the "sovereign enterprise of unreason"?

The sociohistorical origins of modern natural law must be materialistically unmasked; on this point, one can certainly agree with Foucault. What needs to be called into question in turn, though, is the specific direction of that unmasking. In materialist terms, a determinate rather than an abstract negation is mandated.

In Foucault's account the sublimation of madness by the work of art leads to a result that does not simply redound to art's favor. As much as anything, this sublimation represents the secret triumph of unreason over the constraints of bourgeois aestheticism or art for art's sake. For the art or literature in question, as heralded by the work of Goya and Sade, no longer respects the rituals of taste or *politesse* that traditionally accompanied the idea of aesthetic autonomy. Instead, permeated by unreason, the boundaries of the latter now explode from within. As Foucault observes, "After Sade and Goya, and since them, unreason has belonged to whatever is decisive, for the modern world, in any work of art: that is, whatever any work of art contains that is both murderous and constraining." And thus "madness challenged the work of art, reduced it ironically, made of its iconographic landscape a pathological world of hallucinations; that language which was delirium *was not a work of art*. . . . Madness is the *absolute break with the work of art*; it forms the constitutive moment of abolition, which dissolves in time the truth of the work of art."[22]

It is in the work of art that the sovereign enterprise of unreason, which reason falsely believes it has condemned to silence, gains new life in order to indict that world of logic and propriety from which it had been unjustly banished. For Foucault, as for Nietzsche, the moment where the work of art steps out of itself and into the world is a moment of world-historical import. It represents the return of the repressed, the enunciation of a Dionysian truth, a possible sign of the end of reason's long-standing nihilistic reign:

> by the madness which interrupts it, a work of art opens a void, a moment of silence, a question without answer, provokes a breach without reconciliation where the world is forced to question itself. What is necessarily a profanation in the work of art returns to that point, and, in the time of that work swamped in madness, *the world is made aware of its guilt*. Henceforth, and through the mediation of madness, it is *the world that becomes culpable* (for the first time in the Western world) in relation to the work of art; it is now arraigned by the work of art, obliged to order itself by its language, compelled by it to a task of recognition, of reparation, to the task of restoring reason *from* that unreason, and *to* that unreason.[23]

The spirit of aesthetic modernism gives rise to an "adversary culture" in which the traditional value-opposition between reason and its other undergoes a portentous and far-reaching transvaluation.

As is well known, in 1963 Jacques Derrida delivered a provocative critique of *Madness and Civilization*, a critique that Foucault seems to have taken to heart.[24] The binary opposition governing the argumentation of Foucault's 1961 study—that between reason and madness—was misguided, Derrida contended, insofar as it claimed a purity for madness qua other of reason that was, strictly speaking, untenable. In his history of madness, Foucault strove to give voice to "madness itself," to let the "other" itself speak. But, as Derrida points out, the very act of representation necessarily introduces an element of *mediation*—a moment of *différance*—that reveals the idea of a pristine reproduction of "madness as such" to be a grammatological impossibility. Foucault's quest, therefore, for an origin outside of the discourse of reason remains, in the last analysis, ontotheological. Despite itself, the archaeology of madness Foucault seeks to write can only succeed at the price of reinscribing madness within the coordinates of a new discursive regime—that of archaeology itself.

In *The Archaeology of Knowledge* Foucault, it would seem, acknowledges the cogency of this criticism when he observes, "Generally speaking, *Madness and Civilization* accorded far too great a place, and a very enigmatic one too, to what I called an 'experiment,' thus showing to what extent one was still close to admitting an anonymous and general *subject of history*."[25] And thus, the reliance in *Madness and Civilization* on unreason as a type of primordial experiential substrate remains beholden to a prestructuralist hermeneutics of meaning, intentionality, and depth.[26]

But it must be asked: does Foucault, in truth, ever free himself from the aforementioned quest for origins? Could it be that, following Nietzsche, his critique of modernity—in essence, an era of pliable, "docile bodies"—is so thoroughgoing that he leaves himself without a normative *point d'appui* in the here and now, resulting in the archaizing tendencies observed by Derrida? Further, might not such an inclination toward archaism inhere in archaeology itself qua method (or later, in genealogy)?

If we turn now to *The Order of Things* (1966), we notice a remarkably parallel structural dynamic. For once the achaeologist digs far enough beneath the monopoly of signification possessed by the various discursive regimes under investigation (the domains of labor, life, and language), he discovers a bedrock of febrile linguistic immediacy that is capable of challenging the episteme's apparent discursive hegemony. In essence, we have returned to the dialectic of "reason" and its "other" that characterized

Foucault's earlier study. The role played by unreason in the book on madness is now occupied by literature qua *écriture*: the writing of infinity, Barthes' "degré zéro de l'écriture." The latter becomes a type of nonsignifying signification, a new locus of experiential immediacy, the origin (*Ursprung*) toward which nonhegemonic writing should strive.

Hence, coincident with the emergence of the modern episteme circa 1800, there arises the "isolation of a particular language whose peculiar mode of being is 'literary'"—"difficult of access, folded back upon the enigma of its own origin and existing wholly in reference to the pure act of writing."[27] In this way, Foucault explicitly reproduces the argument for "purity" and "origin" that was so prominently featured in *Madness and Civilization*. Literature becomes an indispensable fount of what Foucault calls "radical intransitivity." It becomes the literature of rupture, writing as *transgression*. Transgression of what? Of the linguistic code as an inflexible and constraining embodiment of normativity. It renounces the logic of signification of the various discursive regimes, the necessary relations between word and thing that they seek to establish. It "breaks with the whole definition of *genres* as forms adapted to an order of representations, and becomes merely a manifestation of a language *which has no other law than that of affirming*—in opposition to all other forms of discourse—*its own precipitous existence*."[28]

Released from the instrumentalizing parameters of representation, words are allowed, perhaps for the first time, to engage in the *celebration of their own sovereignty*. Here, Foucault projects the results of Mallarmé's poetics and Nietzsche's philology (his unmasking of the historical, hence, contingent nature of all linguistic expression) back toward romanticism and ahead toward the *nouveau roman*. The enormous archaeological shift between the classical and modern ages has seemingly allowed for the emergence of a space in which *écriture* could flourish. In this way, language took advantage of an hour of provisional epistemological uncertainty in order to reassert its own autonomy, to rediscover (the Heideggerian implications of this characterization are unmistakable) the purity of its own Being: "To the Nietzschean question: 'Who is speaking?,' Mallarmé replies . . . by saying that what is speaking is, in its solitude, in its fragile vibration, in its nothingness, *the word itself*—not the meaning of the word, but *its enigmatic and precarious being*."[29]

In Foucault's eyes such developments are replete with quasi-eschatological significance. For they herald the virtual recovery of a prelapsarian state beyond the trammels of representational signification—hence, beyond discourse—and thus the restoration of the lost unity of language, language in its pristine originality or "plenitude." As Foucault observes, "The whole curiosity of our thought now resides in the question: What is language, how can we find a way round it in order to make it appear in itself, in all its plenitude?"[30] And thus, the advent of "absolute literature" embodies a moment of Nietzschean foreboding, one that presages the "Return" of something originary. It is

> a sign of the approaching birth, or, even less than that, of the very first glow, low in the sky, of a day scarcely even heralded as yet, but in which we can already divine that thought—the thought that has been speaking for thousands of years without knowing what speaking is or even that it is speaking—is about to *re-apprehend itself in its entirety, and to illumine itself once more in the lightning flash of being.* Is that not what Nietzsche was paving the way for when, in the interior space of his language, he killed man and God both at the same time, and thereby promised with the Return the multiple and re-illumined light of the gods?[31]

The "dispersion of language" that is accomplished in complementary ways by Mallarmé and Nietzsche establishes the basis for "the archaeological event we may designate as the disappearance of Discourse."[32] The void of its absence is filled by *écriture*. But this is hardly an event of merely semiological or intralinguistic significance. And it is in this sense that Foucault can claim—anticipating the concept of discursive practice he will employ for the first time in the "Discourse on Language"—that modern thought is "no longer theoretical." Instead, it is a "perilous act"; an insight that is realized most profoundly in the writings of "Sade, Nietzsche, Artaud, and Bataille."[33] The citation of these names suggests that we are once again in the proximity of the thematics of *Madness and Civilization*. The new, nonrepresentational employment of language is the harbinger of an ultimate break with the episteme of the modern age, whose foundational tropes are "history" and "man." To be sure, that episteme lays the basis for its own undoing. For by subjecting "man" to a ceaseless historicization, his essential finitude—the impossibility of being his own Origin or Subject—is laid bare for all to see. This is a contradiction from which the foundationalist mood of the human sciences will never recover. But with man's disappearance, with the abolition of the incurably anthropocentric human sciences—the modern equivalent of what the classical age called Reason—we are provided with "the unfolding of a space in which it is once more possible to think."[34]

The upshot of such portents is something unmistakably positive. They point to an event—"the unfolding of a space in which it is once more possible to think"—that possesses a status akin to what anthropocentric thought would have termed emancipation. Foucault sheds no tears at the thought that, with the overturning of the human sciences, "man would be erased like a face drawn in sand at the edge of the sea."[35] And thus, the "other of reason," as embodied in a variety of nonrepresentational signifying practices whose exponents range from Sade to Nietzsche to surrealism—that is, language as a "perilous act"—remains the source of normativity for Foucault.

AN INTERLUDE ON DISCOURSE AND METHOD

The problem of normativity in Foucault—the basis upon which Foucault opts for those values he values—has already surfaced in connection with Derrida's critique of *Madness and Civilization*. Derrida calls into question Foucault's self-understanding as an advocate of unreason in order to indicate the methodological impossibility of Foucault's achieving what he seeks to achieve: a representation of madness that would surmount the limitations of representation itself. He does not, however, beg to differ with this normative choice per se. Derrida himself stakes out, as it were, a more modest epistemological program: a critique of representation that holds no illusions about the prospects of transcending representation as such. It is in this no-man's-land between the impossibility and the necessity of representation that deconstruction mounts its challenge to linguistic naiveté.

Habermas, in his critique of Foucault, has also raised a number of important questions concerning the normative status of genealogy qua method. Specifically, he has accused Foucault of a "crypto-normativism."[36] In this way, he seeks to identify a tension in Foucault's work between his methodological self-understanding as "felicitous positivist" and the particular value choices he espouses or seems to espouse. For if one indeed embraces a methodological tack that is exclusively descriptive, that shuns considerations of "depth" and "essence" as part of a phenomenological tradition of meaning-bestowing subjectivity that must be jettisoned,[37] then it is far from clear on what basis one might judge or criticize the various power formations that one is investigating or seeking to unmask. Both Habermas and Charles Taylor have raised the question of whether Foucault, given his intrinsic mistrust of the category of "emancipation" (part of a discourse of self-realizing subjectivity that must be avoided), can provide us with any compelling reason as to why we should strive to transcend conditions of domination.[38] For if emancipation is structurally impossible, one can only posit in its stead the eternal return of different power formations, with no hope of getting beyond their cyclical recurrence.

The considerations raised by Habermas and Taylor point to a larger dilemma of Foucault's methodological framework, one that emerges in full only with the genealogical phase of his work, where the primary focus is on the way in which power is produced and reproduced in modern societies; a dilemma, moreover, that is closely related to the normative deficit we have just been discussing. It concerns Foucault's *functionalist definition of power*, for it would seem that functionalism and antinormativism go hand in hand. In a sense, Foucault retains a traditional definition of political legitimacy which he then stands on its head. That is, if the classical functionalist definition of political authority claims that power is legitimate if it is recognized as such by those affected (Weber), Foucault accepts the form but changes the content of this statement, such that power is by definition *illegitimate*. Hence, whereas for Weber authority (*Herrschaft*) is inherently stabilizing and thus a "good," for Foucault, the philosophical anarchist, it is something that by definition must be contested and overturned. Ultimately, however, their positions prove methodologically complementary and only apparently opposed. For Weber is just as incapable of establishing the illegitimacy of socially accepted authority as Foucault proves incapable of establishing its legitimacy.

It is this structural aspect of Foucault's genealogical method, I would like to suggest, that accounts for the normative problems of his thought that have been identified and discussed by thinkers as diverse as Derrida, Habermas, and Taylor. For his functionalist definition of power implies in effect that *power is not something that can be legitimately exercised or wielded*. In the lexicon of genealogy, the term "legitimate political authority" can only stand out as a monumental non sequitur or oxymoron. Consequently, Foucault is methodologically compelled to search for a source of normativity that would be totally heterogeneous to the customary networks of power. Yet, the very existence of such a source is, strictly speaking, ruled out by that same methodology. For as Foucault himself is the first to remind, "Between techniques of knowledge and strategies of power, *there is no exteriority*. . . ."[39]

By the same token, his notion of power as essentially productive, his critique of the traditional juridical definition of power as something that represses or restrains, seriously risks *overgeneralizing the concept of power*, to the point where power is everything and everywhere.[40] Ultimately, according to Foucault's definitions and depictions, power becomes conflated with social action *tout court*; and thus, any act whereby one person influences, persuades, or convinces another turns into an instance of power. But influence, persuasion, and unforced agreement must be analytically separated from power as coercion or the illegitimate exercise of authority. An important distinction must be made between warranted and unwarranted instances of power. In *The History of Sexuality*, volume I, we are told, "*Power is everywhere*; not because it embraces everything, but becasue *it comes from everywhere*"; to the point where, if one carefully follows Foucault's argument, *resistance itself is something that has been produced by power*.[41] Foucault's strikingly original reconceptualization of power as essentially productive is certainly one of the more valuable aspects of his theoretical legacy. Yet if power is indeed omnipresent, if there is essentially no such thing as the legitimate exercise of power, and if, further, those who contest power must necessarily partake of the very mechanisms of power in their struggle to combat it—then their struggles are condemned a priori to reproduce the very thing they are combating. Here, an essentially cynical motif creeps into Foucault's theory of power. At the same time, the foregoing sketch of his theory of power helps explain why, in terms of the structural economy of his theory, Foucault must invoke as a source of resistance an entity (or entities) that exists at a *total remove from* the dominant manifestations of "power-knowledge." In principle, such resistance must assume the form of a primordial, presocialized otherness, such as madness. And this helps explain Foucault's fascination with the trope of "the other of reason" as a subterranean basis of normativity.

The nature of Foucault's functionalist concept of power emerges clearly in his 1974 debate with Noam Chomsky. At issue in the debate is how one can justify civil disobedience (the historical context of the debate being the Vietnam War). In responding to this question, Chomsky invokes the methods of immanent criticism: the constitutional state embodies certain principles of justice and right to which one might appeal under conditions of duress as a set of higher order truths in order to combat specific acts of injustice in the historical present—here, the invasion of a foreign nation in an undeclared war. As Chomsky observes: "To a very large extent existing law represents certain human values, which are decent human values; and existing law correctly interpreted, permits much of what the state commands you not to do"—such as acts of civil disobedience.[42] In essence, Chomsky is appealing to the tradition of modern natural right as embodied in constitutions of the liberal democratic variety. In his view, the essential nature of justice is that it transcends positive law.

For Foucault, however, there exists no such court of appeal or tribunal that one might invoke under such circumstances. Basically, all claims to right are functional; and thus, what one side in a dispute invokes as "right" will be perceived by the other side as a usurpation of "right," and vice versa. In essence, justice, too, is a fiction of intentional subjectivity that is coincident with the age of man. Humanity would be no worse off should it be "erased like a face drawn in sand at the edge of the sea" along with the anthropocentric episteme that has brought it into being.

For Foucault, therefore, the essential distinction between the meaning and validity of statements—and for that matter, of institutions—falls out of account. Hence, the claim in "Nietzsche, Genealogy and History" that "*all knowledge rests upon injustice*": "there is no right, even for the act of knowing, to truth or foundation for truth." Instead, "the instinct for knowledge is *malicious*"—"something *murderous*, opposed to the happiness of mankind."[43] And it is in this spirit that Foucault, discussing the bases of modern politics, recommends his celebrated reversal of Clausewitz: politics is the continuation of war by other means.[44] Social action for Foucault is the antithesis of the Habermasian "orientation toward mutual understanding." Instead, "one's point of reference should not be to the great model of language and signs, but to that of war and battle. The history which bears and determines us has the form of a war rather than that of a language: relations of power, not relations of meaning."[45]

The position he stakes out in response to Chomsky's defense of "justice" must be understood in a similar vein:

> The proletariat doesn't wage war against the ruling class because it considers such a war to be just. The proletariat makes war with the ruling class because, for the first time in history it wants to take power. And because it will overthrow the power of the ruling class it considers such a war to be just. . . . One makes war to win, not because it is just. . . . When the proletariat takes power, it may be quite possible that the proletariat will exert towards the classes over which it has just triumphed, a violent, dictatorial and even bloody power. I can't see what objection one could make to this.[46]

In the preceding passage, Foucault's functionalist conception of justice (and the same could be said for his theories of "truth" and "morality") emerges clearly. Moreover, if we penetrate beyond the (to be sure, anachronistic) *marxisant* rhetorical veneer, we see that in this context Foucault regresses behind Marx, for whom the standpoint of the proletariat was justifiable on the basis of a claim to justice, insofar as it embodied a greater claim to historical universality than its adversary, the bourgeoisie (hence, its status as a "universal class," which, according to Marx, accounted for its historical uniqueness).[47] Since, for Foucault, all claims to justice are merely effects of power and thus serve only to mask determinate power interests, there can be no criteria of legitimacy or right via which the various competing interests might be adjudicated. Political judgment is reduced to the effects of an all-encompassing war of position—hence, Foucault's methodological preference for metaphors drawn from the realm of battle, strategy, and tactics.

To be sure, Foucault consistently expresses solidarity with those groups that have historically suffered from the effects of power. But if, as he claims, considerations of justice play no role in our political judgments and preferences, can this partisanship for the downtrodden ultimately be anything more than a *decision*, and hence, *decisionistic*? And when one blithely extends a Nietzschean cynicism regarding value and meaning to the formal prerequisites of justice—civil liberties, due process, etc.—endorsements of dictatorships that are "violent, dictatorial and even bloody"—such as the one proffered by Foucault in the passage just cited—cannot be far off. But if it is in fact the case that ethical and political disputes are not in the first instance questions of "right," but instead, are best understood in terms of the language of "force, strategic developments, and tactics,"[48] we are essentially thrown back into an a-moral universe in which "the right of the strongest" prevails—and ought to prevail. For in these terms, even a partisanship for the oppressed must remain ungrounded; it is a deduction based on instrumental calculations of force or tactics, and not a question of right. And thus Foucault's theory of power rehabilitates a doctrine of "might makes right" in which the tension between "norm" and "fact" has collapsed. In the words of Hobbes, *Auctoritas non veritas facit legem*.

The allusion to Hobbes, moreover, addresses one of the key problems of genealogy as social theory: the problem of methodological atomism. For as we have seen, with the onset of his genealogical period, Foucault attempts to reconceptualize social theory on the basis of a transfiguration of Clausewitz, in which the rhetoric of power and struggle would supplant a traditional emphasis on norms, values, and rights. It is, above all, this neo-Clausewitzian approach that suggests affinities with Hobbes; however, not with Hobbes the philosopher of political obligation, but Hobbes the theorist of the state of nature qua *bellum omnium contra omnes*—a war of all against all. For Foucault seems to appropriate this Hobbesian model of social action—the prepolitical, social Darwinist Hobbes, as it were—and turn it into the basis for his understanding of the logic of political action in contemporary societies *simpliciter*.[49]

Foucault's embrace of a Hobbesian model of social action is theoretically overdetermined. It follows from his methodological anti-normativism, a standpoint that is reinforced as a result of the material analyses of power that may be found in *Discipline and Punish* and subsequent works, where norm (a term that seemingly encompasses "truth," "value," and "meaning") becomes the equivalent of "normalization." It is precisely such "norms" that coercively permeate and structure the identities of individuals in our modern carceral society. If for Hegel, the logic of normative development leads to "progress in the consciousness of freedom," for Foucault, this verdict must be reversed: beginning with the great reformers of the Enlightenment era (Bentham, Beccaria, etc.), one discovers only increasingly sophisticated techniques of domination. It is in this sense that, from a genealogical perspective, one can speak of norms as being *coextensive with power relations*, as essentially functional. It is a position that Foucault articulates forcefully and unambiguously. As he remarks in "Power and Norm": "the modern sequestration *manufactures norms*. Constitution of labour-power, apparatus of sequestration: disciplinary society, *permanent function of normalization*. That is the series that characterizes our type of society." And further:

> The discourse that will now accompany the disciplinary power is that which grounds, analyzes and specifies the norm in order to make it prescriptive. The discourse of the king can disappear and be replaced by the discourse of the one who sets forth the norm, the one who engages in surveillance, who undertakes to distinguish the normal from the abnormal; that is, through the discourse of the teacher, the judge, the doctor, the psychiatrist, and finally and above all, the discourse of the psychoanalyst. . . . Today, in place of the discourse which is bound up with power, there has come forward a normalizing discourse. That of the human sciences.[50]

Undoubtedly our understanding of the furtive and multifarious character of domination in the modern world has been greatly enhanced as a result of Foucault's concept of a microphysics of power or "bio-power"; a theory whose merit has been to steer us toward manifestations of power that, as Foucault explains, "come from below," and thus fall outside the purview of the juridical model of power, which confuses power with sovereignty. At the same time, there is a risk that, in a specific sense, his theory remains at odds with its own intentions. This is true insofar as it is presented as a critique of power and normalization that implicitly intends to free us from power's grasp. Yet, in self-contradictory fashion, it simultaneously suggests that the goal of emancipating ourselves from power is illusory; that in the final analysis, all we can expect is that one set of coercive practices and controls will be exchanged for another.

However, perhaps it is Foucault's neo-Hobbesian, atomistic concept of social action—his view of the latter as, in essence, a war of all against all—that in effect prevents him from reaching any other conclusion. When society is viewed exclusively from an atomistic standpoint, the prospect of mounting any effective, qualitative opposition to the reigning mechanisms of social control would seem ruled out *ex hypothesi*. For there could not exist the requisite level of social solidarity or intersubjective agreement to permit the attainment of a critical consensus concerning what must be changed and how. Such expectations and hopes would be a priori stifled amid the social fragmentation of the *bellum omnium contra omnes*. Even were such a consensus deemed to be attainable in principle, it would seem condemned in advance to degenerating into a new mode of normalization. Yet such a perspective risks trivializing an entire series of ameliorative and piecemeal political gains—extension of the franchise, reduction of the working day, national health care, and the preservation of basic civil liberties—that no post-totalitarian critical theory of society can afford to ignore. However, the reason Foucault cannot perceive the importance of such incremental gains in "formal freedom" is methodologically overdetermined, on two counts. First, such questions of political freedom hark back to a juridical model of power focusing on questions of sovereignty (essentially, the question of "who rules?"), a model that Foucault seeks to transcend without preserving. Second, his critique of modernity and the human sciences is so uncompromising that the act of thematizing basic human freedoms can only appear as a type of anthropocentric regression—little more than neohumanistic prattle. Either way, such concerns are systematically occluded from the purview of genealogy qua social theory.

THE RETURN OF THE REPRESSED

Earlier we noted that the totalizing character of Foucault's critique of the modern age leaves his theory without any immanent prospects of contestation, resistance, and critique. This was already true of his archaeological phase, where madness qua other of reason undergoes a process of sublimation, only to reappear in the form of "écriture" or "absolute literature." In his genealogical phase, one finds a parallel structural dynamic at work; moreover, the stakes have become even higher. For now Foucault divests himself of the "illusion of autonomous discourse," an erroneous hypostatization of the domains of signification and language, in order to come to terms with the way in which power is institutionalized in the modern world. Here, the dominant models are "discipline"—the systematic training and production of "docile bodies"—and "normalization"—the veritable "incitement to discourse" about sexuality that is responsible for the mistaken belief that we have a sexual nature or essence to express. In both instances, however, the discursive regimes of punishment and sexuality go so far as to produce their own "other," in the same way that madness is constructed by reason.

The modern penal system, for example, is responsible for creating a new social caste of delinquents. In this way, it is able to defuse an inchoate political threat from a series of popular illegalities that surface toward the end of the eighteenth century. The system of punishment is thereby able to alleviate the "great fear" of a revolt among an "outlaw class" of marginal individuals who inhabit the lower echelons of the social order; a fear that, according to Foucault, haunts France from the Empire to the July monarchy.[51] By reconstituting these individuals as "delinquents," the modern penal and legal systems are better able to supervise, manipulate, and control them. And in a similar fashion, the discursive regime of modern sexuality constitutes a new race of "perverts" and "libertines" in order that their wayward practices might be reinscribed among the canons of socially permissible deviance.[52] As Foucault indicates, even the pseudo-oppositional discourse of homosexuality can do no other than articulate its concerns in the language of normalization—of sexuality as a discourse of postconfessional, mandatory truth-telling. Hence, if one carefully traces the logic of the power-resistance dyad, one is inexorably driven to the conclusion—which is Foucault's own—that, "Where there is power, there is resistance, and yet, or rather consequently, *this resistance is never in a position of exteriority in relation to power*. . . . [Resistances] are inscribed in the latter as an irreducible opposite."[53]

Consequently, if the path of immanent contestation vis-à-vis our modern austere institutions and carceral practices has been blocked, one must look to potential sources of opposition that are somehow external to the power-resistance dyad as Foucault has described it. To be sure, throughout Foucault's genealogical phase, a number of tell-tale hints are dropped. For example, in *The History of Sexuality*, one finds a fascinating discussion of the Oriental *ars erotica*, which Foucault counterposes to our own normalizing *scientia sexualis*. According to Foucault, the *ars erotica* represents a "natural" and untroubled mode of sexuality, in which sexual expression is considered not in relation to the permissible and the forbidden, or as network of preexisting social taboos, but *in relation to itself*. As such, it represents a form of sexual practice that is nonalienated and authentic. Moreover, since the techniques of sexual pleasure are not divulged, it remains free of the confessional compulsions of Western sexuality, our so-called incitement to discourse about sex. As Foucault explains:

> In the erotic art, truth is drawn from pleasure itself, understood as a practice and accumulated as experience; pleasure is not considered in relation to an absolute law of the permitted and the forbidden, nor by reference to a criterion of utility, but first and foremost in relation to itself; it is experienced as pleasure, evaluated in terms of its intensity, its specific quality, its duration, its reverberations in the body and soul.

Such practices, Foucault informs us, "transfigure the one fortunate enough to receive [their] privileges: an absolute mastery of the body, a singular bliss, oblviousness to time and limits, the elixir of life, the exile of death and its threats"[54]—Kama Sutra as a pathway to nirvana. It is this uncharacteristically effusive portrait of the *ars erotica* as a type of nonheteronomous, bacchanalian ideal that perhaps best helps us to understand the suggestive, oft-cited appeal with which *The History of Sexuality* itself concludes: "The rallying point for the counterattack against the deployment of sexuality ought not to be sex-desire, but *bodies and pleasures*"—more precisely, "*a different economy of bodies and pleasures.*"[55]

As the remarks just cited suggest, Foucault has never abandoned the vitalistic trope of the other of reason. It was and remains the guiding source of normativity throughout his work. Since discourse by definition remains captive to a thematics of *normalization*, inscribing us in the vernacular of power-knowledge, forcing us "to speak the truth," Foucault's own source of normativity must be *pre*discursive, a type of prelinguistic body language, as it were, an origin that resists the normalizing compulsions of language and socialization. Were any further confirmation necessary of the foundational role this trope plays in his thinking, one need only turn to a 1977 interview with *nouveau philosophe* Bernard-Henri Lévy on the subject of "Power and Sex." Here, Foucault, while trying to distance himself from the "diffuse naturalism" of his earlier work, insists nevertheless on maintaining "the idea that underneath power, with its acts of violence and its artifices, we should be able to rediscover the things themselves in their primordial vitality: behind asylum walls, the spontaneity of madness; in and through the penal system, the fertile unrest of delinquency; beneath sexual prohibitions, the purity of desire."[56]

The vitalistic impulses we have thus far surveyed remain on the genealogical margins until the latter two volumes of *The History of Sexuality*. In stark contrast to *La volonté de savoir* (volume I), the other of reason now occupies center stage. It becomes the analytical focal point, however, in a far from an unmediated sense. It reappears not in the form of presocialized otherness, as did madness in Foucault's early work; nor in the naturalistic guise of the appeal to "a different economy of bodies and pleasures" with which volume I concludes. Instead, it is mediated by a full-blown *aesthetic voluntarism*, whose intellectual antecedents are Nietzsche's doctrine of the will to power and Bataille's theory of sovereignty. For Nietzsche, "the world is a work of art that gives birth to itself." Elsewhere he observes, "I assess a man by the quantum of power and abundance of his will."[57] By combining these insights, one arrives at the standpoint of *aesthetic decisionism* in terms of which Foucault seeks to ground his later position. The "aesthetics of existence" characteristic of both pre-Christian ethics and the modern dandy provides an alternative (or: an alternative "problematization") to the austere normalization of contemporary ethical/sexual practice.

Foucault's unexpected turn to pagan "techniques of self" in volumes two and three of *The History of Sexuality* suggests that the first version of the project, as outlined in *La volonté de savoir*, was conceptually flawed. To be sure, when pressed in interviews to account for the drastic shift in historical focus from modernity to antiquity, he frequently responds in personal-biographical terms.[58] Yet such explanations are less than satisfying, and one cannot help but suspect that his original plan to write "a history of the modern subject" remained unconsummated for more compelling theoretical reasons: above all, a dissatisfaction with the monolithicity of power relations in his work of the mid-1970s, which portrayed the mechanisms of power as essentially unbreachable and inescapable; a scenario which has the perlocutionary effect of condemning all attempts at resistance to failure in advance.

What Foucault finds to admire in pagan ethics is that, for certain privileged individuals, an "aesthetics of existence," the "choice of a beautiful life," is taken to be the focal point of living. As Foucault explains in *The Use of Pleasure*: "What I mean by this phrase are those intentional and voluntary actions by which men not only set themselves rules of conduct, but also seek to transform themselves, to change in their singular being, and to make their life into an oeuvre that carries certain aesthetic values and meets certain stylistic criteria."[59] He elaborates this idea as follows:

> The idea of the *bios* as material for an aesthetic piece of art is something that fascinates me. . . . What strikes me is the fact that in our society, art has become something which is related only to objects and not to individuals, or to life. That art is something which is specialized or which is done by experts who are artists. But couldn't everyone's life become a work of art? Why should the lamp or the house be an art object, but not our life? . . . From the idea that the self is not given to us, I think that there is only one practical consequence: *we have to create ourselves as a work of art.*[60]

Whereas Christian ethics or techniques of self are otherworldly inasmuch as they aim at the *telos* of salvation in the hereafter, Greek ethics are this-worldly insofar as the methods of training—all of which also involve various forms of *askesis* and self-renunciation—aim at an enhancement of the individual's beauty or power in the here and now. In this way, Foucault rehabilitates a quintessentially Nietzschean insight and value judgment. Thus, whereas Greeks ethics are *life-affirming*, Christian ethics are *life-negating*. And in this respect, the "bio-power" that circulates throughout modern disciplinary society represents a continuation of the Christian ethos of subjugation by other means. Greek techniques of self, by contrast, represent for Foucault a kind of privileged (if not entirely unproblematical) model, insofar as they promote a mode of individuation that is non-normalizing. Finally, the Baudelairean dandy, "who makes of his body, his behavior, his passions, his very existence, a work of art," embodies a modern realization of the same non-normalizing ethical precepts.[61]

Hence, Foucault attempts to resolve the aporias of the genealogical model of power by reintroducing the concept of *autonomous subjectivity*—a move that has been the object of both surprise and criticism.[62] Of course, the model of subjectivity Foucault seeks to reclaim is a far cry from the Kantian ideal of self-legislating subjectivity. For to legislate on the basis of maxims that are universally valid would be (as Nietzsche has putatively shown) to relapse into an ethics of normalization. Instead, the model suggested here is the heroic individualism of Nietzsche's superman, whose greatness lies in his capacity to transcend the norm. Moreover, we know that Nietzsche's refabrication of heroic subjectivity is aesthetically grounded. "Art reminds us of states of animal vigor," Nietzsche announces. "Becoming more beautiful as the expression of a victorious will!" he gushes elsewhere—in a spirit that is not at all foreign to the aesthetic voluntarism or sublimated vitalism Foucault endorses as a positive basis of normativity in his later work.[63]

But as we have already intimated, there remain profound and troubling difficulties with Foucault's attempt to introduce this Greco-Nietzschean model as a late remedy for the dilemmas of the genealogical theory of power. Once again he tries, as it were, to leap over these dilemmas rather than to solve them immanently. The appeal to the model of aesthetic self-fashioning seems facile and implausible, especially in contrast with the elaborate and painstakingly detailed descriptions of bio-power in Foucault's preceding works. Can the complex problems of modern self-individuation really be remedied, let alone solved, by way of *a simple assertion of will*, by the "choice of a beautiful life," as Foucault seems to suggest? And if the techniques of carceral subjugation are in fact as all-pervasive and inescapable as Foucault has described them, wherein lie the resources of selfhood upon which we might draw to combat them? Or is the model of aesthetic self-assertion to be reserved solely for the heroic few, who thereby acquire prerogative over the aesthetically displeasing hoi polloi?

In the last analysis Foucault's later embrace of aesthetic self-fashioning founders on an essential point: the attempt to base ethics on aesthetics. His thought necessarily moves in this direction insofar as the theory of bio-power, in neo-Nietzschean fashion, cynically discounts the egalitarian ethos of modernity as conducive only to further disciplinary normalization. It seems, however, that the aestheticization of ethics Foucault seeks to promote is undermined by a new set of contradictions that combine to render it extremely dubious as an alternative theoretical model. For in the last analysis, the idea of reestablishing ethics on the basis of aesthetic criteria leads to a concept of practical philosophy that is, strictly speaking, nongeneralizable. If I view other persons primarily in aesthetic terms—rather than, say, according to the Kantian formula of respecting them as "ends in themselves"—I philosophically underwrite their wanton manipulation: they become in effect material for my own personal aesthetic gratification; they are degraded to the status of bit players in the drama of my own private aesthetic spectacle. For once ethics are predicated on aesthetics, then those actions are prized that aim at effects that are *dramatic*, *spectacular*, and *provocative*—as opposed to those which display "respect for all rational natures." Thereby, a profoundly decisionistic element infiltrates ethical conduct. It is actions that are especially *demonstrative* or *glorious* that are valued primarily, regardless of the specific content or ends of a given act—that is, regardless of whether such an act might be judged "moral" or "immoral" according to conventional ethical standards. Instead of an ethic of reciprocity or brotherliness, Foucault opts for what we might call a dramaturgical model of conduct, in which action becomes meaningful solely qua performative gesture. But this theory risks sanctioning an approach to ethics that is brazenly particularistic and elitist. Formally, it remains only a hair's breadth removed from Nietzsche's rehabilitation of the right of the strongest. With Foucault, however, it is not necessarily the will of the strongest that is legitimated, but instead the "rights of the most beautiful." For this reason, it would seem appropriate to identify Foucault's later advocacy of an "aesthetics of existence" as an aesthetic voluntarism or an aesthetic decisionism; a concluding theoretical gesture which suggests that to the end, and despite his late flirtation with Kant and the philosophical discourse of modernity, his thinking remained mesmerized by the foundational trope of "the other of reason."

The House that Jacques Built: Deconstruction and Strong Evaluation

> The "rationality"—but perhaps that word should be abandoned for reasons that will appear at the end of this sentence—which governs a writing thus enlarged and radicalized, no longer issues from a logos. Further, it inaugurates the destruction, not the demolition but the de-sedimentation, the de-construction, of all the significations that have their source in that of the logos. Particularly the signification of *truth*. . . . That necessary violence responds to a violence that was no less necessary.
>
> —Jacques Derrida, *Of Grammatology*

The unparalleled institutional success deconstruction has achieved in the United States as a methodology of literary analysis would make for an excellent study in the sociology of knowledge. For whereas deconstruction has certainly made significant inroads in the intellectual culture of other Western industrialized nations, its degree of success in the United States has been short of phenomenal. To be sure, it would also be fruitful to subject deconstruction's impact as a mode of literary criticism itself to a deconstructive analysis. For, after all, does not its "transformation via reception" in a North American context represent a paradigmatic instance of several pet deconstructive themes concerning textuality and repetition: translation, iterability, and dissemination? Yet I know of no such efforts to understand the immense cultural influence of deconstruction along these lines.[1] This situation is unfortunate, for in the absence of such attempts at self-understanding, intellectual criticism of deconstruction has often taken the form of a series of ill-willed and intemperate attacks which habitually display little comprehension of the intellectual phenomenon under investigation. Such attempts to belittle deconstruction's achievements usually take on the character of external criticisms which sail wide of the mark and serve only to further the atmosphere of mutual distrust that prevails between deconstruction and its detractors.

The hypothetical study in *Wissenschaftssoziologie* alluded to above would have to account for why deconstruction—whose intellectual star may well be on the wane—ultimately became the disciplinary fixture it did when it did. Such concerns would have to be addressed in terms of both their institutional as well as their larger, cultural ramifications. For example, during the 1960s, when questions of political relevance were to the fore, literary criticism, whose methods were still largely dominated by the textual formalism of the new criticism, underwent a partial cultural eclipse. Criticism, as a result of its endemic disciplinary prejudices in favor of high culture, could not fend off the suspicion of being in league with the established powers; or, at best, of fostering a type of self-indulgent bellettrism that led, in the opinions of some, only to new heights of irrelevance in the midst of a politically charged era. The issue of "relevance," justly or unjustly, became an albatross of literary critical bad conscience.

In many respects, the advent of deconstruction was able not only to restore to the field of literary theory its lost prerogative, but to allow the discipline to stake a hitherto unprecedented claim to *intellectual primacy*. For Derrida's theory of archi-writing, that groundless ground of discourse as such, allowed those who laid claim to his methods to contend that all questions of interpretation rested, unwittingly and parasitically, on deconstructionist premises. That is, if archi-writing were, indeed, the long repressed, uncircumnavigable *origin of signification as such*, then "writing," "*écriture*," could not truly be comprehended apart from the understanding of textual figuration as set forth by deconstruction and its practitioners. Deconstruction's claim to textual "primordiality" would then constitute the unavoidable presupposition of interpretation *tout court*. Since all other disciplines are engaged in the interpretation of texts, and since grammatology, as a type of negative hermeneutics—a hermeneutics of *absence* rather than *presence*—lays bare the genealogical preconditions of *textuality in general*, all interpretation becomes, *nolens volens*, a variant of grammatology/deconstruction. Consequently, were one to analyze deconstruction's considerable institutional success in terms of a Foucauldian "economics of power" (or equally, perhaps, in terms of a Nietzschean logic of "Wille zur Macht"), the manifest attributes of deconstruction qua theory would seem unequivocal and compelling. Moreover, the element of sheer difficulty involved in mastering both Derrida's texts and the intellectual tradition(s) they presuppose may even be viewed as a type of initiation rite that limits access to the position of privileged insight deconstruction has come to represent. Naturally, this difficulty of access also tends to increase the value of the doctrines themselves.

However much insight a sociological analysis of deconstruction's institutional prestige might yield, this framework, too, ultimately falls short of the mark in the manner of other external criticisms of deconstruction. For the claim that the circulation of ideas has its origins in a less exalted, material-institutional sphere can tell us little or nothing about the intrinsic content of the ideas themselves; in the case at hand, about the inherent import and cogency of the deconstructive approach. In fact, its weakness lies precisely in its methodological inability to acknowledge a quasi-autonomous logic of ideas; that is, the fact that, in order to be understood, questions of truth and meaning also demand recourse to the immanent techniques of interpretation. And in this regard, one of the most serious limitations of the sociology of knowledge is that questions of "right" cannot be decided on the basis of questions of "fact." That an idea or set of ideas undergoes a prior sociohistorical determination and becomes "accepted," far from being inherently damnable, is merely to specify the concrete preconditions for the social genesis of knowledge as such. Thus, genealogy is a necessary but not a sufficient condition of historical understanding. What we also need to know are the reasons or grounds why the successful institutional realization of certain ideas should be favored and that of others opposed. And this is a task that calls for an analysis on the level of meaning or immanent criticism.

What I shall attempt in the discussion that follows is an immanent criticism of deconstruction; that is, one that takes the claims of deconstruction as an approach to textual analysis or cultural criticism seriously. The question of deconstruction's status as an "approach to textual analysis or cultural criticism" is itself far from uncontroversial. Surveying the literature, one often gains the impression that the movement's progenitor, Jacques Derrida, has a conception of deconstruction's uses and limitations that may be significantly at odds with the dominant modes in which it has been received to date. That deconstruction begins, in a quasi-Heideggerian spirit, as a critique of metaphysics, and has achieved renown in the first instance as an approach to literary criticism is perhaps the most important illustration of the vagaries of its North American reception. While there is no doubt a fruitful tension at issue here, it seems that, at the same time, Derrida's followers have very often made stronger claims on behalf of deconstruction—especially with regard to its potentially revolutionary cultural consequences—

than would Derrida himself. For when pressed (in interviews, public statements, and position papers), Derrida tends to be extremely circumspect concerning the wider "civilizational" implications of his theories. On the other hand, however, he has shown himself on no few occasions enamored of and fascinated by a new "apocalyptical tone recently adopted in philosophy."[2]

I believe that Derrida's pronounced ambiguity regarding the possible revolutionary cultural consequences of deconstruction—an ambiguity that results in a seemingly contradictory posture of extreme theoretical circumspection, on the one hand, and a radical propheticism, on the other—is the defining characteristic of deconstruction as a whole. One might even go so far as to say that deconstruction *lives within this ambiguity*; or, that to understand it fully is to understand what deconstruction is essentially about. At base, it reflects the essential ambiguity or tension in our relation to the tradition of Western metaphysics; and, for Derrida, following Heidegger, this ambiguity necessarily extends to the entirety of our intellectual heritage (although, importantly, both Heidegger and Derrida grant exceptional status to certain poets), which is profoundly structured and determined by the history of metaphysics. In a far from trivial sense, the whole of deconstruction represents an extended meditation on the nature of this ambiguity: a meditation on the seemingly contradictory imperative of *the need to go beyond the history of metaphysics* and the simultaneous *impossibility* of *really* "going beyond." Deconstruction, knowingly and proudly, operates within the parameters that have been opened up by this void. In Derrida's view—to paraphrase Foucault—it opens up a space in which it is once again possible to think; that is, to think "non-metaphysically." (But can this really be done?)

In this connection, a patented trope of Heideggerian provenance is of great relevance: his characterization of the present age as one which is afflicted by a kind of *double forsakenness*: the absence of the gods who have fled and the not-yet of the gods to come. For Heidegger, who was thoroughly familiar with the "apocalyptical tone" identified by Derrida, this condition of double forsakenness bespeaks the "end of metaphysics" (*die Vollendung der Metaphysik*). And although the era of Western metaphysics has definitely played itself out (cataclysmically, in view of the immeasurable historical catastrophes that have characterized the era of its "consummation"), the conditions of a *postmetaphysical era*, while they may be discerned, are far from being realized.

Derrida is a direct heir of the foregoing Heideggerian diagnosis of the historical present (*Zeitdiagnose*). He is the self-conscious legatee of the

Heideggerian quest for a viable mode of thinking or doing philosophy in a postmetaphysical age. And while he distances himself appropriately from the "homey" (*heimisch*) character of Heidegger's philosophical metaphorics, which, he suspects, are still too redolent of a "metaphysics of presence" that Heidegger has elsewhere called into question, he is simultaneously convinced of the preeminent value of the "uncircumventable Heideggerian meditation."[3] Thus, just as Heidegger appeals for "another beginning,"[4] Derrida confidently evokes the project of "an *other* writing, with all the implied risks."[5]

The intellectual filiations between Heidegger and Derrida are essential, not merely from the standpoint of the history of ideas, but for the sake of understanding the centrality of the Heideggerian critique of metaphysics to Derrida's post-philosophical project. On the one hand, it would be hard to conceive of two thinkers more temperamentally opposed. The philosophy of the later Heidegger, driven by despair over a nihilistic modernity, and despite its trenchant criticisms of "onto-theology," never sheds the longing for a forgotten origin, a lost condition of primordiality, in which mortals and gods dwelled in blissful mutual proximity or *Nähe*. His celebrated *Fehlleistung* or slip in the *Spiegel* interview, to the effect that contemporary humanity has fallen so far that "only a god can save us!" must be understood as an expression of extreme intellectual disorientation—*Ratlosigkeit*—given the paucity of intellectual choices presented by the modern world. The aesthetic sensibility of modernity, with its malformities and dissonances, is so far anathema to him that his alternatives remain either a neoclassicist monumentalism (one, moreover, that goes far toward explaining his attraction to German fascism [cf. his discussion of the Greek temple in "The Origin of the Work of Art"]), or an endorsement of "poetic revealing" in which Hölderlin—a Teutonic Homer, the "voice of the Volk"[6]—makes it possible to recoup the lost teleology of Greco-Germanic Dasein. Derrida, conversely, revels in the disintegrations and slippages of modernity, to the point where these appear as the virtual historical precondition for the emergence of deconstruction as a critique of the language of "presence": that is, as a critique of the entire gamut of naive philosophical pieties concerning the possibility of a "transcendental signified" or the self-evidence of meaning. For him, therefore, Mallarmé becomes, as it were, a deconstructionist *avant la lettre*. The iconoclastic poetic sensibility that has served as the point of departure for many of his finer essays—on Artaud, Bataille, Sollers, as well as Mallarmé—would be summarily banned from Heidegger's pan-German pantheon of *grosse Dichter*.

Nevertheless, it might be said that both Heidegger and Derrida share a certain postmodern sensibility. But here one must be extremely precise as to the conceptual implications of what is probably the most overused term in contemporary cultural criticism. Heidegger and Derrida are postmodern to the extent that both maintain a view of the history of philosophy that culminates in a shared understanding of the indigence of the historical present qua "modernity." Since the history of philosophy is covalent with the history of metaphysics (or, for Derrida, the history of logocentrism), and since it is the Cartesian/metaphysical gesture of "enframing" (*das Gestell*) that defines the essence of modernity (in Heideggerian parlance, it describes the dominant modality in which Being "comes to presence"), both thinkers are postmodern to the extent that they are both "post-philosophical." Only a resolutely *post-philosophical culture* promises a world in which our relation to metaphysics—above all, our relation to the necessary linkages between *violence* and *metaphysics* ("in a classical philosophical opposition we are not dealing with the peaceful coexistence of a *vis-à-vis*, but rather with a *violent hierarchy*," observes Derrida)[7]—would be qualitatively "other," "different." In sum, Heidegger's avowed *antimodernism* and Derrida's implicit *postmodernism* converge on a shared object of criticism: modernity as the site par excellence of a metaphysics of presence. In the case of both thinkers, therefore, the critique of philosophy merges with a withering critique of the historical present.

■ ■ ■ ■ ■ ■

From the beginning, Derrida has always insisted that "deconstruction . . . is not *neutral*. It *intervenes*."[8] What we need to investigate, though, is *how* it intervenes; on what basis it can claim a position of privilege or methodological primordiality as a mode of intervention—not only as a method of interpreting texts, but in the multifarious situations and experiences of daily life. For, indeed, Derrida has repeatedly insisted that deconstruction, far from being a textual idealism in which Being would be reduced to the problem of signification, has perpetually challenged the naive belief in the integrity of signification; that is, the cherished philosopheme that "signs" are neutral and unproblematical purveyors of "meaning." Instead, deconstruction, as a result of this ceaseless and unremitting assault on the delusions of semiological transparency, actually serves to explode the boundaries of textuality per se. And thus, foremost among the idealisms that deconstruction seeks to expose is precisely that of the autonomy of the text.

Yet the charge of "linguistic idealism" has probably been the accusation most frequently leveled against deconstruction over the years. It is the core of Michel Foucault's response, in a later edition of *Histoire de la folie à l'age classique*, to Derrida's essay, "Cogito and the History of Madness."[9] Derrida's approach to criticism, argues Foucault, remains exclusively *textual*. As an interpreter and critic, he leads us into the text from which, in turn, *we never emerge*. Themes and concerns that transcend the parameters of textuality—above all, those that are related to questions of social reality, institutions, and *power*—remain fully imperceptible from the standpoint of this rarefied, hyperlinguistic framework.

In a similar vein, Edward Said wonders aloud whether Derrida's approach to criticism, by virtue of its emphasis on fissures, absences, and the impossibility of determining meaning with any semblance of certainty, does not "[muddle] traditional thought beyond the possibility of its usefulness." "The effect of such [deconstructionist] logic (*the mise en abime*)," he continues, "is to reduce everything that we think of as having some extratextual leverage in the text to a textual function." He concludes unsparingly: "Derrida's key words [hymen, différance, trace, supplement, etc.] . . . are unregenerate signs: he says that they cannot be made more significant than signifiers are. In some quite urgent way, then, there is something frivolous about them, as all words that cannot be accommodated to a philosophy of serious need or utility are futile or unserious."[10] (However harsh such remarks may seem, they may, ironically, be in perfect accord with Derrida's own self-understanding, which is centered around the notion of signification as "play").

In *Tropics of Discourse*, Hayden White sets forth a number of similar criticisms, which culminate in the charge that Derrida is "imprisoned in structuralism's hypostatized labyrinth of language."[11] Finally, for Russell Berman, the political implications of deconstruction—pseudo-radical rhetorical posturing notwithstanding—are deeply conservative: "It marks the termination of the radicalism of the sixties: preserving the radicalism as tropic gesture but bringing it to an end as social practice." Viewed sociologically, deconstruction represents a "reification of radicalism" that is profoundly consonant with the era of neoconservative political stabilization and apathy:

> For it is, after all, "always already" only verbal radicalism; hence the rallying cry that there is nothing beyond the text. Far from trying to change the world, deconstruction does not even want to interpret it but smugly abolishes it instead, writing it off as a figment of the imagination of language. . . . [The] "young conservatism" of deconstruction encompasses elements that resonated closely with

> the new powers-that-be: a rejection, indeed denunciation of emancipatory projects, a return (with some notable exceptions) to an increasingly restrictive canon of texts, a reconstruction of literary studies as an elitist undertaking, and, especially the insistence on a definitive separation of literature from politics; the only revolution it imagines is the revolution in the literary text.[12]

To be sure, there is no a priori reason why an interpretive approach whose privileged terrain of operation is that of philosophical and literary discourse should feel compelled to proffer judgments about the domain of institutional life or "objective spirit" (Hegel). Yet Derrida himself, on a number of prominent occasions, insists not only that deconstruction is adequate to such a task, but that, in the contemporary cultural context, it even represents a type of critical *via regia*. In opposition to the charges raised by Foucault, Said, et al., he has maintained that deconstruction has always problematized or called into question the traditional binary opposition between "exterior" and "interior," sign and referent, text and non-text; and that, conversely, an unthinking empiricism that naively insists on the indubitable "reality of the real," is in truth little better than an uncritical idealism. In fact, the real error lies with those who seek to attribute a type of primordial, evidential status to concepts such as "social reality" and "power," as if they were somehow entities existing "out there," merely waiting to be seized by us; as if we could somehow simply *bypass the problematic of representation* and allow beings, as it were, to speak for themselves (perhaps in a manner akin to Marx's technique in *Capital* I, where he observes: "Could commodities themselves speak, they would say: Our use-value may be a thing that interests men. It is no part of us as objects.");[13] as if the problems of language, signification, and writing, that Derrida has mapped out in so many places and in such painstaking detail, could simply be effaced by virtue of an insouciant return to the pregrammatological distinctions between "ideal" and "real," "text" and "non-text." All discourse, all representation, must pass through the filter of différance. There is no escape from the diacritical imperatives of archi-writing, the logic of supplementarity. To believe and desire differently—as do Foucault, Said, and others who have raised similar charges against deconstruction—is to succumb to a retrograde metaphysical longing for unmediated presence; a longing that is perennially subverted and withheld by the alterity of the trace.

Derrida's response to the charge of "pan-textualism" may be gleaned in part through his notion of the "general text"; a concept that intends the opposite of what it may seem to imply on first view. For to speak of a "general text" does not mean that the entire "world" is a "text," a panoply of signs, a book to be read. Instead, it describes an obverse condition: the bounds of the text (in the narrow sense) won't hold; by virtue of the logic of signification, it necessarily overflows its margins, such that the traditional distinction between "inside" and "outside" no longer obtains. In this respect and unavoidably, "text" and "world" mutually inform each other; they act as communicating vessels, as it were. As he observes:

> What I call *text* is also that which "practically" inscribes and overflows the limits of such a [purely conceptual, theoretical] discourse. *There is* such a general text everywhere that (that is, everywhere) this discourse and its order (essence, sense, truth, meaning, consciousness, ideality, etc.) are *overflowed,* that is, everywhere that their authority is put back into the position of a *mark* in a chain that this authority intrinsically and illusorily believes it wishes to, and does in fact, govern. . . . What is produced in the current trembling is a reevaluation of the relationship between the general text and what was believed to be, in the form of reality (history, politics, economics, sexuality, etc.), the simple, referable exterior of language or writing, the belief that this exterior could operate from the simple position of cause or accident. What are apparently simply "regional" effects of this trembling, therefore, at the same time have a nonregional opening, destroying their own limits and tending to articulate themselves with the general scene, but in new modes, without any pretension to mastery.[14]

Consequently, according to Derrida's own critical self-understanding, the general text that is at issue in all deconstructive criticism opens upon the field of history proper. Deconstruction seeks to show that history (or, at least, temporality), rather than possessing the status of an excluded or marginalized other (an *hors texte*), operates within the interior of the text itself, vitiating its claim to self-referential exclusivity. And it is precisely insofar as it constantly calls into question the deluded idealism of the predominant philosophical discourse, insofar as it ruthlessly unmasks the belief that categories such as "truth," "consciousness," and "meaning" *really do govern,* that deconstruction, in Derrida's view, finds itself allied with the project of an *authentic materialist criticism*—"authentic" inasmuch as it does not become merely an "inverted idealism." Or, as Derrida affirms: "It seems to us that the itinerary of a deconstruction of logocentric discourse inevitably encounters the materialist text, which has long been the historical text repressed-suppressed by logocentric discourse (idealism, metaphysics, religion) taken as the discourse of a ruling ideology in its different historical forms."[15]

Lest there remain any residual ambivalences concerning the ultimate compatibility of deconstruction with the concerns of materialist criticism, Derrida, at least on one occasion, goes to no small lengths to spell out his position:

> There have been several misinterpretations of what I and other deconstructionists are trying to do. It is totally false to suggest that deconstruction is a suspension of reference. Deconstruction is always deeply concerned with the "other" of language. I never cease to be surprised by critics who see my work as a declaration that there is nothing beyond language, that we are imprisoned in language; it is, in fact, saying the exact opposite. *The critique of logocentrism is above all else the search for the "other" and the "other of language."* Every week I receive critical commentaries and studies on deconstruction which operate on the assumption that what they call "post-structuralism" amounts to saying that there is nothing beyond language, that we are submerged in words—and other stupidities of that sort. Certainly, deconstruction tries to show that the question of reference is much more complex and problematic than traditional theories supposed. It even asks whether our term "reference" is entirely adequate for designating the "other." The other, which is beyond language and which summons language, is perhaps not a "referent" in the normal sense which linguists have attached to this term. But to distance oneself thus from the habitual structure of reference, to challenge or complicate our common assumptions about it, does not amount to saying that there is *nothing* beyond language.[16]

Thus, as Derrida points out, to problematize reference, to call into question the way in which the "presence" of the "other" of language is, typically, *merely assumed*, is not the same thing as canceling reference in toto. The avowal just cited is fruitful because it helps us understand the weaknesses of similar accusations that have been leveled against deconstruction: for example, that its unrelenting investigation of the conditions of possibility of truth and meaning has rendered these concepts obsolete and dysfunctional; and that Derrida's abandonment of such categorial mainstays of the Western tradition can only lead to the most extreme form of intellectual nihilism.[17] But here, too, Derrida would be quick to remind that a rigorous questioning of such philosophical truisms—their conceptual displacement and refashioning as performed by deconstruction—is far from equivalent to their simple disqualification. Moreover, if one takes seriously his point about the dangers of a logocentric culture—that is, about the metaphysical violence, hierarchy, and coercion that goes hand in hand with this culture—it is the deconstruction of such categories alone that will permit our partial emancipation from their tyrannical yoke.

It is worth noting that here, too, Derrida shares a diagnosis of the historical present with Nietzsche and Heidegger. In full accordance with Nietzsche's understanding of "European Nihilism,"[18] he believes that it is not so much the *critique* of Western values (idealism, metaphysics, religion) that leads to nihilism or the precipice of meaninglessness, rather it is those values themselves *that are already nihilistic* and that have driven us headlong toward the abyss. Along with Heidegger, he believes that the "decline of the West" is, in the first instance, a crisis of *metaphysical provenance* or of logocentrism; and thus, not only does the "principle of reason" "constitute the verbal formulation of a requirement present since the dawn of Western science and philosophy, it provides the impetus for a new era of purportedly 'modern' reason, metaphysics, and technoscience."[19] Subjective reason as "enframing" or Heideggerian *Gestell* comes to hold sway over an entire epoch—"modernity." However, what is troubling about this position is the suspicion that Derrida, while pursuing this Nietzschean-Heideggerian intellectual lineage, has uncritically assimilated the standpoint of a total critique of modernity; a standpoint that renders all immanent criticism of modernity virtually superfluous. It is this position, moreover, that may help to account for Derrida's fascination with philosophy's recent "apocalyptical tone."

As we have seen, Derrida insists that deconstruction, as a critique of metaphysics, idealism, and dialectical illusion, far from being incompatible with a materialist criticism, actually serves to expose philosophical discourse to what is heterogeneous to language. Or, as he observes at one point: "Deconstruction is not an enclosure in nothingness, but an openness towards the other."[20] Yet the question must seriously be posed: how far in fact does deconstruction actually go in this direction? How suitable are its methods for the understanding of extralinguistic themes and problems? And thus, when we take a closer look at what Derrida himself actually means by "materiality," "otherness," and so forth, it is difficult to remain satisfied with all the assurances he has provided concerning deconstruction's seriousness of purpose.

For in those few passages in which he directly confronts the problem of deconstruction's understanding of extralinguistic reality—of what it would mean for deconstruction actually to get "outside of the text"[21]—the results are less than reassuring. In such instances one is led to conclude that deconstruction equates "materiality" and "reference" exclusively with certain *grammatological tropes*: spacing, supplementarity, différance; and that the only material elements it is capable of recognizing are those that determine the figural properties of the text. It is in this spirit that Derrida observes—

in an aside that is only too revealing—that "spacing/alterity" constitute "the materialist moment *par excellence*, heterogeneity." Hence, for Derrida, "*The irreducibility of spacing is the irreducibility of the other*."[22] Yet, when we habitually speak about otherness, heterogeneity, alterity, and the like, we do not mean something like the ineliminability of the trace—those insurmountable slippages between the referential pretensions of everyday language and "écriture" or "archi-writing" in the Derridean sense, which constantly subverts those pretensions. We practice instead a suspension of disbelief in the trace (for Derrida, of course, this "suspension of disbelief" is the original sin of metaphysics), which allows for the practical efficacy of language as a medium of coordinating human action. To be sure, this everyday "suspension of disbelief" tends to minimize the rhetorical and figurative dimensions of language—precisely those dimensions to which deconstruction is most sensitive. However, it seems that deconstruction is so profoundly wedded to a by now familiar litany of nonconceptual determinants of discourse, that the "material" points of reference it *claims* to be able to recoup remain, in the last analysis, *unrecoverable*. In other words, one must seriously inquire as to whether deconstruction has not in fact problematized objectivity and reference to the point where, given the demanding network of differential coordinates it has established, such concepts have essentially lost their meaning.

(There is, of course, a fascinating paradox at issue here. For wouldn't Derrida be immediately tempted to respond that the loss of meaning, in the form of stale and familiar *Evidenz*, is precisely what deconstruction seeks to accomplish; and that the net results of this maneuver are in some sense "freeing"? Yet one cannot, it seems, have it both ways: a radical problematization of meaning and reference without a corresponding diminution of what it is that these concepts signify. Ultimately, Derrida would have to show how the deconstructive "remarking" of these concepts constitutes an overall *enhancement*—however this term might be understood—of what our habitual notions of meaning and reference entail. He would have to show convincingly that, in the aftermath of the deconstructive "double séance," our world-relations are not referentially and semantically impoverished, but *enriched*. But doesn't this suggest that deconstruction would have to provide us with something like an [Hegelian] *Aufhebung* or a *relève* vis-à-vis our traditional concepts of meaning and reference—the very thing whose possibility it strenuously denies?)

■ ■ ■ ■ ■ ■

Unlike Jean-François Lyotard, Derrida has intentionally avoided associating deconstruction with the postmodern turn in criticism and the arts.[23] Nevertheless, it would be difficult to deny that his thinking coincides in several crucial respects with what might be called the "anticivilizational ethos" of postmodern culture; "anticivilizational" inasmuch as it remains convinced that the dominant values of modern culture—self-positing subjectivity, ethical universalism, and, more generally, the tyranny of holistic thinking—have failed us profoundly and are in need of a radical "unmaking." It is in this spirit that, in an interesting commentary on the postmodern situation, Ihab Hassan has aptly characterized postmodernism as a movement of "unmaking":

> It is an antinomian moment that assumes a vast unmaking in the Western mind—what Michel Foucault might call a post-modern *episteme*. I say "unmaking" though other terms are now *de rigeur*: for instance, deconstruction, decentering, disappearance, dissemination, demystification, discontinuity, *différance*, dispersion, etc. Such terms express an ontological rejection of the traditional full subject, the *cogito* of Western philosophy. They express, too, an epistemological obsession with fragments or fractures, and a corresponding ideological commitment to minorities in politics, sex and language. To think well, to feel well, to act well, to read well, according to the *episteme* of unmaking, is to refuse the tyranny of wholes; totalization in any human endeavor is potentially totalitarian.[24]

Unsurprisingly, several terms of Derridean provenance—deconstruction, dissemination, and *différance*—figure prominently in Hassan's description. Indeed, the general affinities between Hassan's characterization and Derrida's project are far from superficial. For from his earliest works, Derrida explicitly ties deconstruction to a certain demystification of Western ethnocentrism, which is based on the primacy of metaphysics qua logocentrism—"the imperialism of the logos," "the scientificity of science."[25] Grammatology, as the unmaking of metaphysics, must be viewed as a product of "the system whose dislocation is today presented as such"; and in this respect, it "shows signs of liberation all over the world, as a result of decisive efforts" that are "necessarily discreet, dispersed, and almost imperceptible." As a science of writing, grammatology promotes "the wanderings of a way of thinking that is faithful and attentive to the ineluctable world of the future which proclaims itself at present, beyond the closure of knowledge." However, he continues, "The future can only be anticipated in the form of an *absolute danger*. It is that which breaks absolutely with constituted normality and can only be proclaimed, *presented*, as a sort of *monstrosity*"[26]—a monstrosity, that is, from the standpoint of the logocentric habits of thought that are currently predominant. For the future to which Derrida alludes—or, as he terms it at one point, "the death of the civilization of the book"[27]—is one that will have essentially gone ***beyond*** such habits of thought; that is, beyond the relationship of speech to writing, of signifier to signified, of presence to absence, that such habits have traditionally entailed and demanded. If this future appears on the horizon as an "absolute danger," it is because it comes upon us, like a Heideggerian *Seinsgeschick*, without warrantability or guarantee: its discourse on method can never be written. And if it must, in the manner of Lévi-Strauss' *bricoleur*, of necessity still make use of the concepts and terms it has deconstructed (since the notion of an absolute break with metaphysics is itself a species of dialectical illusion), it will operate with these concepts *sous rature*.

For someone who is so often accused of the sins of textual idealism, Derrida seems to go to no small lengths to situate deconstruction's emergence historically in terms of the reigning zeitgeist. However, it seems there is certainly another way to interpret the contemporary mood of dislocation and decentering, one which suggests that the epochal paradigm shift identified by Derrida should be greeted with skepticism and reserve rather than a yea-saying, neo-Nietzschean *amor fati*. For the trend toward cultural disintegration noted by Derrida, one which accounts for his flirtation with a certain postapocalyptical sensibility, may at the same time express a condition of acute cultural impoverishment. It may signify the fact that the bonds of human solidarity are becoming frayed beyond repair. It might in part reflect a logic of *total reification*: the fact that a culture that prizes exchange value over use value, abstract over concrete labor, the simulacrum over the thing itself, has reached a virtual point of no return. If the "legitimacy of the modern age" (Blumenberg) is contingent on a program of self-justification—this, after all, is the essence of the Kantian formula of autonomy, "man's emergence from self-incurred immaturity" or the ability "to use one's own understanding without the guidance of another"[28]—then the transition to postmodernity, cautiously heralded by Derrida, may in fact presage a new era of heteronomy: an era of passive submission, in which the central dilemmas of collective human endeavor are belittled as the vestiges of an atavistic urge for "self-possession" or "presence."

Thus, the desedimentation of established cultural practices—which are grounded in a nonplayful, anthropo-logical violence—that Derrida views as a possible sign of liberation may equally be viewed as a manifestation of loss, of *dis-orientation*, in a far from untroubling sense. Doesn't this alternative interpretation of the postmodern condition, moreover, accord more with the grim, postapocalyptical scenario depicted in the opening passages of Alasdair MacIntyre's *After Virtue*? Here, MacIntyre envisages a civilization—ours—so lacking in normative coherence (or, one might say, self-presence) that it succumbs to a type of cultural aphasia: a radical incapacity for self-orientation. For in the thought experiment with which MacIntyre's study begins, he asks us to imagine a society in which, following a series of environmental catastrophes, "science" is held accountable: "Widespread riots occur, laboratories are burnt down, physicists are lynched, books and instruments are destroyed." It is almost as though MacIntyre has reinterpreted Derrida's portentous remarks concerning "the death of the civilization of the book" with the totalitarian movements of the mid-twentieth century in mind. Later on, he continues, some enlightened survivors attempt to reconstruct scientific knowledge on the basis of the few traces that have survived. But this attempt is unsuccessful, for all that they possess are *fragments*: "a knowledge of experiments detached from any knowledge of the theoretical context which gave them significance; parts of theories unrelated either to the other bits and pieces of theory which they possess or to experiment; instruments whose use has been forgotten; half-chapters from books, single pages from articles, not always fully legible because torn and charred."[29] And in a harsh (and probably unjust) indictment of contemporary interpretive methodologies, MacIntyre goes on to tell us that were such a hypothetical scenario to come to pass, the reigning philosophical schools—phenomenology, existentialism, and, above all, analytic philosophy (whose techniques are primarily descriptive, hence, non-normative)—*would barely notice the difference*: "All the structures of intentionality would be what they are now. The task of supplying an epistemological basis for these false simulacra of natural science would not differ in phenomenological terms from the task as it is presently envisaged. A Husserl or a Merleau-Ponty would be as deceived as a Strawson or a Quine."[30]

But the truly provocative aspect of MacIntyre's imaginative excursus lies in his suggestion that it is far from entirely fictive. Instead, were we to substitute *moral* for *scientific* knowledge in the foregoing parable, we would have a fairly accurate representation of the current disarray of contemporary moral theory. Or, as MacIntyre asserts:

> The hypothesis which I wish to advance is that in the actual world which we inhabit the language of morality is in the same state of grave disorder as the language of natural science in the imaginary world which I described. What we

possess, if this view is true, are the fragments of a conceptual scheme, parts which now lack those contexts from which their significance derived. We possess indeed simulacra of morality, we continue to use many of the key expressions. But we have—very largely, if not entirely—lost our comprehension, both theoretical and practical, of morality.[31]

There are many aspects of MacIntyre's argument with which one could easily disagree—for example, the hyperbolic description of the contemporary moral impasse. For when MacIntyre says "morality," he really means Hegelian *Sittlichkeit*: a conception of ethical life that is modeled after the Greek polis and in which the moral choice of the individual is rigidly circumscribed as a result of his or her social role. Hence, in such nonegalitarian societies, one's capacity for moral excellence or "virtue" is narrowly defined by one's position in the social hierarchy. Part of the dilemma of moral autonomy which is coincident with the advent of modernity and the emancipation of the individual from the prescriptive hierarchies of traditional society is the problem of legitimate moral disagreement. Hence, one cannot simultaneously valorize the rights of individual conscience (it was Socrates' embodiment of this principle that, for Hegel, explains the demise of the "ethical totality" of the Greek polis) and expect to achieve the level of near automatic moral consensus that tends to characterize premodern societies. Although freedom of conscience, which under conditions of modernity comes to supplant Aristotelian "virtue," certainly increases the risks of moral dissensus, it also opens up for the first time the prospects of an authentic ethical pluralism.

At the same time, MacIntyre's neo-Aristotelian account of our present-day ethical quandary is far from baseless. However, he would like to hold the legitimate demands of a modern ethical pluralism responsible for a lack of normative cohesion that must instead be traced back to a different source: the conflicting moral imperatives that derive from the cultural split between *bourgeois* and *citoyen*. For as inhabitants of modern society, there is a constant tension between the demands of ethical solidarity (familial, religious, political), which require that we treat other persons as *ends in themselves*, and those of occupational life or "civil society," which mandate that we act strategically, and thus treat other persons fundamentally as *means*.

Be that as it may, I think that if we accord a certain heuristic value to MacIntyre's fable of contemporary moral decay, it poses significant problems for a framework such as Derrida's. Bluntly put: it may well be that the current historical hour requires a labor of reconstruction rather than deconstruction. Of course, Derrida has always insisted that deconstruction, far from being a purely negative or nihilistic endeavor, in no way rules out the realization of "positive" results, whose attainment would be implicit in the practice of "remarking." But, in truth, the affinities between deconstruction and the contemporary spirit of "unmaking" are so profound that it becomes extremely difficult, if not at times impossible, to imagine concretely the type of "positivities" deconstruction would freely embrace. The deconstruction of traditional conceptual oppositions and hierarchies—mind and body, presence and absence, nature and culture, essence and appearance, and so forth—does not, purportedly, leave us with a result that is merely "negative." The metaphysical oppositions remain, for, in a strict sense, they are *insurmountable*, there is no getting "outside"; nevertheless, they have become permanently altered, different, and thus nonidentical with themselves in their prior, unreflective, logocentric incarnation. They have been deconstructively re-marked.

But this process of remarking raises a welter of disconcerting questions about the status and direction of deconstructive remarking itself. For we need to know more about the motives, the grounds, and the ends that determine the process of deconstructive reinscription. We need to know more about the nature of the new postmetaphysical positivities that this procedure might yield. In lieu of a convincing response to such questions, deconstruction cannot help but seem, on this essential point, profoundly weak. For one suspects that it has too readily imbibed the Heideggerian equivalence between *Grund* and *Abgrund*; that is, the notion that reason is ultimately an *abyss*. Hence, its fascination with abyss-al (abys-mal?) "nonconcepts"—the hymen, *différance*, and the trace. But is this an abyss from which one can reemerge, in conceptually plausible fashion, to remake a metaphysically impoverished world? When one, in an oversimplifying fashion (one that may indeed be more characteristic of the purveyors of deconstruction than of Derrida himself), equates "Grund" (ground or reason) with metaphysical violence, one potentially loses something indispensable: *the capacity to make significant distinctions*. By subjecting "ground" to the by now familiar deconstructive "double gesture" ("overturning" and "displacement"), does one not potentially lose the capacity to discriminate between warranted and unwarranted assertion? And by rendering this distinction problematical, "out of play" (*hors jeu*), have we not lost something truly essential? That is, isn't this a distinction that merits strengthening rather than "displacement"? And thus, Derrida's "fixation on metaphysics, and the pressing need he sees to battle its ideal essences at every turn divert his attention and energies from the real task of postmetaphysical thought." As opposed to the by now familiar deconstructive meditations on the "abyss," the latter would be defined by the attempt "to reconstruct the notions of reason, truth, objectivity, and the like in nonfoundationalist terms."[32]

Aristotle, one will recall, in the *Politics* had the following to say about *logos*: "*Logos* serves to declare what is advantageous and what is the reverse, and it therefore serves to declare what is just and what is unjust. It is the peculiarity of man, in comparison with the rest of the animal world, that he alone possesses a perception of good and evil, of the just and the unjust, and of other similar qualities."[33] In its sweeping indictment of logocentrism, by treating its occidental preeminence as little more than an incurable social pathology, doesn't deconstruction risk losing contact with an indispensable capacity for theoretical discernment: a capacity for distinguishing between "what is just and what is unjust" which, according to Aristotle, more than anything else accounts for our humanity. Moreover, doesn't that indictment itself succumb, following Heidegger and in a far from trivial manner, to a profoundly metaphysical, "essentializing" gesture: the "violent" hypostatization of an entire, variegated, tension-filled epoch in the history of thought—metaphysics—as "logocentric"? "All metaphysicians," observes Derrida,

> from Plato to Rousseau, Descartes to Husserl, have proceeded in this way, conceiving good to be before evil, the positive before the negative, the pure before the impure, the simple before the complex, the essential before accidental, the imitated before the imitation, etc. And this is not just *one* metaphysical gesture among others, it is *the* metaphysical exigency, that which has been the most constant, most profound and the most potent.[34]

Yet "metaphysics" may not be the origin and ground of the contemporary cultural impasse or crisis. (For reasons that I can only hint at in the context at hand, I would like to suggest that the origins and grounds of this crisis are "historical" rather than "metaphysical"; and that Derrida, by following Heidegger in attributing such sovereign world-historical efficacy to "metaphysics," thereby indeed lapses into a type of "idealism." In the case of both thinkers, the problem is the same: the history of philosophy becomes a philosophy of history.) Moreover, it may be the case that a widespread postmetaphysical philosophical skepticism has led to a paralyzing cynicism concerning the capacity of thought for *strong evaluation*; that is, concerning its ability to distinguish between good and bad, the positive and the negative, the essential and the accidental. Thus, as the philosopher Richard Bernstein has remarked, "'The danger today does not come from the utopian impulse of metaphysics but rather from the various attempts to kill off metaphysics.'"[35] Derrida, to be sure, is too sophisticated to believe that we could ever be done with metaphysics, no matter how desirable that end might ultimately be. Unfortunately, though, his thought has provided the conceptual impetus for a contingent of more literal-minded kindred spirits—as is apparent, for example, if we return to Ihab Hassan's remark, cited above, concerning the integral relation between "totalitarianism" and "totalization"; or, the equation of "totality" with "terror" with which Lyotard concludes *The Postmodern Condition*.[36] This postmetaphysical sensibility, moreover, has resulted in the proliferation of a feckless pluralism, a denatured "perspectivism" (if there is one thing of which one cannot accuse perspectivism's progenitor, Nietzsche, it is an incapacity for "strong evaluation"), an avoidance of conceptual "hierarchies" to the point where, ultimately, all points of view are deemed equally valid. Or else, one discovers a complementary tendency to embrace the "other" of reason merely because it is "other"—the "bad" instead of the "good," the "negative" rather than the "positive," the "accidental" rather than the "essential." But, as Derrida would probably be the first to point out, to favor such a move is merely to succumb to an *inverse metaphysics*—in the same way that Heidegger accuses Nietzsche of practicing an "inverted Platonism."[37]

To take Derrida seriously would mean to appreciate the essential tension that defines the preconditions for genuine postmetaphysical thinking: the simultaneous necessity of going beyond metaphysics coupled with the impossibility of ever really "going beyond." As Derrida observes:

> There is no sense in doing without the concepts of metaphysics in order to shake metaphysics. We have no language—no syntax and no lexicon—which is foreign to this history; we can pronounce not a single destructive proposition which has not already had to slip into the form, the logic and the implicit postulations of precisely what it seeks to contest.[38]

Or as Derrida, in an unambiguous allusion to Heideggerian *Denken*, remarks in another context: "'Thought' requires *both* the principle of reason *and* what is beyond the principle of reason, the *arkhe* and an-archy. Between the two, the difference of a breath or an accent, only the *enactment* of this 'thought' can decide."[39]

And yet one must be sure that deconstruction's patented "double gesture" does not turn into a "double bind." We must ascertain what it means to fulfill this Beckettesque program of going beyond without ever really getting beyond. In other words, in the case of deconstruction, what is the difference that makes a difference once one enters the purgatory zone between the end of philosophy and the beginning of an *écriture* that has never yet been? Or, to pose the same question in different terms, does Derrida's dread of a "metaphysics of presence"—which is something that must be "avoided" but which it is ultimately impossible to "surmount"—ultimately betray an incapacity to "take a position," despite his forceful claim that "deconstruction . . . is not *neutral.* It *intervenes.*"[40] And thus, despite Derrida's many well-placed reservations about the tradition of Western rationalism, one must be wary about falling into a reverse dogmatism: a dogmatism of the negative. It is undoubtedly in this vein that Edward Said has suggested that "the supreme irony of what Derrida has called logocentrism is that its critique, deconstruction, is as insistent, as monotonous and as inadvertently systematizing as logocentrism itself";[41] in the predictability of its results, it risks becoming merely the inverse image of what it criticizes: the dogmatism of "undecidability."

I believe that no one has addressed these questions with more subtlety and insight than Richard Bernstein:

> Derrida knows all too well that there is no ethics or politics—or even metaethics or metapolitics—without "taking a position." But few have written more persuasively and imaginatively than he has about all the snares and traps that await us in "taking a position"—how easily we can fall back into the metaphysics of presence and the dream of a fixed center that he has sought so valiantly to question; how a self-deceptive violent dogmatism awaits those for whom *archai* do not tremble. But even if we learn this lesson over and over again, we are still left with the unanswered question: *how can we "warrant" (in any sense of the term) the ethical-political "positions" we do take?* This is *the* question that Derrida never satisfactorily answers. What is worse, despite the overwhelming evidence of his own moral passion and his willingness and courage in "taking positions," he seems to call into question the very possibility of "warranting" ethical-political *positions.* Or rather, it is not clear how Derrida understands the *practice* of warranting our ethical-political positions. What are we to do after we realize that all *archai* tremble? It is almost as if Derrida wants to bring us out of the wilderness, wants to *überwinden* the violent "history of the West" without providing us with an orientation for avoiding the abyss of nihilism that he so desperately wants to avoid. We lack what he himself calls a *mochlos*—a lever—for displacing the history of violence. He presumably points us toward the promised land of a *post-metaphysical* ethics and politics without adumbrating its geography.[42]

Of course, it would be foolish to insinuate that the notion of "engagement" or "taking a position" could somehow become a touchstone for authentic philosophizing. But Derrida himself has described the methodological intentions of deconstruction in terms of furnishing the "protocols of vigilance for a new *Aufklärung*."[43] He has spoken allusively (and elusively), in a barely veiled prophetic mode, of "the yet unnameable which is proclaiming itself . . . under the species of the nonspecies, in the formless, mute, infant, and terrifying form of monstrosity";[44] an event of qualitative rupture whose advent he ties (in a manner reminiscent of Yeats' "The Second Coming") to the loss of the "center"—of the consolation and security the latter has traditionally provided for Western culture. This event, moreover, allows for the breakthrough of a

> Nietzschean *affirmation*, that is the joyous affirmation of the play of the world and of the innocence of becoming, the affirmation of a world of signs without fault, without truth, and without origin which is offered to an active interpretation. *This affirmation then determines the noncenter otherwise than as loss of the center*. And it plays without security. For there is a *sure* play: that which is limited to the *substitution* of *given* and *existing*, *present*, pieces. In absolute chance, affirmation also surrenders itself to *genetic* indetermination, to the *seminal* adventure of the trace.[45]

In passages such as these, Derrida implies that there *is* such a thing as genuine transgression, that by embracing "free play" or "the seminal adventure of the trace," one can indeed transcend the "double bind." But it is difficult to square such uncharacteristic effusion with his many other more temperate assessments of the prospect of "overcoming metaphysics."[46]

A prophetic mode is also apparent in his tantalizing appeal, in the course of a fascinating meditation on the "politics of friendship," to a democracy that has never yet been; one in which the concept of friendship would accede to the measurelessness of its truth, a truth that would be beyond the traditional homo-fraternal and phallogocentric schema.[47] Yet since deconstruction rules out of play the "data" accrued by the social sciences, insofar as they are still determined by the "principle of reason," hence, *logocentric*—for "they never touch upon that which, in themselves, continues to be based on the principle of reason and thus on the essential foundation of the modern university. They never question scientific normativity, beginning with the value of objectivity or of objectivation, which governs and authorizes their discourse"[48]—its investigations of "democracy," the "university," and "hierarchy" in general remain, as a matter of principle, *empirically uninformed*. Instead, as others have pointed out,[49] its researches are paradoxically confined to the "close reading" of certain canonical texts and thinkers—Aristotle, Hegel, Husserl, Heidegger, and so forth; a situation, moreover, that has given rise to a current of vigorous protest from within the ranks against deconstruction's patent refusal "to open onto an 'outside' constituted by ethico-political contingencies."[50]

In questioning whether deconstruction possesses sufficient conceptual resources for the tasks of contemporary cultural criticism, we are led back to the motif of strong evaluation. This theme suggests that the best account of the present sociohistorical situation is *not* the Heideggerian theme of the "end of metaphysics." Instead, it takes pains to delineate an immanent, this-worldly sociohistorical diagnosis of crisis tendencies in the modern world, one in which the Weberian concept of "rationalization" figures prominently. Weber addresses this problem in terms of the triumph of rational-purposive over substantive reason (*Zweck-* vs. *Wertrationalität*); and he explains this situation in terms of the dilemmas of a capitalist-bureaucratic culture that is increasingly oriented toward the values of productive efficiency as opposed, for example, to a belief in humanity as an end in itself. He defines this dilemma succinctly in a passage from "Science as a Vocation," where he explains that the worldview of modern science "gives us an answer to the question of what we must do if we wish to master life technically. It leaves quite aside, or assumes for its purposes, whether we should and do wish to master life technically and whether it ultimately makes sense to do so."[51] In other words, under rule of the "performance principle" (H. Marcuse) of late capitalism, a preoccupation with instrumental mastery—mastery over nature and over the intersubjective human world—predominates to the exclusion of our ability to reflect on *ends*—a concern that was traditionally the province of metaphysics. In the antimetaphysical age inaugurated by modern positivism (from Comte to the Vienna Circle), such concerns have been stigmatized as "prescientific"—hence, irrational.

An orientation toward strong evaluation aims at recovering our capacity for rational reflection on ends (*telei*). It entails the construction of vocabularies and discourses—languages of *qualitative evaluation*—that better enable us to articulate the values we prize and the type of people we would like to be; an intellectual project that, because of its profound teleological resonances, its emphasis on qualitative judgment and the themes of self-realization, would, for deconstruction, undoubtedly remain excessively *metaphysical*. An appreciation of strong evaluation entails a prejudice (a "rational prejudice," as it were) in favor of the values of *cultural reflexivity* through which we establish *second order concepts*. For it is one thing to have—as do all individuals and cultures—tastes and preferences, likes and dislikes. It is quite another to cultivate a second order evaluative framework on whose basis one coherently determines and grounds one's preferences, likes, and dislikes. When Marx talks about overcoming socially necessary illusion or "false consciousness," when the early Heidegger talks about surmounting the reified conceptual universe of *Alltäglichkeit* ("everydayness") and acceding to self-transparency or "authenticity" (albeit in terms that are excessively a-historical and decisionistic), it is our capacity for strong evaluation that is at stake. As Charles Taylor has observed, "The question at issue concerns which is the truer, more authentic, more illusion-free interpretation and which on the other hand involves a distortion of the meanings things have for me." At issue is the conviction that "it is more honest, courageous, self-clairvoyant, hence a higher mode of life, to choose in lucidity than it is to hide one's choices behind the supposed structure of things"—as threatens to occur, for example, with the later Heidegger's "destining of Being" or Derrida's *différance*. And thus, "the strong evaluator envisages his alternatives through a richer language. The desirable is not only defined for him by what he desires, or what he desires plus a calculation of consequences; it is also defined by a qualitative characterization of desires as higher and lower, noble and base, and so on."[52]

One must seriously doubt whether an intellectual approach such as Derrida's, one that stakes so much on the negative moment of going beyond a "metaphysics of presence," is capable of attaining such levels of insight. "Presence," as embodied in the values of history, politics, and individual self-fulfillment, is also something that must be renewed and preserved. Thus, the omnipresent fear of a relapse into metaphysics can quickly turn into a paralyzing incapacity for qualitative intellectual judgment. Or, as an astute critic of deconstruction has suggested: "If deconstruction prevents us from asserting or stating or identifying anything, then surely one ends up, not with 'differance,' but with indifference, where nothing is anything, and everything is everything else?"[53]

Derrida has never hesitated to point out the "positional" or "strategic" character of his theoretical interventions. Thus, he observes, "It seemed strategically useful at a given moment to say, for example, 'a body is text, the table is text, the market—Wall Street, etc.—is text.' Or else, 'nuclear arms are text.' That seemed strategically useful at a given moment." But he goes on to remark that "there is no single strategy. Since a strategy is dictated by places really, and therefore by forces and individuals who are inscribed in these places, what may be strategically opportune here at one moment, is no longer opportune there at another moment."[54] In this way, deconstruction issues its own forthright invitation to self-criticism. It is an initiative that should be seized. This would mean that the future of deconstruction as a discourse of cultural criticism may well depend on a certain *in-fidelity*; an infidelity that testifies to the fact that its advocates have taken up this invitation to self-criticism in earnest.

Notes

Preface

1. See Theodor Adorno, "Cultural Criticism and Society," in *Prisms*, translated by S. Weber (London: Neville Spearman, 1967). A new English edition appeared in 1985 from MIT Press. Adorno's other three volumes of cultural criticism were: *Eingriffe* (1963), *Ohne Leitbild* (1967), and *Stichworte*, which appeared after his death in 1969. The four volumes have been published as an ensemble bearing the title "Kulturkritik und Gesellschaft" in Adorno's *Gesammelte Schriften*, vols. 10(1) and 10(2) (Frankfurt: Suhrkamp, 1977). English translations of all three are scheduled to appear in the European Perspectives series of the Columbia University Press.

2. Thomas Mann, *Betrachtungen eines Unpolitischen* (Frankfurt: Fischer, 1956).

3. Adorno, *Prisms*, p. 19.

4. Hauke Brunkhorst, *Der Intellektuelle im Lande der Mandarine* (Frankfurt: Suhrkamp, 1987), p. 81. On this point, see also the important study by Fritz Stern, *The Failure of Illiberalism* (New York: Knopf, 1972).

5. Walter Benjamin, "The Work of Art in the Age of Mechanical Reproduction," in *Illuminations*, edited by Hannah Arendt, translated by H. Zohn (New York: Schocken, 1969), p. 242.

6. Adorno, *Prisms*, p. 23.

7. Ibid., p. 34.

8. Ibid., p. 23.

9. Benjamin, "The Work of Art in the Age of Mechanical Reproduction," p. 256. Or, as Adorno remarks in a similar vein, "The 'eternal values' of which cultural criticism is so fond reflect the perennial catastrophe"; *Prisms*, p. 25.

10. All of the preceding citations are from Benjamin, "Theses on the Philosophy of History," in *Illuminations*, pp. 254–261.

11. Adorno, *Prisms*, p. 34.

12. Ibid.

13. Ibid., p. 27.

14. For an important discussion of Marcuse's intellectual indebtedness to Heidegger, see Alfred Schmidt, "Existential Ontology and Historical Materialism in the Work of Herbert Marcuse," in *Marcuse: Critical Theory and the Promise of Utopia*, edited by R. Pippen et al. (South Hadley, Mass.: Bergin and Garvey, 1988). For a revealing, systematic comparison of Heidegger and Adorno, see Hermann Mörchen, *Macht und Herrschaft im Denken von Heidegger und Adorno* (Stuttgart: Klett-Cotta, 1980).

15. See the account in Martin Jay, *Marxism and Totality: The Adventures of a Concept from Lukács to Habermas* (Berkeley: University of California Press, 1984); see, above all, chapter 9, "Henri Lefebvre, the Surrealists and the Reception of Hegelian Marxism in France," pp. 276ff.

16. See Luc Ferry and Alain Renaut, *French Philosophy of the Sixties: An Essay on Antihumanism* (Amherst: University of Massachusetts Press, 1990).

17. This is, of course, the title of Ludwig Klages' interminable, yet inordinately influential 1928 work, *Geist als Widersacher der Seele* (The Intellect as Antagonist of the Soul) (Bonn: Bouvier, 1966).

18. Peter Sloterdijk, *Kritik der zynischen Vernunft*, 2 vols. (Frankfurt: Suhrkamp, 1983); English translation: *Critique of Cynical Reason* (Minneapolis: University of Minnesota Press, 1987). For other significant instances of the reception of poststructuralist theory in Germany, see H. Böhme and G. Böhme, *Das Andere der Vernunft* (Frankfurt: Suhrkamp, 1983); and Wolfgang Welsch, *Unsere postmoderne Moderne* (Weinheim: VCH, Acta Humaniora, 1988). For a good illustration of the uses to which Foucault has been put in Germany, see E. Erdmann, R. Forst, and A. Honneth, eds., *Ethos der Moderne: Foucaults Kritik der Auflärung* (Frankfurt: Campus, 1990).

19. See Alexis de Tocqueville, *Democracy in America*, vol. II, translated by P. Bradley (New York: Vintage, 1945), pp. 3ff.

20. In *The Sea-Change: The Migration of Social Thought, 1930–1945* (New York: Harper and Row, 1975), H. Stuart Hughes dates the beginnings of this momentous intellectual shift with the arrival of the European émigrés seeking a refuge from fascism in the 1930s and 1940s. See also J. C. Jackman and C. M. Borden, eds., *The Muses Flee Hitler: Cultural Transfer and Adaptation, 1930–1945* (Washington, D.C.: Smithsonian Institution Press, 1983).

21. Sigmund Freud, *The Standard Edition of the Complete Psychological Works of Sigmund Freud*, translated by James Strachey (London: Hogarth Press, 1953), vol. 2, p. 305.

22. Ibid., vol. 22, p. 80.

23. G. W. F. Hegel, *Hegel's Aesthetics*, translated by T. M. Knox (Oxford: Oxford University Press, 1975), pp. 148–150.

24. See Georg Lukács, "The Nature and Form of the Essay," in *Soul and Form*, translated by A. Bostock (Cambridge, Mass.: MIT Press, 1974); and Theodor Adorno, "The Essay as Form," in *Notes to Literature*, vol. 1, translated by Shierry W. Nicholsen (New York: Columbia University Press, 1991).

25. Letter to Walter Benjamin of March 18, 1936, in R. Taylor, ed. *Aesthetics and Politics* (London: New Left Books, 1977), p. 123.

A Note on Man Ray's *Imaginary Portrait of D. A. F. de Sade*

1. "Henry Miller: Recollections of Man Ray in Hollywood," in Arturo Schwarz, *Man Ray: The Rigour of Imagination* (New York: Rizzoli, 1977), p. 322.

2. Simon Schama, *Citizens* (New York: Simon and Schuster, 1989), p. 391.

3. See Bataille, "La Souveraineté," in *Oeuvres complètes* (Paris: Gallimard, 1970), pp. 245–455.

4. Cited in Schwarz, *Man Ray*, p. 186.

5. In order to understand the complexity of Man Ray's views about Sade, one must also take into account a later painting based on earlier sketches, *Aline et Valcour* (1950), which takes the marquis' political novel of the same name as its point of departure. The novel itself has to do with a fictive African country, Butua, where "sadism" has become a type of state religion: here, freedom consists in the systematic subjugation of women for the sake of the pleasure of men, human sacrifice, and cannibalism. In an interview, Man Ray remarked that he considered *Aline et Valcour* the most important of Sade's novels due to its prescient treatment of the problem of political power. "Sade showed what you could do if you had power," remarked Man Ray. See Pierre Bourgeade, *Bonsoir, Man Ray* (Paris: Pierre Belfond, 1972), p. 78. Man Ray's painting itself, like the *Imaginary Portrait*, is far from untroubling. The image consists of a faceless mannequin reclining beside a woman's severed, blindfolded head, which has been placed in a bell jar and is resting on a book (Sade's novel?). The surrealist fetishization of femal membra disjecta—a Sadean inheritance—is undoubtedly one of the more dubious aspects of their artistic legacy.

Introduction: Thrasymachus' Ghost

1. Agnes Heller, *A Radical Philosophy*, translated by James Wickham (Oxford: Basil Blackwell, 1984), p. 21.

2. Max Weber, "Science as a Vocation," in *From Max Weber: Essays in Sociology*, edited by H. Gerth and C. W. Mills (New York: Oxford University Press, 1946), p. 155.

3. Ibid., p. 143. Or, as Weber observes in the same connection: "Who—aside from certain big children who are indeed found in the natural sciences—still believes that the findings of astronomy, biology, physics, or chemistry could teach us anything about the

meaning of the world? If there is any such 'meaning,' along what road could one come upon its tracks? If these natural sciences lead to anything in this way, they are apt to make the belief that there is such a thing as the 'meaning' of the universe die out at its very roots."

4. Manfred Frank, *Die Grenzen der Verständigung: Ein Geistergespräch zwischen Habermas und Lyotard* (Frankfurt: Suhrkamp, 1988), p. 20.

5. Max Horkheimer and Theodor Adorno, *Dialektik der Aufklärung* (Frankfurt: Fischer, 1969), p. 6; *Dialectic of Enlightenment*, translated by J. Cumming (New York: Herder and Herder, 1972), p. xvi.

6. Theodor Adorno, *Negative Dialektik* (Frankfurt: Suhrkamp, 1973), p. 27; Theodor Adorno, *Negative Dialectics*, translated by E. B. Ashton (New York: Seabury, 1973), p. 15.

7. Edmund Burke, *Reflections on the Revolution in France* (Garden City, N.Y.: Anchor, 1973), p. 70.

8. Marquis de Sade, *Histoire de Juliette*, vol. III (Holland, 1797), pp. 78, 282.

9. Ibid., vol. IV, pp. 4, 7; cited in Horkheimer and Adorno, *Dialectic of Enlightenment*, pp. 98–99.

10. Maurice Blanchot, *Lautréamont et Sade* (Paris: Minuit, 1963), p. 41.

11. Friedrich Nietzsche, *The Genealogy of Morals*, translated by Walter Kaufmann (New York: Vintage, 1967), p. 45.

12. Georges Bataille, *Literature and Evil*, translated by Alistair Hamilton (New York: Urizen, 1973), p. 89.

13. Nietzsche, *Genealogy of Morals*, p. 42; Friedrich Nietzsche, *The Will to Power*, translated by Walter Kaufmann and R. J. Hollingdale (New York: Vintage, 1967), no. 382.

14. Blanchot, *Lautréamont et Sade*, p. 21. Nietzsche's call for the "barbarians of the twentieth century" may be found in *The Will to Power*, no. 868: "A master race can grow up from terrible and violent beginnings only. Problem: where are the barbarians of the twentieth century? Obviously, only after tremendous social crisis will they loom and consolidate themselves. It will be those elements which are capable of the greatest rigor towards themselves and able to vouch for the longest and strongest will." As Karl Löwith correctly observes, "This political program is not to be found on the periphery but at the center of Nietzsche's philosophy." See Löwith, *Nature, History, and Existentialism* (Evanston: Northwestern University Press, 1966), p. 14.

15. Blanchot, *Lautréamont et Sade*, p. 33.

16. Horkheimer and Adorno, *Dialectic of Enlightenment*, p. 100.

17. Jean-François Lyotard, *The Postmodern Condition: A Report on Knowledge*, translated by G. Bennington and B. Massumi (Minneapolis: University of Minnesota Press, 1984), p. 81; emphasis added.

18. Martin Jay, "The Morals of Genealogy: Or is There a Post-Structuralist Ethics?" *The Cambridge Review* 110 (1989):71.

19. Peter Dews, *Logics of Disintegration: Post-structuralist Thought and the Claims of Critical Theory* (London: Verso, 1987), p. 230.

20. Jay, "The Morals of Genealogy," p. 70.

21. See Jacques Derrida, "The Principle of Reason: The University in the Eyes of Its Critics," *Diacritics* XIX (1983):3–20.

22. Jay, "The Morals of Genealogy," p. 74.

23. Derrida, "The Principle of Reason," p. 16. I discuss this aspect of Derrida's work in chapter 9.

24. See Karl-Otto Apel, *Understanding and Explanation*, translated by Georgia Warnke (Cambridge, Mass.: MIT Press, 1984).

25. See Bryan Wilson, ed., *Rationality* (New York: Harper and Row, 1970).

26. J. Hillis Miller, *The Ethics of Reading* (New York: Columbia University Press, 1987), p. 58.

27. For an important discussion of the ambiguous methodological status of the "discursive regime" in Foucault, see Manfred Frank, *What is Neostructuralism?*, translated by Sabine Wilke and Richard Gray (Minneapolis: University of Minnesota Press, 1988), pp. 102ff.

28. Philippe Lacoue-Labarthe, *Heidegger, Art and Politics*, translated by C. Turner (Oxford: Basil Blackwell, 1990), p. 95. For a criticism of this position, see Richard Wolin, *The Politics of Being: The Political Thought of Martin Heidegger* (New York: Columbia University Press, 1990), pp. 156ff.; and Luc Ferry and Alain Renaut, *Heidegger and Modernity*, translated by F. Philip (Chicago: University of Chicago Press, 1990). See also Nancy Fraser, "The French Derrideans: Politicizing Deconstruction or Deconstructing Politics," in *Unruly Practices: Power, Discourse and Gender in Contemporary Social Theory* (Minneapolis: University of Minnesota Press, 1989), pp. 69ff.

29. It is worth pointing out that toward the end of his life Michel Foucault seemed to return to the ideal of aesthetic self-fashioning as an alternative to Christian and modern-legalistic conceptions of the self. See "What is Enlightenment?" and "On the Genealogy of Ethics: An Overview of Work in Progress," in P. Rabinow, ed., *The Foucault Reader* (New York: Pantheon, 1984). It is this late move in the direction of aesthetic self-fashioning that Jay seems to have in mind when he warns about "the aesthetic modernist gesture of forgetting the victim so long as the gesture is beautiful" in the passage cited above.

30. Jean-Luc Nancy, *La Communauté désoeuvrée* (Paris: Christian Bourgois, 1986). Also relevant in this connection is Maurice Blanchot's *La Communauté inavouable* (Paris: Minuit, 1983).

31. Georges Bataille, "The Notion of Expenditure," in *Visions of Excess: Selected Writings, 1927–1939*, edited by Allan Stoekl (Minneapolis: University of Minnesota Press, 1985), pp. 117, 118. But as Bataille recognizes elsewhere (e.g., *The Accursed Share* [Cambridge, Mass.: MIT Press, 1989]), such "primitive" instances of nonproductive consumption do have an end beyond themselves: they serve very much to reinforce and preserve inherited power relations.

32. Benjamin, "The Work of Art in the Age of Mechanical Reproduction," in *Illuminations*, p. 242.

33. Georges Bataille, *Oeuvres complètes*, vol. VII (Paris: Gallimard, 1970), p. 461.

34. Georges Bataille, "The Psychological Structure of Fascism," in *Visions of Excess*, pp. 145, 143.

35. Frank, *What is Neostructuralism?*, p. 184.

36. John Rajchman, *Michel Foucault: The Freedom of Philosophy* (New York: Columbia University Press, 1984), pp. 122–123; emphasis added. See also Rajchman's attempt to expand these insights in "Ethics after Foucault," *Social Text* (Winter 1985):165–183.

37. Reiner Schürmann, "Political Thinking in Heidegger," *Social Research* 45 (1978):191–221.

38. Lyotard, *The Postmodern Condition*, p. 10.

39. Seyla Benhabib, "Epistemologies of Postmodernism," *New German Critique* 33 (1984):113.

40. Jean-François Lyotard, *Just Gaming*, translated by W. Godzich (Minneapolis: University of Minnesota Press, 1985), pp. 14, 17. One could well dispute Lyotard's claim in the remarks cited that, in the case of Aristotle, the prudent individual "judges without criteria." For one thereby attributes a quasi-Nietzschean position to Aristotle (as occurs in the continuation of the passage in question) that could hardly be more foreign to his way of thinking. In fact, Aristotle explicitly confirms what Lyotard denies in the context at hand, namely, that *phronesis* or judgment takes its bearings from the *sensus communis*, from the values of the *polis* or the community. And in this respect (as Alisdair MacIntyre has recognized in *After Virtue*), Aristotelian *phronesis* and Nietzsche's decisionism could not be more opposed.

41. Frank, *What is Neostructuralism?*, p. 82.

42. Lyotard, *The Postmodern Condition*, p. xxiv.

43. See Jürgen Habermas, *The Philosophical Discourse of Modernity*, translated by F. Lawrence (Cambridge, Mass.: MIT Press, 1987), pp. 322–323:

> Inasmuch as communicative agents reciprocally raise validity claims with their speech acts, they are relying on the potential of assailable grounds. Hence, a moment of *unconditionality* is built into *factual* processes of mutual understanding—the validity laid claim to is distinguished from the social currency of a de facto established practice and yet serves it as the foundation of an existing consensus. The validity claimed for propositions and norms transcends spaces and times, *"blots out" space and time*; but the claim is always raised *here and now*, in specific contexts, and is either accepted or rejected with factual consequences for action. Karl-Otto Apel speaks in a suggestive way about the entwinement of the real communication community with an ideal one.

As Axel Honneth shows in "An Aversion Against the Universal: A Commentary on Lyotard's *Postmodern Condition*," *Theory, Culture and Society* 2(3) (1985):154, Lyotard's objections to Habermas' discourse ethic "are largely based on a mistaken interpretation of Habermas' and (Apel's) principle of dialogue free of domination as a procedure for the repressive unification of all particular interests and needs, instead of seeing in it a way of communicatively testing the degree to which such interests and needs can be generalised. The procedure of discourse ethics does not have its final goal in the determination of common needs, as Lyotard supposes, but rather in intersubjective agreement about just those social norms which allow it to realise differing interests and needs within the common relations of social life." I raise a number of criticisms of the idealizing presuppositions of Habermas' discourse ethic in chapter 1.

44. Walter Benjamin, *Reflections*, translated by E. Jephcott (New York: Harcourt Brace, 1978), p. 289.

45. Ibid., p. 300.

46. Ibid.

1 ■ Critical Theory and the Dialectic of Rationalism

1. Theodor Adorno, *Kierkegaard: Construction of the Aesthetic*, translated by Robert Hullot-Kentor (Minneapolis: University of Minnesota Press, 1989).

2. Richard Hamilton, *Who Voted for Hitler?* (Princeton: Princeton University Press, 1982).

3. See Max Horkheimer, "Die gegenwärtige Lage der Sozialphilosophie und die Aufgaben eines Instituts für Sozialforschung," in *Sozialphilosophische Studien* (Frankfurt: Fischer, 1981). An English translation, "The State of Contemporary Social Philosophy and the Tasks of an Institute for Social Research," may be found in S. Bronner and D. Kellner, eds., *Critical Theory and Society* (New York: Routledge, 1989), pp. 25–36.

4. Martin Jay, *The Dialectical Imagination: A History of the Frankfurt School and the Institute for Social Research* (Boston: Little, Brown, 1973), pp. 60–63.

5. Michael Löwy, "Le Marxisme rationaliste de l'école Frankfort," *L'homme et la société*, no. 65–66 (July-December 1982):45–64.

6. Max Horkheimer, "The Latest Attack on Metaphysics," in *Critical Theory*, translated by M. J. O'Connell (New York: Seabury, 1972), p. 132.

7. Karl Marx and Friedrich Engels, "Manifesto of the Communist Party," in *The Marx-Engels Reader*, edited by R. Tucker (New York: Norton, 1978).

8. The classical discussion of these new Leviathan-like social formations in the literature of Critical Theory may be found in Pollock's important essay, "State Capitalism" (1940), reprinted in the A. Arato and E. Gebhardt, eds., *The Essential Frankfurt School Reader* (Oxford: Blackwell, 1978), pp. 71–94.

9. Karl Marx, *Capital*, vol. I (New York: International Publishers, 1967), p. 20.

10. Max Horkheimer, "Traditional and Critical Theory," in *Critical Theory*, p. 213 (reading "vernunftige" as "rational" rather than "reasonable").

11. Herbert Marcuse, "Philosophy and Critical Theory," in *Negations*, translated by J. Shapiro (Boston: Beacon Press, 1968), p. 134.

12. Ibid., p. 135.

13. Jay, *The Dialectical Imagination*, p. 47.

14. See the discussion of these themes in the "Alienated Labor" section of the

"Economic and Philosophic Manuscripts of 1844," in *The Marx-Engels Reader*, pp. 70ff.

15. Paul Ricoeur, *Freud and Philosophy* (New Haven: Yale University Press, 1976).

16. Marcuse, "Philosophy and Critical Theory," pp. 135–136.

17. G. W. F. Hegel, *Reason in History* (Indianapolis: Bobbs-Merrill, 1953), p. 24.

18. Karl Marx, "Contribution to the Critique of Hegel's *Philosophy of Right*: Introduction," in *The Marx-Engels Reader*, p. 60.

19. Marcuse, "Philosophy and Critical Theory," pp. 141–142.

20. On this point, see Heller, A *Radical Philosophy*.

21. Marcuse, "Philosophy and Critical Theory," pp. 150–151.

22. Ibid., p. 153.

23. Ibid., p. 155; translation altered.

24. For a more contemporary discussion of the inherent link between truth and life conduct in Greek philosophy, see Heller, A *Radical Philosophy*, passim.

25. Max Horkheimer, "The Social Function of Philosophy," in *Critical Theory*, p. 257.

26. Just how radical is the Kantian theory of autonomy? For a provocative reading—and one that is by no means unsympathetic—that sees Kant's emphasis on the "primacy of practical reason" as foreshadowing a doctrine of revolutionary will that progresses from Fichte, Marx, and Bolshevism, to post-World War II Third World liberation movements, see Charles Taylor, "Kant's Theory of Freedom," in *Philosophy and the Human Sciences: Philosophical Papers*, vol. 2 (Cambridge: Cambridge University Press, 1985), pp. 318–337.

27. For a recent discussion of this theme, see Russell Jacoby, "The Greening of the University," *Dissent* (Spring 1991):286–293.

28. Horkheimer, "The Social Function of Philosophy," pp. 264, 266–267.

29. Ibid., p. 266.

30. Ibid., p. 268.

31. Max Horkheimer, *The Eclipse of Reason* (New York: Seabury, 1974), pp. 4, 11.

32. See the comprehensive history of this category and its relationship to Western Marxism by Jay, *Marxism and Totality*.

33. See Max Horkheimer, *Die Sehnsucht nach dem ganzen Anderen* (Hamburg: Furche, 1970).

34. Herbert Marcuse, *One-Dimensional Man* (Boston: Beacon Press, 1964), p. 207.

35. Ibid., p. 207.

36. Herbert Marcuse, *Eros and Civilization* (New York: Vintage, 1962), p. 107.

37. Theodor Adorno, "Die Aktualität der Philosophie," in *Gesammelte Schriften* I (Frankfurt: Suhrkamp, 1973), pp. 325–344. English translation in *Telos* 31 (1977):120–133.

38. See Susan Buck-Morss, *The Origin of Negative Dialectics* (New York: Free Press, 1977).

39. See Benjamin, *Illuminations*, p. 254. I have explored the relationship between

the philosophies of history of Benjamin and the authors of *Dialectic of Enlightenment* in my study *Walter Benjamin: An Aesthetic of Redemption* (New York: Columbia University Press, 1982), pp. 266ff.

40. Horkheimer and Adorno, *Dialectic of Enlightenment*, pp. 13–14.

41. Adorno, *Negative Dialectics*, pp. 12–13.

42. Marcuse, *Eros and Civilization*, pp. 110, 109.

43. Jürgen Habermas, "What is Universal Pragmatics?" in *Communication and the Evolution of Society*, translated by T. McCarthy (Boston: Beacon PRess, 1979), pp. 1–68.

44. Jürgen Habermas, *The Theory of Communicative Action*, vol. II, translated by T. McCarthy (Boston: Beacon Press, 1987).

45. See the criticisms of Habermas by Agnes Heller, "Habermas and Marxism," in *Habermas: Critical Debates*, edited by J. Thompson and D. Held (Cambridge, Mass.: MIT Press, 1982), and Charles Taylor, "Language and Society," in *Communicative Action: Essays on Jürgen Habermas's* The Theory of Communicative Action, edited by A. Honneth and H. Joas (Cambridge, Mass.: MIT Press, 1991).

46. The constituents of happiness in postcapitalist society were an important concern during the early years of Critical Theory. In this regard, two essays stand out as important: Marcuse's "On Hedonism," in *Negations*, pp. 159–200; and Horkheimer's "Egoismus und Freiheitsbewegung," in *Kritische Theorie* (Frankfurt: Fischer, 1968), pp. 385–465.

47. Jürgen Habermas, *Philosophical-Political Profiles*, translated by F. Lawrence (Cambridge, Mass.: MIT Press, 1983), p. 158 (translation emended).

2 ■ The Frankfurt School: From Interdisciplinary Materialism to Philosophy of History

1. The story of the Institute's founding has been told by Jay in *The Dialectical Imagination*, pp. 3–41; and more recently by Rolf Wiggershaus, *Die Frankfurter Schule: Geschichte, Theoretische Entwicklung, Politische Bedeutung* (Munich: Hanser, 1986), pp. 19–49 (an English translation of Wiggershaus' important book is forthcoming from MIT Press).

2. See Fritz Ringer, *The Decline of the German Mandarins* (Cambridge, Mass.: Harvard University Press, 1969).

3. At the same time, their Jewishness was always a factor which the Institute members themselves attempted to consistently downplay. See the interview with Leo Lowenthal, "The Utopian Moment is Suspended," in *An Unmastered Past*, edited by Martin Jay (Berkeley: University of California Press, 1987). See also Jay, *The Dialectical Imagination*, p. 32: "What strikes the current observer is the intensity with which many of the Institute's members denied, and in some cases still deny, any meaning at all to their Jewish identities."

4. Cf. Wiggershaus, *Die Frankfurter Schule*, pp. 147–148.

5. Horkheimer, "Die gegenwärtige Lage der Sozialphilosophie," pp. 33–46. For one of the best general discussions of the early research program of the Frankfurt School, see Wolfgang Bonss, *Einblick der Tatsachen: Zur struktur und Veränderung empirischer Sozialforschung* (Frankfurt: Suhrkamp, 1982), especially pp. 154ff.

6. Immanuel Kant, *Critique of Pure Reason*, translated by N. K. Smith (London: Macmillan, 1933), B 75, A 51.

7. For the historical background of this concept and the seminal role it plays in the development of Western Marxism, see Jay, *Marxism and Totality*.

8. It is perhaps worthy of note that in his preface to *Studies on Authority and the Family*, Horkheimer explicitly acknowledges Lynd's landmark 1929 study, *Middletown*, as an influential precursor of the Institute's 1936 undertaking.

9. See Apel, *Understanding and Explanation*.

10. Max Horkheimer, "Notes on Science and the Crisis," in *Critical Theory*, p. 4.

11. Citations from Horkheimer, "Die gegenwärtige Lage der Sozialphilosophie," pp. 39, 40, 41.

12. Cited in *The Marx-Engels Reader*, p. 144.

13. On Horkheimer's early conception of the relationship between philosophy and social theory, see Jürgen Habermas, "Bemerkungen zur Entwicklungsgeschichte des Horkheimerschen Werkes," in *Max Horkheimer heute: Werk und Wirkung*, edited by A. Schmidt and N. Altwicker (Frankfurt: Fischer, 1986).

14. Horkheimer, "Traditional and Critical Theory," p. 231.

15. Max Horkheimer, "Zum Rationalismusstreit in der gegenwärtigen Philosophie," *Zeitschrift für Sozialforschung* 3 (1934):26.

16. This is one of the main theses of Helmut Dubiel's study, *Theory and Politics: Studies in the Development of Critical Theory* (Cambridge, Mass.: MIT Press, 1985). As Dubiel remarks, "We systematically assume that Horkheimer understood his ideas about a theory of 'dialectical presentation,' scattered throughout his early essays, as a methodological reflection on the interdisciplinary research done by his colleagues." However, Dubiel goes on to caution that this description represents an "idealization" that was by no means adhered to strictly in the day-to-day conduct of business at the Institute.

17. Jay, *The Dialectical Imagination*, p. 26.

18. Erich Fromm, "The Method and Function of Analytic Social Psychology," in *The Essential Frankfurt School Reader*, edited by A. Arato and E. Gebhardt (Oxford: Basil Blackwell, 1978), p. 483.

19. For another good example of the application of Fromm's approach, see Theodor Adorno, "Freudian Theory and the Pattern of Fascist Propaganda," in *The Essential Frankfurt School Reader*, pp. 118–137.

20. Erich Fromm, *The Working Class in Weimar Germany: A Psychological and Sociological Study* (Cambridge, Mass.: Harvard University Press, 1984). This study was never published by the Institute, primarily because Horkheimer felt it was not in a

sufficiently finished form. Fromm disagreed, and the dispute over the matter was one of the major reasons behind the break between Fromm and the Institute in the late 1930s. Jay describes the nature of this controversy in *The Dialectical Imagination*, p. 117. There is a very thorough review of Fromm's study (which only first appeared in German in 1980) by Wayne Gabardi (*New German Critique* 41 [1987]:166ff.) that sheds additional light on the Institute's relations with Fromm.

21. Jay, *The Dialectical Imagination*, p. 117.

22. Erich Fromm, "Sozialpsychologischer Teil," in *Studien über Autorität und Familie* (Paris: F. Alcan, 1936), p. 100.

23. For an important critique of the uncritical reliance of the critical theorists on the bourgeois family, and the idea of "rational paternal authority" that is its necessary concomitant, as a type of model, see Jessica Benjamin, "Authority and the Family Revisited; or, A World Without Fathers?" *New German Critique* 13 (1978):35–68.

24. Fromm, "The Method and Function of Analytic Social Psychology," p. 122.

25. For an earlier discussion of this theme in Fromm's work, see "Die sozialpsychologische Bedeutung der Mutterrechttheorie," *Zeitschrift für Sozialforschung* 2 (1934).

26. Jay, *The Dialectical Imagination*, p. 131.

27. See the remarks in ibid., p. 130: "Critical Theory . . . was unremittingly hostile to pure induction as a methodology."

28. Wiggershaus, *Die Frankfurter Schule*, p. 173.

29. Marcuse, *Negations*, p. 19.

30. Vichy France is an apparent exception to this claim. But of course this was a regime whose survival was dependent on the presence of an occupying foreign power.

31. Wiggershaus, *Die Frankfurter Schule*, p. 297.

32. See Max Horkheimer, *Dawn and Decline*, translated by M. Shaw (New York: Seabury, 1978), pp. 119–240.

33. A similar point has been raised by Habermas in "Bemerkungen zur Entwicklungsgeschichte des Horkheimerischen Werkes," p. 174: "That Horkheimer brings theology into play, if only hypothetically, is only logical once the [Frankfurt School] philosophy of history had lost not only its historical basis, but rather, generalized as a totalizing critique of reason, threatened to destroy its own foundations."

3 ■ Mimesis, Utopia, and Reconciliation: A Redemptive Critique of Adorno's *Aesthetic Theory*

1. Leo Lowenthal, "The Utopian Motif is Suspended" (interview conducted with Martin Lüdke), *New German Critique* 38 (Spring-Summer 1986):105–111. It has also appeared in Lowenthal's autobiography, *An Unmastered Past*, edited by Martin Jay (Berkeley: University of California Press, 1987), pp. 237–246.

2. For the best account of this generation and its various programs, see Michael Löwy, *Rédemption et Utopie* (Paris: PUF, 1988).

3. In a private conversation, Lowenthal identified Bloch's *Geist der Utopie* and Lukács' *Theorie des Romans* as the two works that most influenced his own early development.

4. Lowenthal, "The Utopian Motif," p. 111.

5. Translated in English as "Religious Rejections of the World and Their Directions," in *From Max Weber*, pp. 323–359.

6. Ibid., p. 342.

7. It may seem paradoxical to attribute "systematic intentions" to the author of *Negative Dialectics*. However, it should be kept in mind that despite his pronounced aversion to *l'esprit de system, l'esprit systematique* was not a concept entirely alien to his way of thinking: from Rolf Tiedemann's "Nachwort" to *Aesthetic Theory*, we learn that Adorno intended to compose a major treatise on moral philosophy upon completion of the latter work. Had this intention not been cut short by his death in 1969, Adorno's three major works would have corresponded to the subject matter of Kant's three *Critiques*.

8. Horkheimer and Adorno, *Dialectic of Enlightenment*, pp. 14, 9.

9. Adorno, *Negative Dialectics*, p. 321.

10. Ibid., p. 15.

11. Ibid., pp. 12–13.

12. Adorno, *Aesthetic Theory*, pp. 122, 124.

13. Ibid., pp. 122–123.

14. Ibid.

15. Ibid., pp. 190, 192; emphasis added.

16. Horkheimer and Adorno, *Dialectic of Enlightenment*, p. 40.

17. Cf. Walter Benjamin, "The Mimetic Faculty," in *Reflections*, edited by Peter Demetz (New York: Harcourt Brace, 1978), pp. 333–336.

18. Horkheimer and Adorno, *Dialectic of Enlightenment*, p. 30.

19. Adorno, *Aesthetic Theory*, p. 183.

20. Ibid., pp. 183, 184.

21. Ibid., p. 196.

22. Although the true intellectual historical origins of his outlook on philosophy and history go back to two profoundly Benjaminian essays from the early 1930s. See "Die Aktualität der Philosophie" and "Die Idee der Naturgeschichte," both in Theodor Adorno, *Gesammelte Schriften* I (Frankfurt: Suhrkamp, 1974), pp. 325–344, 345–365.

23. On the relation between Adorno and negative theology, see F. Grenz, *Adornos Philosophie in Grundbegriffen* (Frankfurt: Suhrkamp, 1974).

24. Jürgen Habermas, "Questions and Counterquestions," in *Habermas and Modernity*, edited by Richard J. Bernstein (Cambridge: Polity Press, 1985), pp. 200–202.

25. Peter Bürger, "The Decline of the Modern Age," *Telos* 62 (Winter 1984–1985):117–130.

4 ■ Carl Schmitt, Political Existentialism, and the Total State

1. Carl Schmitt, "Der Führer schützt das Recht—zur Reichstagsrede Adolf Hitlers vom 13. Juli, 1934," *Deutsche Juristen-Zeitung* 39 (1934); "Die Verfassung der Freiheit," *Deutsche Juristen-Zeitung* 40 (1935).

2. Carl Schmitt, *Political Theology*, translated by G. Schwab (Cambridge, Mass.: MIT Press, 1985; to be cited henceforth in the text as PT); *The Crisis of Parliamentary Democracy*, translated by E. Kennedy (Cambridge, Mass.: MIT Press, 1985; henceforth cited in the text as CPD); and *Political Romanticism*, translated by Guy Oakes (Cambridge, Mass.: MIT Press, 1986).

3. Carl Schmitt, *The Concept of the Political*, translated by G. Schwab (New Brunswick, N.J.: Rutgers University Press, 1976).

4. Representative critical studies of Schmitt's work in the postwar years include J. Fijalkowski, *Die Wendung zum Führerstaat: Ideologische Komponenten in der politische Philosophie Carl Schmitts* (Köln: Westdeutscher Verlag, 1958); H. Hofmann, *Legitimität gegen Legalität: Der Weg der politischen Philosophie Carl Schmitts* (Neuwied and Berlin: Luchterhand, 1964); C. von Krockow, *Die Entscheidung: Eine Untersuchung über Ernst Jünger, Carl Schmitt, und Martin Heidegger* (Stuttgart: Enke, 1958). For a bibliography of Schmitt's work and secondary literature, see P. Tommissen, "Carl Schmitt Bibliographie," in *Festschrift für Carl Schmitt zum 70. Geburtstag*, edited by H. Barion et al. (Berlin: Duncker und Humblot, 1959); as well as an "Ergänzungliste" also by Tommissen in *Epirrhosis: Festgabe für Carl Schmitt*, 2 vols., edited by H. Barion et al. (Berlin: Duncker und Humblot, 1968). The two last-named volumes generally contain essays that are supportive of Schmitt's ideas. See also *Der Fürst dieser Welt: Carl Schmitt und die Folgen*, vol. 1, edited by J. Taubes (Munich and Zurich: Fink, 1983).

5. Most noteworthy in this respect was a special issue of the journal *Telos* 72 (1987) devoted to Schmitt's work. For other English-language literature on Schmitt, see George Schwab, *The Challenge of the Exception* (Berlin: Duncker und Humblot, 1970); see also Schwab's Introduction to Schmitt, *Political Theology*; Ellen Kennedy, Introduction to Schmitt, *The Crisis of Parliamentary Democracy*; and Joseph Bendersky, *Carl Schmitt: Theorist for the Reich* (Princeton, N.J.: Princeton University Press, 1983). Unlike the discussions of Schwab and Kennedy, Bendersky's study has the merit of confronting Schmitt's deep Nazi involvements, as well as his at times vicious anti-Semitism, head on. However, he reaches the unsatisfactory conclusion that Schmitt, far from being a "convinced Nazi," merely underwent a series of extensive political compromises in the 1930s for the sake of self-preservation. Hence, his Nazism and anti-Semitism were "insincere." Unsurprisingly, both Schwab (*Canadian Journal of Political and Social Theory* 4/2 [Spring-Summer 1980]) and Kennedy (*History of Political Thought* 4/3 [Winter 1983]) have written very positive reviews of Bendersky's work, endorsing his conclusions concerning the insincerity of Schmitt's Nazism. A salutary contrast to this "hall of mirrors" semblance of unanimity is Martin Jay's review of Bendersky in the

Journal of Modern History 53/3 (September 1984). See also Gordon Craig's review of Bendersky, "Decision, Not Discussion," in *Times Literary Supplement*, August 13, 1983.

6. Karl Löwith, "Der okkasionelle Dezionismus von Carl Schmitt," first published in the *Internationale Zeitschrift für Theorie des Rechts* 9 (1935) under the pseudonym Hugo Fiala. It has recently been republished in Löwith, *Heidegger: Denker in dürftiger Zeit* (Stuttgart: Metzler, 1984), pp. 32–71. Philosophical use of this peculiar term, "occasionalism," may be traced back to Malebranche's polemic with Descartes in *De la recherche de la verité* (1674–1675). There, in opposition to the Cartesian view that the body, as influenced by the soul, is responsible for its own movement, Malebranche argues that the true principle of the movement of bodies is to be found in God alone. Bodily movements are thus "occasioned" by a higher, divine, causality.

7. To be sure, from existentialism one can also derive a very different political philosophy—e.g., that of Jean-Paul Sartre (who was at least equally influenced in his early work by the "rationalist" phenomenology of Husserl). At issue is a determinate version of German existentialism in vogue during the interwar years that facilitated the rejection of liberal-democratic political paradigms and a preference instead for ones that were distinctly fascistic.

8. See Ringer, *The Decline of the German Mandarins*; Stern, *The Failure of Illiberalism*; and more recently, Brunkhorst, *Der Intellektuelle im Land der Mandarine*; and J. Herf, *Reactionary Modernism* (New York: Cambridge University Press, 1984). Herf's study, which contains a section on Schmitt, is especially relevant in the present context, since he convincingly details the worldview held in common by thinkers such as Schmitt, Jünger, Spengler, and Heidegger.

9. As a result of this shared emphasis on the concept of decision, Löwith perceives distinct parallels between the existential philosophy of Heidegger and the political existentialism of Schmitt. He observes: "It is no way accidental if in C. Schmitt a political decisionism, which corresponds to the existential philosophy of Heidegger, transposes the Heideggerian 'potentiality-for-Being-a-whole' of an always particular existence to the 'totality' of the authentic state, itself always particular." See Löwith, "The Political Implications of Heidegger's Existentialism," in *The Heidegger Controversy: A Critical Reader*, edited by Richard Wolin (New York: Columbia University Press, 1991), pp. 167–185.

10. "War is an intoxication beyond all intoxication, an unleashing that breaks all bonds. It is a frenzy without caution and limits, comparable only to the forces of nature. In combat the individual is like a raging storm, the tossing sea, the raging thunder. He has melted into everything. He rests at the dark door of death like a bullet that has reached its goal. And the purple waves dash over him. For a long time he has no awareness of transition. It is as if a wave slipped back into the flowing sea." Ernst Jünger, *Kampf als inneres Erlebnis* (Berlin: E. S. Mittler, 1922), p. 57.

11. Oswald Spengler, *Der Untergang des Abendlandes*, vol. 2 (Munich: C. H. Beck, 1923), p. 1007.

12. Carl Schmitt, *Der Begriff des Politischen* (Berlin: Duncker und Humblot, 1963), p. 49; emphasis added (hereafter cited in the text as BP).

13. Carl Schmitt, *Gesetz und Urteil* (Berlin: Beck, 1912), p. 69.

14. Carl Schmitt, *Der Wert des Staates und die Bedeutung des Einzelnen* (Tübingen: Mohr, 1914), pp. 108, 74.

15. See Schwab, *The Challenge of the Exception*, pp. 37–43.

16. Kennedy, Introduction to *The Crisis of Parliamentary Democracy*.

17. The Neumann quotes are from *Behemoth: The Structure and Practice of National Socialism, 1933–44* (New York: Oxford University Press, 1967), pp. 47, 43. Recently, Ellen Kennedy has argued that many of the positions of Neumann himself—as well as the Frankfurt School's critique of liberalism in general—were borrowed without acknowledgment from Schmitt's own critique of "parliamentarianism." See Kennedy, "Carl Schmitt and the Frankfurt School," *Telos* 71 (1987). While it is true that Neumann and Otto Kirchheimer attended Schmitt's lectures in Berlin in the late 1920s, Kennedy makes a travesty of an originally worthwhile insight by attempting to view the Frankfurt School in general as a type of covert "Carl Schmitt Society." In trying to work the positions of Horkheimer, Marcuse, and even Walter Benjamin, into the bargain, this Schmitt-obsession takes on absurd proportions. After the extremely thorough rejoinders by Martin Jay, Alfons Söllner, and Ulrich Preuss in the same issue of *Telos*, there seems to be little left of Kennedy's original claim concerning the Frankfurt School's furtive reliance on Schmittian paradigms.

18. H. Saner, "Grenzsituation," *Historisches Wörterbuch der Philosophie*, vol. 3 (Basel: Schwab, 1974), p. 877.

19. See Michael Löwy, *Georg Lukács: From Romanticism to Bolshevism* (London: New Left Books, 1977).

20. Schmitt concludes the first chapter of *Political Theology* with a laudatory reference to an unnamed nineteenth-century theologian (Kierkegaard) who demonstrated "the vital intensity possible in theological reflection." He cites the following remarks from *Repetition*: "Endless talk about the general becomes boring; there are exceptions. If they cannot be explained, then the general also cannot be explained. The difficulty is usually not noticed because the general is not thought about with passion but with a comfortable superficiality. The exception on the other hand thinks the general with passion."

21. See Schmitt, "Das Zeitalter der Neutralisierungen und Entpolitisierungen," reprinted in the 1932 edition of *Der Begriff des Politischen*.

22. These remarks are especially important, insofar as in the revisionist literature, Schmitt is typically portrayed as a supporter of the "legitimate constitutional authority"; a claim which is used to account both for his reputed support for Weimar democracy, as well as his later support for the Nazis. However, as the preceding citation shows clearly, the question of "legitimacy" is a matter of total indifference to Schmitt. Yet, for Schmitt, this is not a matter of "subjective conviction," but follows of necessity from the inner logic of his political thought, whose emphasis on a "decision created out of nothingness" pointedly excludes all respect for legitimate order.

23. The trenchancy of Schmitt's indictment of bouregois liberalism has, unsurprisingly, won Schmitt his admirers on the political left as well as the right. To be sure, the argument that the true ends of democracy have been vitiated by the particularism of economic interests will have a distinctly familiar ring to adherents of the Marxist tradition. Schmitt's critique is indisputably valid in many respects. It is the motives behind his criticism and the alternative model of politics he has in mind that remain highly dubious. For examples of supportive considerations of Schmitt by left-wing intellectuals, see Ulrich Preuss, "Zum Begriff des Politischen bei Carl Schmitt," in *Politische Verantwortung und Bürgerloyalität* (Frankfurt: Fischer, 1984); and Paul Hirst, "Carl Schmitt's Decisionism," *Telos* 72 (1987):15–26.

Schmitt's justification of "plebiscitarian dictatorship" suggests parallels with Max Weber's advocacy of a "plebiscitarian leader-democracy," which alone would surmount the irresistible tendency toward bureaucratic stagnation that afflicts the modern industrial world. The best discussion of this concept in Weber may be found in Wolfgang Mommsen, *The Age of Bureaucracy: Perspectives on the Sociology of Max Weber* (New York: Harper and Row, 1974), pp. 72–94.

24. See, for example, Schmitt's discussion of Jacobinism in *The Crisis of Parliamentary Democracy*, p. 27. Thus Schmitt has no difficulties in accepting the most extreme implications of Jacobin "substitutionism." Or, as he remarks in ibid., one "can never reach an absolute, direct identity that is actually present at every moment. A distance always remains between real equality and the results of identification. The will of the people is of course always identical with the will of the people, whether a decision comes from the yes or no of millions of voting papers, or from a single individual who has the will of the people even without a ballot, or from the people acclaiming in some way." Hence, according to Schmitt's logic, once one accepts the precept that there is an inevitable hiatus between the popular will and its political embodiment or expression, once it is realized that one can never have an "absolute identity" between these two components, "dictatorship" becomes as authentic a realization of democracy as any other.

25. See Schmitt's remarks in *Der Begriff des Politischen*, p. 35: "A world in which the possibility of struggle [*Kampf*] has disappeared without a trace would be a world without the distinction between friend and enemy and consequently a world without politics."

26. Schmitt, "Reich, Staat, Bund" (1933), reprinted in *Positionen und Begriffe* (Hamburg: Hanseatische Verlaganstaltung, 1940), p. 198.

27. Schmitt, "Das Zeitalter," p. 93.

28. Ibid.

29. Schmitt, "Die Wendung zum totalen Staat," *Europaische Revue* 7 (April 1941):241–243.

30. Schmitt, "Weiterentwicklung des totalen Staat in Deutschlands," in *Verfassungsrechtliche Aufsätze* (Berlin: Duncker und Humblot, 1973).

31. Stephen Holmes has addressed this issue as follows: "The notion that [Schmitt] was equally hostile to the right and the left isn't altogether credible. Prior to the seizure

of power, he considered the Nazis 'immature'—able to make Germany ungovernable, but unable to govern it themselves. He disliked them mainly because he feared they would create disorder that communists, in turn, might exploit. He also opposed attempts to revise the Weimar constitution for this reason, not because he was loyal to it or thought it good (all his constitutional writings are devoted to displaying its fundamental incoherence), but because he feared that upending basic institutions in a crisis could create opportunities for a communist coup." *New Republic*, August 22, 1988:33.

32. See Bendersky, "The Expendable *Kronjurist*: Carl Schmitt and National Socialism, 1933–36," *Journal of Contemporary History* 14 (1979):312.

33. Schmitt, *Staat, Bewegung, Volk* (Hamburg: Hanseatische Verlaganstaltung, 1933), p. 7.

34. Ibid., p. 11.

35. See Neumann, *Behemoth*, pp. 65–66.

36. Schmitt, "Die deutsche Rechtwissenschaft im Kampf gegen den judischen Geist," *Deutsche Juristen-Zeitung* 20 (1936):1197.

37. Schmitt, *Der Leviathan in der Staatslehre des Thomas Hobbes* (Hamburg: Hanseatische Verlagsanstalt, 1938), p. 108.

38. Ibid., p. 109.

39. Both Schwab and Bendersky attempt to justify Schmitt's loyalty to the Nazis using the following argument: "By opting for National Socialism Schmitt merely transferred his allegiance to the newly constituted legal authority, and this was not incompatible with his belief in the relation between protection and obedience." The citation is from Schwab, *The Challenge of the Exception*, p. 106. Bendersky cites Schwab's reasoning with approval in "The Expendable *Kronjurist*," p. 312.

40. Schmitt, *Staat, Bewegung, Volk*, p. 45.

41. Ibid., p. 46.

42. Paul Piccone and G. L. Ulmen, "Introduction to Carl Schmitt," *Telos* 72 (1987):14.

43. Schmitt, *Ex Captivitate Salus: Erfahrungen der Zeit, 1945–47* (Köln: Greven, 1950).

44. The letter of Heidegger to Schmitt of August 22, 1933 is reprinted in *Telos* 72 (1987):132.

45. See Richard Wolin, "French Heidegger Wars," in Wolin, ed., *The Heidegger Controversy*, pp. 282–310.

5 ■ Merleau-Ponty and the Birth of Weberian Marxism

1. "An Unpublished Text by Maurice Merleau-Ponty: A Prospectus of His Work," in J. Edie, ed., *The Primacy of Perception* (Evanston: Northwestern University Press, 1964), pp. 6, 3.

2. Claude Lefort, "Editor's Preface," in *The Prose of the World*, translated by J. O'Neill (Evanston: Northwestern University Press, 1973), p. xix.

3. Jay, *Marxism and Totality*, p. 361. A few pages later in the same work, Jay presents the issues at stake in a more even-handed way: "The harsh critic of all anti-empirical, essentialist systems, the bitter opponent of all idealist 'high-altitude thinking,' the advocate of irreducible historical ambiguities had allowed himself to turn the proletariat of his imagination into the transcendental ground of his historical optimism." Ibid., p. 371.

4. James Miller, *History and Human Existence: From Marx to Merleau-Ponty* (Berkeley: University of California Press, 1979), p. 206.

5. See Edmund Husserl, *The Crisis of the European Sciences and Transcendental Phenomenology* (Evanston: Northwestern University Press, 1970).

6. See Husserl, "Philosophy as Rigorous Science," in *Phenomenology and the Crisis of Philosophy*, edited by Quentin Lauer (New York: Harper, 1965).

7. For an intelligent reading of Merleau-Ponty's work in terms of this theme, see Alphonse de Waehlens, *Une philosophie de l'ambiguité: L'Existentialisme de Maurice Merleau-Ponty* (Louvain: Publications Universitaires de Louvain, 1968); also see F. Alquié, "Une philosophie de l'ambiguité," *Fontaine* 59 (1947):47–70.

8. See Husserl, *Ideas*, translated by R. B. Gibson (London: Allen and Unwin, 1931), pp. 54–58.

9. See Hans-Georg Gadamer, "The Phenomenological Movement," in *Philosophical Hermeneutics*, translated by D. E. Linge (Berkeley: University of California Press, 1976), pp. 130–181.

10. Merleau-Ponty, *The Phenomenology of Perception*, translated by C. Smith (New York: Routledge, 1962), p. vii.

11. Ibid., p. 154; emphasis added.

12. For a good discussion of his status within the phenomenological movement, see Herbert Speigelberg, *The Phenomenological Movement* (The Hague: M. Nijhoff, 1976), vol. 2, pp. 516–562.

13. Merleau-Ponty, *The Phenomenology of Perception*, p. 150.

14. Ibid., p. 154.

15. Merleau-Ponty, *Humanism and Terror* (Boston: Beacon Press, 1969), p. xv.

16. Ibid., p. xiii.

17. See Ernst Bloch, *Geist der Utopie* (Frankfurt: Suhrkamp, 1964), p. 302.

18. Merleau-Ponty, "A Note on Machiavelli," in *Signs*, translated by R. McCleary (Evanston: Northwestern University Press, 1964), p. 214.

19. Ibid., p. 223.

20. Merleau-Ponty, *Humanism and Terror*, p. xvii.

21. Ibid., p. xviii.

22. Ibid., p. xxi.

23. Ibid., p. xix.

24. Ibid., p. xxi.

25. Arthur Koestler, *The Yogi and the Commissar* (New York: Macmillan, 1946), pp. 3–14.

26. Cited in Merleau-Ponty, *Humanism and Terror*, pp. 163–164.

27. Sartre recounts Merleau-Ponty's political development in *Situations* (New York: Braziller, 1965), pp. 156–226.

28. Merleau-Ponty, *Adventures of the Dialectic*, translated by J. Bien (Evanston: Northwestern University Press, 1973), p. 4. All subsequent page references to this work will appear in the text in parentheses.

29. For a very effective defense of Sartre against the charge of "ultra-Bolshevism," see Simone de Beauvoir, "Merleau-Ponty et le pseudo-sartrisme," *Les Temps Modernes* 114–115 (June-July 1955).

30. For a fuller account of these two figures and their roles within the Western Marxist legacy, see Jay, *Marxism and Totality*, chapters 2 and 12.

31. *Karl Marx: Early Writings*, edited by T. Bottomore (New York: McGraw-Hill, 1964), p. 155.

32. For an excellent discussion of this distinction, see Agnes Heller, *A Theory of History* (London: Routledge, 1982).

33. An impressive critique of the historicist mentality of Ranke, Dilthey, and Droysen can be found in Hans-Georg Gadamer, *Truth and Method* (New York: Continuum, 1975), pp. 153–213.

34. Max Weber, *Gesammelte Aufsätze zur Wissenschaftslehre* (Tübingen: Mohr, 1922), p. 154. Cited in Merleau-Ponty, *Adventures of the Dialectic*, p. 26.

35. G. W. F. Hegel, *Science of Logic* (London: Allen and Unwin, 1929), p. 73.

6 ■ Sartre, Heidegger, and the Intelligibility of History

1. For a more detailed treatment of these issues, see my recent study, *The Politics of Being: The Political Thought of Martin Heidegger* (New York: Columbia University Press, 1990).

2. Otto Pöggeler, *Der Denkweg Martin Heideggers*, 2d ed. (Pfullingen: Neske, 1983), p. 335.

3. Heidegger, *Hölderlins Hymne "Der Ister." Gesamtausgabe* 53 (Frankfurt: Klosterman, 1984), p. 106.

4. Cited in Hugo Ott, *Martin Heidegger: Unterwegs zu seiner Biographie* (Frankfurt: Campus, 1988), pp. 316–317.

5. Sartre, *L'Etre et le Néant* (Paris: Gallimard, 1950), p. 134. "La réalité humaine est souffrante dans son être, parce qu'elle surgit à l'être comme perpétuellement hantée par une totalité qu'elle est sans pouvoir l'être, puisque justement elle ne pourrait atteindre l'en-soi sans se perdre comme pour-soi. Ell est donc par nature conscience malheureuse, sans dépassement possible de l'état de malheur."

6. Ibid., pp. 707–708.

7. Ibid., p. 321.

8. Ibid., pp. 721–722.

9. It is precisely on this basis that one can account for Sartre's well-known, paradoxical

claim, "Jamais nous n'avons été plus libres que sous l'occupation allemande." But as Sartre goes on to explain: "Puisque le venin nazi se glissait jusque dans notre pensée, chaque pensée juste était une conquête, puisqu'une police toute-puissante cherchait à nous contraindre au silence, chaque parole devenait précieuse comme une déclaration de principe; puisque nous étions traqués, chacun de nos gestes avait le poids d'un engagement. Les circonstances souvent atroces de notre combat nous mettaient enfin à même de vivre, sans fard, sans voile, cette situation dechirée et insoutenable qu'on appelle la condition humaine." See *Sartre: Un film réalisé par Alexandre Astruc et Michel Contat* (Paris: Gallimard, 1977), pp. 71–72.

10. Jean-Paul Sartre, "The Itinerary of a Thought," in *Between Marxism and Existentialism* (New York: William Morrow, 1974), pp. 33–34.

11. Jean-Paul Sartre, *The Words* (New York: Braziller, 1964), pp. 251–252.

12. Jean-Paul Sartre, *On a raison de se révolter* (with P. Gavi and P. Victor) (Paris: Gallimard, 1974), p. 24.

13. Francis Jeanson, *Le problème morale et la pensée de Sartre* (Paris: Seuil, 1965), p. 354.

14. Jean-Paul Sartre, *Critique de la raison dialectique* (Paris: Gallimard, 1960), p. 29.

15. Simone de Beauvoir, *The Prime of Life*, translated by Peter Green (Cleveland: World Publishers, 1962), p. 282. According to the recent testimony of Hans-Georg Gadamer, Sartre's interest in Heidegger was not reciprocated: Heidegger cut open only forty pages of *L'Etre et le Néant* before giving the book away to Gadamer. See Gadamer, "Das Sein und das Nichts," in *Sartre: Ein Kongress*, edited by Traugott König (Hamburg: Rowohlt, 1988), p. 37.

16. Jean-Paul Sartre, *Les Carnets de la drôle de guerre* (Paris: Gallimard, 1983), pp. 224, 227.

17. Sartre, *L'Etre et le Néant*, p. 587.

18. Ibid., p. 635.

19. "Heidegger's Politics: An Interview with Herbert Marcuse," in *Marcuse: Critical Theory and the Promise of Utopia*, edited by Robert Pippin et al. (South Hadley, Mass.: Bergin and Garvey, 1988), pp. 96–97. For another essay that makes a point very similar to the one by Marcuse just cited, see Guenther Stern (Anders), "The Pseudo-Concreteness of Heidegger's Philosophy," *Philosophy and Phenomenological Research* 9 (1948):337–370. For one of the best articles on the early Marcuse's indebtedness to Heidegger, see Alfred Schmidt, "Historisme, histoire et historicité dans les premiers écrits de Herbert Marcuse," *Archives de Philosophie* 52/3 (Juillet-Septembre 1989):369–383.

20. Sartre, *Cahiers pour une morale* (Paris: Gallimard, 1983), pp. 15, 14.

21. Ibid., p. 14.

22. Sartre, "The Itinerary of a Thought," p. 35.

23. Jean-Paul Sartre, *L'Existentialisme est un humanisme* (Paris: Nagel, 1966), p. 22.

24. Marx, *The Eighteenth Brumaire of Louis Bonaparte* (Moscow: Progress, 1972), p. 10. Sartre cites this remark by Marx in *Critique de la raison dialectique* (Paris: Gallimard, 1960), p. 131.

25. Sartre, *L'Existentialisme est un humanisme*, pp. 24, 27.

26. Sartre, "Matérialisme et révolution," *Situations* III (Paris: Gallimard, 1949), p. 201.

27. Sartre, *Cahiers pour une morale*, p. 16.

28. Sartre, *Qu'est-ce que la littérature?* (Paris: Gallimard, 1948), p. 73.

29. Ibid., p. 79.

30. Ibid., pp. 55, 78, 79.

31. Sartre, *L'Existentialisme est un humanisme*, p. 92.

32. Heidegger, "Überwindung der Metaphysik," *Vorträge und Aufsätze* (Pfullingen: Neske, 1954), pp. 67–69.

33. Sartre, *Cahiers pour une morale*, p. 13.

34. Hans Blumenberg, *Legitimacy of the Modern Age* (Cambridge, Mass.: MIT Press, 1983), p. 192.

35. Martin Heidegger, *Holzwege* (Frankfurt: Klostermann, 1950), p. 263.

36. Jürgen Habermas, *Der philosophische Diskurs der Moderne* (Frankfurt: Suhrkamp, 1985), p. 140.

37. This is a position embraced by Jacques Derrida in "Heidegger, l'enfer des philosophes," *Le Nouvel Observateur* (6–12 November 1987):170–174.

38. See Lacoue-Labarthe, *La fiction du politique* (Strasbourg: Presses des Universités de Strasbourg, 1987). See also Derrida's *De l'esprit: Heidegger et la question* (Paris: Editions Galilée, 1987). For a more detailed discussion of the texts by Lacoue-Labarthe and Derrida, see Wolin, *The Politics of Being*, pp. 155–160. See also Richard Wolin, "French Heidegger Wars," in Richard Wolin, ed., *The Heidegger Controversy: A Critical Reader* (New York: Columbia University Press, 1991), pp. 282–310.

39. Heidegger, in his various apologiae, always claimed that his intention as rector had been to preserve the autonomy of the university against external political encroachments (see *Das Rektorat 1933/34: Tatsachen und Gedanken* [Frankfurt: Klostermann, 1983]). We now know the opposite to be the case: under Heidegger's supervision, Freiburg University was delivered over wholesale to the Nazi *Führerprinzip* (with Heidegger himself apparently helping to draft the *Gleichschaltung* legislation). See Ott, *Martin Heidegger*, pp. 187ff.

40. See the commentaries by Maurice Blanchot, Emmanuel Levinas, and Philippe Lacoue-Labarthe in the *Nouvel Observateur* dossier of 22–28 Janvier 1988, pp. 41ff.

41. "Agriculture is today a motorized food industry, in essence the same as the manufacture of corpses in gas chambers and extermination camps, the same as the blockade and starvation of countries, the same as the manufacture of atomic bombs." Cited by Wolfgang Schirmacher, *Technik und Gelassenheit* (Freiburg and Munich: Alber, 1983), p. 25.

42. It must be pointed out that Derrida has formulated an important critique of the

later Heidegger's longing for "origins" in "Les fins de l'homme," *Marges de la philosophie* (Paris: Editions de Minuit, 1972).

43. Heidegger, *Das Rektorat 1933/34*, p. 25.

44. Heidegger, *Was heisst Denken?* (Tübingen: Niemayer, 1954), p. 65.

45. This is also the sense in which Sartre interprets Heidegger's important lecture of 1930, "Über das Wesen der Wahrheit," in the recently published *Vérité et existence* (Paris: Gallimard, 1989).

46. Martin Heidegger, "Brief über den Humanismus,"in *Wegmarken* (Frankfurt: Klostermann, 1967), p. 210.

47. Ibid., p. 222.

48. Ibid., p. 210.

49. Heidegger, *Einführung in die Metaphysik* (Frankfurt: Klostermann, 1983).

50. Heidegger, "Only a God Can Save Us," in Richard Wolin, ed., *The Heidegger Controversy: A Critical Reader* (New York: Columbia University Press, 1991), p. 111.

51. For example, see Helmuth Plessner, *Die verspätete Nation* (Frankfurt: Suhrkamp, 1974) and Ralf Dahrendorf, *Society and Democracy in Germany* (New York: Norton, 1979).

52. André Gorz, "Sartre and Marx," *New Left Review* 37 (May-June 1966).

53. Sartre, *Critique de la raison dialectique*, p. 248.

7 ■ Recontextualizing Neopragmatism: The Political Implications of Richard Rorty's Antifoundationalism

1. Daniel Bell, *The End of Ideology* (New York: Free Press, 1962). That some fourteen years later Bell wrote an equally interesting work entitled *The Cultural Contradictions of Capitalism* (New York: Harper, 1976) might indicate that the "end of ideology" was not as final as he initially believed.

2. Richard Rorty, "The Priority of Democracy to Philosophy," in *Reading Rorty*, edited by A. Malachowski (Oxford: Blackwell, 1990), p. 286.

3. The issue at stake here, the historical and political preconditions of a specific mode of thought, is a complex one, which I in no way wish to simplify. Rorty himself has been alarmed by the amount of criticism he has received for the purportedly neoconservative implications of his philosophical doctrines (cf. his essay "Thugs and Theorists," *Political Theory* 15[4] [November 1987]:575*n*3). To his credit, he has retained his sense of humor throughout these assaults. Claiming that he has received an equal amount of "flak" from the right for his abandonment of "universal and objective values," he observes, "Such flak had helped convince me I was on the right track" (ibid., p. 574).

4. In a subsequent essay, "Solidarity or Objectivity?" (in *Post-Analytic Philosophy*, edited by Cornel West and John Rajchman [New York: Columbia University Press, 1985], pp. 3–19), Rorty goes to some lengths—which are not entirely convincing—to show that he is not a relativist—i.e., someone who believes that all values are of equal

merit—but an "ethnocentric": he considers the values of his *own* culture to be the best, and is aware that there is no way to turn this standpoint into a universally valid maxim. But all Rorty offers us here (in the context of a debate with Hilary Putnam) is sleight of hand: if one generalizes his belief in ethnocentrism (the claim that every culture bases its conception of what is best in terms of its own parochial value scheme), one ends up with nothing less than full-blown cultural relativism (for example, both Hitler and the Ayatollah Khomeini were avowed ethnocentrics, which places Rorty in bad company).

5. One of the major deficiencies of his book is that Rorty fails to address promising new efforts to formulate a nonfoundationalist universalism by philosophers such as Jürgen Habermas, Karl-Otto Apel, and Hilary Putnam. In his more recent work, Rorty has tried somewhat to remedy this oversight. See, for example, his review of Habermas' *The Philosophical Discourse of Modernity* ("Posties") in the *London Review of Books*, 3 September 1987. See also the comparison of Habermas and Foucault (in which Rorty expresses his partisanship for Habermas' liberal politics and Foucault's social constructivist epistemology) in *Contingency, Irony, and Solidarity* (Cambridge: Cambridge University Press, 1989), pp. 61ff.

6. Rorty, *Philosophy and the Mirror of Nature* (Princeton, N.J.: Princeton University Press, 1979), p. 328.

7. Jacques Derrida, *Of Grammatology*, translated by G. Spivak (Baltimore: Johns Hopkins University Press, 1976), p. 158.

8. On this point, see Charles Taylor's essay, "Rorty in the Epistemological Tradition," in *Reading Rorty*, p. 260. Regarding Rorty's claim concerning the impermeability of cultural contexts or worldviews, Taylor remarks: "I don't think this is something you can know about in advance of trying. How could you know in general that this kind of question can't be adjudicated by reasoned argument with a view to truth? Well you could know this if you had a lot of confidence in some general theory of what knowing was."

9. Thomas McCarthy, "Philosophy and Social Practice: Avoiding the Ethnocentric Predicament," in *Zwischenbetrachtungen: Im Prozess der Aufklärung*, edited by Axel Honneth et al. (Frankfurt: Suhrkamp, 1989), p. 195.

10. Rorty, "Pragmatism and Philosophy," in *The Consequences of Pragmatism* (Minneapolis: University of Minnesota Press, 1982), p. xlii.

In "Truth and Freedom: A Reply to Thomas McCarthy" (*Critical Inquiry* 16 [Spring 1990]:636), Rorty observes:

> Like Habermas and Karl-Otto Apel, McCarthy sees my refusal to take on the job of answering Hitler as a sign of irresponsible "decisionism" or "relativism." But I have always (well, not always, but for the last twenty years or so) been puzzled about what was supposed to count as a knockdown answer to Hitler. . . . Would it answer him to say that his views are incompatible with the construction of a society in which communication is undistorted, and that his refusal of a voice to his opponents contradicts the presupposition of his own communicative acts?

> What if Hitler rejoins that to interpret truth as a product of free and open encounters rather than what emerges from the genius of a destined leader begs the question against him? (What if, in other words, he goes Heideggerian on us?) Richard Hare's view that there is no way to "refute" a sophisticated, consistent, passionate psychopath—for example, a Nazi who would favor his own elimination if he himself turned out to be Jewish—seems to me right, but to show more about the idea of "refutation" than about Nazism.

Here, it seems, that Rorty entirely misses the meaning of "refutation," which is not only an empirical question (i.e., a matter of persuading an interlocutor of the correctness of one's standpoint), but also *ideal*: that is, we can certainly provide good reasons—both moral and historical—as to why democracy, rather than the whims of a malevolent genius, is preferable as a basis for social organization and political rule. In this sense, the parochial self-justifications of the authoritarian ruler or the passionate psychopath are certainly open to refutations that are cogent and convincing, even were they not empirically accepted by the parties one is seeking to convince. Moreover, according to Rorty's self-avowed cultural parochialism, there would be no fair or just basis for bringing war criminals to trial at Nuremburg. Inevitably, such trials are merely a variant of "victor's justice"—which is precisely what many German conservatives and neo-Nazis have argued all along.

11. Rorty, *Philosophy and the Mirror of Nature*, p. 373; emphasis added.

12. See Charles Taylor, "What is Human Agency?" in *Human Agency and Language: Philosophical Papers* I (Cambridge: Cambridge University Press, 1985). In retrospect, this essay seems the germ cell of Taylor's challenging recent work, *Sources of the Self* (Cambridge, Mass.: Harvard University Press, 1989).

13. Fredric Jameson, "Postmodernism or the Cultural Logic of Late Capitalism," *New Left Review* 146 (1984):53–92. In this essay, Jameson felicitously conveys the central distinction at issue—that between modernism and postmodernism—by way of contrasting Van Gogh's *Peasant Shoes* with *Diamond Dust Shoes* of Andy Warhol.

14. See Richard Bernstein, "Rorty's Liberal Utopia," *Social Research* 57(1) (Spring 1990):56–58: "In the final analysis, Rorty has little more to say than that we will or will not find a vocabulary attractive. Whatever our response, it is itself a matter of historical contingencies. The 'logic' of Rorty's strategy comes down to making the adoption of a vocabulary *a matter of taste about which there can be no rational debate*. . . . For it is Rorty who says that anything can be made to look good and bad by redescription. Any vocabulary can be made to look attractive if one is clever and imaginative enough" (emphasis added).

15. Rorty, *Philosophy and the Mirror of Nature*, p. 333.

16. Rorty, "Solidarity or Objectivity," p. 10.

17. Rorty, *Philosophy and the Mirror of Nature*, pp. 378, 360.

18. Ibid., p. 389.

19. Rorty, "Pragmatism and Philosophy," p. xl.

20. Habermas, "Philosophy as Stand-In and Interpreter," in *After Philosophy: End or Transformation*, edited by K. Baynes et al. (Cambridge, Mass.: MIT Press, 1987); and Richard Bernstein, "Philosophy in the Conversation of Mankind," in *Philosophical Profiles* (Philadelphia: University of Pennsylvania Press, 1986).

21. On this point, Richard Bernstein (ibid., pp. 53–54) observes: "Sometimes it seems as if Rorty himself is guilty of a version of the 'Myth of the Given'—as if social practices are the sort of thing that are *given*, and that all we need to do is to look and see what they are. But surely this is an illusion. To tell us, as Rorty does over and over again, that 'to say the True and Right are matters of social practice' or that 'justification is a matter of social practice' or that 'objectivity should be seen as conformity to norms of justification we find about us' will not do. We want to know how we are to understand 'social practices,' how they are generated, sustained, and pass away. But even more important we want to know how they are to be *criticized*."

22. See Rorty, *Contingency, Irony, and Solidarity*, especially chapter 3 ("The Contingency of a Liberal Community"). See also the excellent critique by Nancy Fraser, "Solidarity or Singularity: Richard Rorty between Romanticism and Technocracy," in *Unruly Practices* (Minneapolis: University of Minnesota Press, 1989).

23. Bernstein, "Philosophy in the Conversation of Mankind," p. 49.

24. Hegel, *The Phenomenology of Spirit*, translated by A. V. Miller (Oxford: Oxford University Press, 1977), p. 47 (translated slightly altered).

25. See, for example, the following essays: Cornel West, "Afterword: The Politics of American Neo-Pragmatism," in *Post-Analytic Philosophy*, pp. 260–275; Frank Lentricchia, "Rorty's Cultural Conversation," *Raritan* 3 (1983):136–141; William Connolly, "Mirror of America," *Raritan* 3 (1983):124–135; Rebecca Comay, "Interrupting the Conversation: Notes on Rorty," *Telos* 69 (Fall 1986); see also the critique by Richard Bernstein, "One Step Forward, Two Steps Backward," *Political Theory* 15(4) (1987):538–563.

26. Cf. Rorty, "The Priority of Democracy to Philosophy"; "Postmodern Bourgeois Liberalism," *Journal of Philosophy* (1983):583–589; as well as "Thugs and Theorists."

27. Rorty, "The Priority of Democracy to Philosophy," p. 281.

28. See Alasdair MacIntyre, *After Virtue* (South Bend, Ind.: University of Notre Dame Press, 1981); Michael Sandel, *Liberalism and the Limits of Justice* (Cambridge: Cambridge University Press, 1982); for works by Charles Taylor, see *n*. 12 above.

29. On this point, see Bernstein, "Rorty's Liberal Utopia," p. 48: "If the objector persists and maintains that all Rorty is doing is affirming his own idiosyncratic ethnocentric prejudices, Rorty does not deny this. His response is that, of course, he is being ethnocentric, but some forms of ethnocentrism are better than others, namely, the ethnocentrism of 'we' liberal ironists 'who have been brought up to distrust ethnocentrism.'"

30. Rorty, "The Priority of Democracy to Philosophy," p. 288.

31. Ibid., p. 290

32. Bernstein, "One Step Forward," pp. 538–563.

33. Bernstein, "Rorty's Liberal Utopia," p. 67.

34. Rorty, *The Consequences of Pragmatism*, p. 207.

35. Ibid., pp. 210, 207.

36. Rorty, "Postmodern Bourgeois Liberalism," p. 585.

37. The following discussion of Dewey is based on *The Public and Its Problems*, in *The Later Works*, vol. 2, edited by J. A. Boydston (Carbondale: Southern Illinois University Press, 1981), pp. 307ff.

38. Weber, *The Protestant Ethic and the Spirit of Capitalism* (New York: Scribner, 1958), p. 182.

39. Horkheimer, *The Eclipse of Reason* (New York: Seabury, 1974), p. 51.

40. Rorty, *Contingency, Irony, and Solidarity*, p. 63.

41. Ibid.

42. Richard Rorty, "From Logic To Language to Play: A Plenary Address to the InterAmerican Congress," *Proceedings and Addresses of the American Philosophical Association* 59 (1986):752.

8 ■ Michel Foucault and the Search for the Other of Reason

1. Michel Foucault, "Truth and Power," in *The Foucault Reader*, edited by Paul Rabinow (New York: Pantheon, 1984), p. 72.

2. Ibid., p. 74.

3. Ibid., p. 63.

4. Ibid., pp. 66–67.

5. For an excellent discussion of Foucault and the Frankfurt School which came to my attention rather late in the writing of the present chapter, see Thomas McCarthy, "The Critique of Impure Reason: Foucault and the Frankfurt School," *Political Theory* 18(3) (1990):437–469.

6. Foucault, "What is Enlightenment?," in *The Foucault Reader*, p. 38.

7. Immanuel Kant, "An Answer to the Question: What is Enlightenment?," in *Kant's Political Writings*, edited by Hans Reiss (Cambridge: Cambridge University Press, 1970), p. 54.

8. Foucault, "The Art of Telling the Truth," in *Foucault: Politics, Philosophy, Culture*, edited by L. Kritzman (New York and London: Routledge, 1988), p. 88.

9. Ibid., p. 95. The essay in question appeared in the May 1984 issue of *Magazine littéraire*.

10. Jürgen Habermas, "Taking Aim at the Heart of the Present," in *Foucault: A Critical Reader*, edited by David C. Hoy (Berkeley: University of California Press, 1986), p. 108.

11. Michel Foucault, *Madness and Civilization* (New York: Random House, 1965), p. 278; emphasis added.

12. In "The Discourse of Language" (1970; reprinted in *The Archaeology of Knowledge* [New York: Pantheon, 1972]), Foucault describes genealogy as dealing with "the series of effective formation of discourse: it attempts to grasp it in its power of affirmation

. . . the power of constituting domains of objects, in relation to which one can affirm or deny true or false propositions." He continues: "Let us call these domains of objects positivist and, to play on words yet again, let us say that, if the critical style is one of studied casualness, then the genealogical mood is one of *felicitous positivism*" (p. 234).

13. Michel Foucault, *Discipline and Punish*, translated by A. Sheridan (New York: Pantheon, 1977), p. 31.

14. Foucault, "Truth and Power," p. 57; emphasis added.

15. Foucault, *Madness and Civilization*, p. 269. See also the discussion of "surveillance and judgment," pp. 251ff., which also foreshadows important themes from *Discipline and Punish*.

16. Foucault, *Madness and Civilization*, p. 278.

17. Ibid., p. 281.

18. Ibid.

19. Ibid., p. 283. For more on the relation between Sade and Nietzsche as key contributors to the ethics and ethos of modernity, see the classical account by Max Horkheimer and Theodor Adorno ("Juliette or Enlightenment and Morality") in *Dialectic of Enlightenment*.

20. Ibid., p. 285.

21. Sade, *Histoire de Juliette*, vol. V, p. 322. In the remarks just cited, there is a further irony: Francavilla comes across as an advocate of the "science of population control" which, for Foucault, signals the origin of our modern "disciplinary society."

22. Ibid., pp. 285–287; emphasis added.

23. Ibid., p. 288; emphasis added.

24. Jacques Derrida, "Cogito and the History of Madness," in *Writing and Difference*, translated by Alan Bass (Chicago: University of Chicago Press, 1978).

25. Foucault, *The Archaeology of Knowledge*, p. 16; emphasis added.

26. For more on this point, see H. Dreyfus and P. Rabinow, *Michel Foucault: Beyond Structuralism and Hermeneutics* (Chicago: University of Chicago Press, 1982), pp. 12–13.

27. Foucault, *The Order of Things* (London: Tavistock, 1970), p. 300.

28. Ibid.; emphasis added.

29. Ibid., p. 305; emphasis added.

30. Ibid., p. 306.

31. Ibid.; emphasis added.

32. Ibid., p. 307.

33. Ibid., p. 328.

34. Ibid., p. 342.

35. Ibid., p. 387.

36. See Habermas, *The Philosophical Discourse of Modernity*, p. 276.

37. See Foucault, "Truth and Power," p. 59: "I don't believe the problem can be solved by the phenomenologists, fabricating a subject that evolves through the course of history. One has to dispense with the constitutive subject, to get rid of the subject

itself, that is to say, to arrive at an analysis which can account for the constitution of the subject within a historical framework. And this is what I would call genealogy. . . ."

38. Charles Taylor, "Foucault on Freedom and Truth," in *Foucault: A Critical Reader*, pp. 69–102.

39. Foucault, *The History of Sexuality* (New York: Pantheon, 1978), p. 98; emphasis added.

40. Nancy Fraser has appropriately criticized this dimension of Foucault's work in *Unruly Practices*, when she observes: "The problem is that Foucault calls too many different sorts of things power and simply leaves it at that. Granted, all cultural practices involve constraints. But these constraints are of a variety of different kinds and thus demand a variety of different normative responses. . . . Foucault writes as if oblivious to the existence of the whole body of Weberian social theory with its careful distinctions between such notions as authority, force, violence, domination, and legitimation. Phenomena which are capable of being distinguished via such concepts are simply lumped together. . . . As a consequence, the potential for a broad range of normative nuances is surrendered, and the result is a certain normative one-dimensionality." Ibid., p. 32.

41. Foucault, *The History of Sexuality*, p. 93.

42. Michel Foucault and Noam Chomsky, "Human Nature: Justice versus Power," in *Reflexive Water: The Basic Concerns of Mankind*, edited by Fons Elder (London: Souvenir, 1974), p. 178. Chomsky continues: "And in fact there are interesting elements of international law, for example, embedded in the Nuremburg principles and the United Nations Charter, which permit, in fact, I believe, *require* the citizen to act against his own state in ways which the state will falsely regard as criminal."

43. *The Foucault Reader*, p. 95; emphasis added.

44. See Foucault, "Two Lectures," in *Power/Knowledge*, edited by C. Gordon (New York: Pantheon, 1980), p. 90: "The role of political power . . . is perpetually to reinscribe this relation [of force] through a form of unspoken warfare; to reinscribe it in social institutions, in economic inequalities, in language, in the bodies themselves of each and everyone of us."

45. Foucault, "Truth and Power," p. 56. For another important text of the same period where Foucault explains his understanding of power as a form of war, see "Power and Norm," in *Michel Foucault: Power, Truth, Strategy*, edited by M. Morris and P. Patton (Sydney: Feral, 1979). As Foucault remarks at one point (p. 60): "Power is won like a battle and lost in just the same way. At the heart of power is a war-like relation and not that of an appropriation."

46. Foucault and Chomsky, "Human Nature," pp. 182–185. Foucault supplements the foregoing citation with the following claim: "If you like, I will be a little bit Nietzschean about this; in other words, it seems to me that the idea of justice in itself is an idea which in effect has been invented and put to work in different types of societies as an instrument of a certain political and economic power or as a weapon against that power. But it seems to me that, in any case, the notion of justice itself functions within a society of classes as a claim made by the oppressor class and as a justification for it."

47. See, above all, Karl Marx, "Contribution to the Critique of Hegel's *Philosophy of Right*: Introduction," in *The Marx-Engels Reader*, pp. 16–26. Needless to say, the cogency of Marx's theory of history is not at issue here. Instead, we are concerned with a methodological point.

48. Foucault, "Truth and Power," p. 56.

49. See Axel Honneth, *Kritik der Macht* (Frankfurt: Suhrkamp, 1984), p. 176: "Foucault proceeds on the basis of a specific conception of social action; his basic model is the strategic intersubjectivity of struggle . . . [i.e.,] the Hobbesian claim for an original struggle of all against all." Honneth goes on to raise an extremely pertinent question: on the basis of this atomist/bellicist understanding of social action, how would social cohesion be possible? Doesn't Foucault's neo-Hobbesian concept of society as a war of all against all suggest social relations that would be predicated on anomie? And thus, how could a social order predicated on interminable struggle and conflict actually institutionalize and stabilize itself? It is not clear that Foucault ever effectively answered such questions.

50. Foucault, "Power and Norm," pp. 65–66, emphasis added. To be sure, there are strong precedents for such a functionalist understanding of the concept of norm in the tradition of sociological theory. And in support of the claims he makes in the passages cited, Foucault appends a discussion of the employment of the term in Durkheim's understanding of the relation between "norm" and "society." It would be fruitful to contrast Foucault's understanding of Durkheim with Habermas' discussion of "The Rational Structure of the Linguistification of the Sacred," in *The Theory of Communicative Action*, vol. II, pp. 77–111.

Finally, in *The Philosophical Discourse of Modernity*, Habermas has raised an apparently valid objection to Foucault's misleading identification of the human sciences as an exclusively "normalizing discourse," which is the underlying assumption of *The Order of Things* (especially the concluding chapter on "Man and His Doubles"). Habermas' point is that insofar as the human sciences today have a predominantly *interpretive* rather than *positivistic* self-understanding, they transcend the normalizing practices of, say, nineteenth-century scientific sociology (Auguste Comte, etc.).

51. Foucault, *Discipline and Punish*, pp. 275ff.

52. Foucault, *The History of Sexuality*, pp. 39ff.

53. Ibid., pp. 95–96; emphasis added.

54. Ibid., pp. 57–58.

55. Ibid., pp. 157, 159; emphasis added. For Foucault's later self-criticism of the discussion of the *ars erotica* in *The History of Sexuality*, see "On the Genealogy of an Ethics: An Overview," *The Foucault Reader*, pp. 347–348.

56. Foucault, "Power and Sex," in *Politics, Philosophy, Culture*, pp. 117–118; translation slightly altered. Here, Foucault seems to ascribe a primarily heuristic value to such methods of classification. As he continues: "At times, such simplifications are necessary. Such a dualism can be provisionally useful, to change the perspective from time to time and move from *pro* to *contra*."

57. Nietzsche, *The Will to Power*, nos. 796, 382.

58. See, for example, his account of the change of plan in "The Concern for Truth" (1984), in *Politics, Philosophy, Culture*, p. 255: "I changed my mind. When a piece of work is not also an attempt to change what one thinks and even what one is, it is not very amusing. I did begin to write two books in accordance with my original plan, but I very soon got bored. It was unwise of me to embark on such a project and run counter to my usual practice." These remarks should be interpreted in relation to Foucault's description of writing as an act of "self-transformation," in "The Minimalist Self," in ibid., pp. 3ff.

59. Foucault, *The Use of Pleasure* (New York: Pantheon, 1984), pp. 10–11.

60. Foucault, "On the Genealogy of Ethics," pp. 348, 351; emphasis added.

61. Foucault, "What is Enlightenment?" pp. 41–42.

62. See, for example, Maria Daraki, "Foucault's Journey to Greece," *Telos* 67 (Spring 1986):87–110. Leo Bersani, "Pedagogy and Pederasty," *Raritan* (Summer 1985).

63. Nietzsche, *The Will to Power*, nos. 802, 800.

9 ■ The House that Jacques Built: Deconstruction and Strong Evaluation

1. Some of these questions are touched on in the context of a very interesting interview with Derrida entitled "Deconstruction in America," in *Critical Exchange* 17 (Winter 1985):1–33. For an intriguing "deconstruction of deconstruction," which attempts to point out deconstruction's rather fawning institutional conformism despite its radical anti–institutional self-understanding, see Jeffrey Mehlman, "Writing and Difference: The Politics of Literary Adulation," *Representations* 15 (Summer 1986).

2. Jacques Derrida, "Of an Apocalyptical Tone Recently Adopted in Philosophy," *Semeia* XXIII (1982):63–97. Of course, as is the case with all of his "positions," Derrida's endorsement of the "apocalyptical tone" is far from unqualified.

3. Jacques Derrida, *Positions*, translated by Alan Bass (Baltimore: Johns Hopkins University Press, 1981), p. 47.

4. See Martin Heidegger, "Overcoming Metaphysics," in Richard Wolin, ed., *The Heidegger Controversy: A Critical Reader* (New York: Columbia University Press, 1991), p. 77: "With Nietzsche's metaphysics, philosophy is completed. That means: it has gone through the sphere of prefigured possibilities. . . . But with the end of philosophy, thinking is not also at its end, but in transition to another beginning."

5. Derrida, *Positions*, p. 53.

6. An expression used by Heidegger in "Hölderlin and the Essence of Poetry," in *Existence and Being* (South Bend, Ind.: Gateway, 1949), p. 288.

7. Derrida, *Positions*, p. 41; emphasis added.

8. Ibid., p. 93.

9. Michel Foucault, *Histoire de la folie à l'age classique* (Paris: Gallimard, 1972), pp. 583–603; English translation: "My Body, This Paper, This Fire," *Oxford Literary*

Review 4 (1979):9–28. Jacques Derrida, "Cogito and the History of Madness," in *Writing and Difference*, pp. 31–63.

10. Edward Said, *The World, the Text, and the Critic* (Cambridge, Mass.: Harvard University Press, 1983), pp. 203, 204, 207.

11. Hayden White, *Tropics of Discourse* (Baltimore: Johns Hopkins University Press, 1978), p. 280.

12. Russell Berman, "Troping to Pretoria: The Rise and Fall of Deconstruction," *Telos* 85 (1990):5–7.

13. Marx, *Capital* I, p. 83.

14. Derrida, *Positions*, pp. 59–60, 91.

15. Ibid., p. 61.

16. Derrida, "Deconstruction and the Other," in *Dialogues with Contemporary Continental Thinkers*, edited by Richard Kearney (Manchester: Manchester University Press, 1984), pp. 123–124.

17 This is a charge that has been explicitly raised against Derrida by Hans-Georg Gadamer. As Gadamer observes: "As far as [Derrida] is concerned, the concept of truth which is implied in harmonious agreement and which defines the 'true' opinion of what something means, is itself a naive notion that ever since Nietzsche, we can no longer accept." See Gadamer, "Reply to Jacques Derrida," in *Dialogue and Deconstruction: The Gadamer-Derrida Encounter*, edited by Diane Michelfelder and Richard E. Palmer (Albany: State University of New York Press, 1989), p. 56.

18. See Nietzsche, *The Will to Power*, pp. 5–83.

19. Derrida, "The Principle of Reason: The University in the Eyes of its Pupils," *Diacritics* XIX (1983):8. Derrida continues (p. 12): "One can no longer distinguish between technology on the one hand and theory, science and rationality on the other. The term techno-science has to be accepted, and its acceptance confirms the fact that an essential affinity ties together objective knowledge, the principle of reason, and a certain metaphysical determination of the relation to truth. We can no longer—and this is finally what Heidegger recalls and calls on us to think through—we can no longer dissociate the principle of reason from the very idea of technology in the realm of their modernity." But the Heideggerian critique of modern reason proves incapable of distinguishing between *practical and instrumental reason*: the former is viewed as merely a subspecies of the latter. On this view, which Derrida appears to adopt with few reservations, the difference between the Kantian commandment that we treat all rational natures as "ends in themselves" and the scientific-cybernetic view of utopia as the "administration of things" falls out of account.

20. Derrida, "Deconstruction and the Other," p. 124.

21. An allusion to Derrida's oft-cited epithet in *Of Grammatalogy*, p. 158, that "there is nothing outside the text."

22. Derrida, *Positions*, pp. 92–93, 94; emphasis added.

23. Of late this seems to be changing. Over the last several years he has taken an increasing interest in postmodern architectural theory and practice; and two leading

postmodern architects, Peter Eisenman and Bernard Tschumi, have explicitly embraced deconstructive principles. For more on Derrida's relation to contemporary postmodern architectural currents, see *Architectural Design* 58(3/4) (1988).

24. Ihab Hassan, "The Critic as Innovator: The Tutzing Statement in X Frames," *Amerikastudien* 22(1) (1977):55; cited in Albrecht Wellmer, "On the Dialectic of Modernism and Postmodernism," *Praxis International* 4 (1984):338.

25. Derrida, *Of Grammatology*, p. 3.

26. The preceding citations may be found in ibid., pp. 4–5.

27. Ibid., p. 8.

28. Kant, "An Answer to the Question," p. 54.

29. MacIntyre, *After Virtue*, p. 1ff.

30. Ibid., p. 2.

31. Ibid.

32. Thomas McCarthy, "The Politics of the Ineffable: Derrida's Deconstructionism," in *Hermeneutics and Critical Theory in Politics and Ethics*, edited by Michael Kelly (Cambridge, Mass.: MIT Press, 1990), pp. 155–156. I believe that one of the most important issues addressed by McCarthy's article is deconstruction's neo-Heideggerian aversion to the social sciences and empirical inquiry in general, which Derrida, in an exclusionary gesture, dismisses as essentially logocentric, and hence metaphysical (e.g., in "The Principle of Reason," p. 16).

33. Aristotle, *Politics*, I, ii.

34. Derrida, "*Limited Inc* a b c . . . ," in *Glyph* 2 (1977):236.

35. Richard Bernstein, "Metaphysics, Critique, Utopia," *Review of Metaphysics* 42 (December 1988):272.

36. Lyotard, *The Postmodern Condition*, p. 82: "Under the general demand for slackening and appeasement," observes Lyotard, "we can hear the mutterings of the desire for a return of terror, for the realization of the fantasy to seize reality. The answer is: Let us wage a war on totality; let us be witnesses to the unpresentable; let us activate the differences and save the honor of the name."

37. See Heidegger, "Overcoming Metaphysics," p. 74: "The reversal of Platonism, according to which for Nietzsche the sensuous becomes the true world and the suprasensuous becomes the untrue world, is thoroughly caught in metaphysics. This kind of overcoming of metaphysics, which Nietzsche has in mind in the spirit of nineteenth-century positivism, is only the final entanglement in metaphysics, although in a higher form. It looks as if the 'meta,' the transcendence to the suprasensuous, were replaced by the persistence in the elemental world of sensuousness, whereas actually the oblivion of Being is only completed and the suprasensuous is let loose and furthered by the will to power."

38. Derrida, "Structure, Sign, and Play in the Discourse of the Human Sciences," in *Writing and Difference*, pp. 280–81.

39. Derrida, "The Principle of Reason," pp. 18–19.

40. Derrida, *Positions*, p. 93.

41. Said, "Opponents, Audiences, Constituencies, and Community," in *The Anti-Aesthetic: Essays on Postmodern Culture*, edited by H. Foster (Port Townsend: Bay Press, 1983), p. 143.

42. Richard Bernstein, "Serious Play: The Ethical-Political Horizon of Jacques Derrida," *Journal of Speculative Philosophy* 1(2) (1987):112. I would like to thank Richard Bernstein for being good enough to show me Derrida's epistolary response to "Serious Play."

43. Derrida, "The Principle of Reason," p. 19.

44. Derrida, "Structure, Sign, and Play," p. 293.

45. Ibid., p. 292.

46. I believe that two of Derrida's most forceful statements of the impossibility of going beyond metaphysics may be found in the Levinas and Bataille critiques in *Writing and Difference* ("Violence and Metaphysics: An Essay on the Thought of Emmanuel Levinas" and "From Restricted to General Economy: A Hegelianism without Reserve"). For the gist of both critiques points to the impossibility of escaping the relationship between "metaphysics" and "violence," that is, of genuinely surmounting the onto-theological determinants of thought.

47. Derrida, "The Politics of Friendship," *Journal of Philosophy* LXXXV(12) (1988):632–645. I am basing my characterization in part on a yet unpublished, longer version of this essay.

48. Derrida, "The Principle of Reason," p. 16.

49. This point is made, for example, by Andreas Huyssen in "Mapping the Postmodern," *New German Critique* 33 (Fall 1984):39, who observes: "Thus it is no coincidence that the politically weakest body of French writing (Derrida and the late Barthes) has been privileged in American literature departments over the more politically intended projects of Foucault and Baudrillard, Kristeva and Lyotard." It has also been noted by Thomas McCarthy, in "The Politics of the Ineffable," p. 161: "In a manner reminiscent of Heidegger's 'essential thinking,' his approach devaluates the usual procedures of empirical and normative inquiry as being, one and all, shot through with the metaphysics of presence. Their place is taken by the deconstructive reading of selected texts. . . ."

50. Gayatri Spivak, in *Les fins de l'homme: a partir du travail de Jacques Derrida*, edited by J-L. Nancy and P. Lacoue-Labarthe (Paris: Galilée, 1981), p. 514; cited by Nancy Fraser in "The French Derrideans: Politicizing Deconstruction or Deconstructing Politics," *New German Critique* 33 (Fall 1984):130. See also Spivak, "Speculations on Reading Marx: After Reading Derrida," in *Post-Structuralism and the Question of History* (Cambridge: Cambridge University Press, 1987), pp. 30–62.

51. Weber, *From Max Weber*, p. 144.

52. Taylor, "What is Human Agency?" pp. 27, 33, 23.

53. "Dialogue with Jacques Derrida," in Kearney, *Dialogues with Contemporary Continental Thinkers*, p. 114.

54. Derrida, "Deconstruction in America," pp. 15, 21.

Index